Electronic Commerce

If your organization is to move successfully into the electronic age it must address the following questions:

- What is your next generation business-to-business trading relationship structure?
- Which business models are relevant for the Internet?
- How do you create a successful marketing strategy?
- What is the appropriate marketing programme?
- How do you implement the necessary changes?
- What will be the future of business-to-business electronic commerce?

This book will help you to answer these questions to ensure you can take advantage of the unprecedented opportunities on offer in the business-to-business trading environment rather than have the competition take advantage of you.

Electronic Commerce

Strategies and Models for Business-to-Business Trading

PAUL TIMMERS

JOHN WILEY & SONS, LTD

Chichester · New York · Weinheim · Brisbane · Singapore · Toronto

Paperback edition 2000
Copyright © 1999 by John Wiley & Sons Ltd,
Baffins Lane, Chichester,
West Sussex PO19 1UD, England

National	01243 779777
International	(+44) 1243 779777

e-mail (for orders and customer service enquiries):
cs-book@wiley.co.uk
Visit our Home Page on http://www.wiley.co.uk
or http://www.wiley.com

Other Wiley Editorial Offices

John Wiley & Sons, Inc., 605 Third Avenue,
New York, NY 10158-0012, USA

WILEY-VCH Verlag GmbH, Pappelallee 3,
D-69469 Weinheim, Germany

Jacaranda Wiley Ltd, 33 Park Road, Milton,
Queensland 4064, Australia

John Wiley & Sons (Canada) Ltd, 22 Worcester Road,
Rexdale, Ontario M9W 1L1, Canada

John Wiley & Sons (Asia) Pte Ltd, 2 Clementi Loop #02-01,
Jin Xing Distripark, Singapore 129809

Library of Congress Cataloging-in-Publication Data

Timmers, Paul.
   Electronic commerce : strategies and models for business-to-
business trading / Paul Timmers.
       p.   cm. – (Wiley series in information systems)
   Includes bibliographical references and index.
   ISBN 0-471-72029-1 (hardback : alk. paper)
   1. Electronic commerce.   2. Industrial marketing.   I. Title.
HF5548.32.T55   1999
658.8′00285–dc21   99-37219
                                                           CIP

British Library Cataloguing in Publication Data

A catalogue record for this book is available from the British Library

ISBN 0-471-49840-8

Typeset in 10/12 pt Times by C.K.M. Typesetting, Salisbury, Wiltshire
Printed and bound in Great Britain by Biddles Ltd, Guildford and King's Lynn
This book is printed on acid-free paper responsibly manufactured from sustainable
forestation, for which at least two trees are planted for each one used.

For Kizito

Contents

Foreword   xi

Preface   xiii

About the Author   xvii

Acknowledgements   xix

1 Introduction   **1**
    Objectives   1
    Book Structure   1

2 Key Features of Internet Electronic Commerce   **3**
    Electronic Commerce—Definition and Market   3
    The Internet for Business   7
        Online/Immediate/24-Hour Availability   9
        Ubiquity   11
        Global   12
        Local   14
        Digitization   15
        Multimedia   15
        Interactivity   16
        One-to-one   17
        Network Effects and Network Externalities   17
        Integration   18
        Intranets, Extranets and the Public Internet   19
    Building Assets to Create Customer Benefits   19
        Cost Base: Lower Transaction Costs and Better Prices   21

Time to Market   22
Brand Image   23
Market Share and Market Access   23
Customer Orientation   24
Quality   25
Customer Loyalty and Switching Costs   26
Functional Integration   27
Network Integration   27
Innovation Orientation—New Products and Services   27
Innovation Orientation—New Business Models   28
Summary   29

3 Business Models for Electronic Commerce   31
Value-chain Analysis and Business Model Architectures   32
Current Business Models   35
E-shops   35
E-procurement   36
E-malls   36
E-auctions   37
Virtual Communities   38
Collaboration Platforms   38
Third-party Marketplaces   39
Value-chain Integrators   39
Value-chain Service Providers   40
Information Brokerage, Trust and Other Services   40
Classification   41
Trends and Evolution   42
Summary   45

4 Business-to-Business Electronic Commerce Cases   47
Introduction and Overview of Selected Cases   47
Marshall Industries: A New Channel with Added Value   49
Business   49
Customers   49
Products and Services   50
Competition   51
Marketing Strategy   51
Summary—Marketing Model   52
Fedex: From Logistics to Generic Electronic Business Services   52
Business   52
Products and Services   53
Customers   54
Competition   54
Marketing Strategy   55
Summary—Marketing Model   55
Industry.Net: Pioneering an Internet Industry Marketplace   55
Business   55
Products and Services   56
Customers and Benefits   57
Competition   57

Marketing Strategy 59
Summary—Marketing Model 59
Amazon Associates and Advantage: Opening Up the Value Chain 60
  Business 60
  Products and Services 62
  Customers 62
  Competition 64
  Marketing Strategy 65
  Summary—Marketing Model 66
Citius Belgium: From EDI to Internet Marketplace 66
  Business—Customers—Competition 67
  Marketing Strategy 74
  Marketing Mix 76
  Summary—Marketing Model 79
Tradezone: Internet for Third-party Market Access 80
  Business—Customers—Competition 80
  Marketing Strategy 84
  Marketing Mix 87
  Summary—Marketing Model 90
  Postscript 90
Global Engineering Network/Industrial Cooperation System:
  Collaboration and Trading in Design and Manufacturing 90
  Business—Customers—Competition 90
  Marketing Strategy 100
  Marketing Mix 101
  Summary—Marketing Model 103
Infomar: Reorganizing an Auction-based Market 103
  Business—Customers—Competition 103
  Marketing Strategy 109
  Marketing Mix 111
  Summary—Marketing Model 114
Summary 114

5 **Markets and Competition** **115**
Industry Structure 116
  Industry Competition 116
  Suppliers' Power 120
  Customers' Power 121
  New Entrants 121
  Substitutes 122
  Generic Competitive Strategies 123
  Industry Structure—Summary 125
Transaction Costs 126
  Introduction 126
  Citius 127
  Tradezone 128
  GEN 129
  Infomar 130
  Frequency Revisited 131
Internal and External Business Organization 132
  Internal Business Organization 132

External Organization—Disintermediation   133
External Organization—Value Networks and Dynamic
   Markets   135
Summary   137

6 Marketing Strategies and Programmes   **139**
Traditional B-to-B Marketing   139
Segmentation and Targeting   141
Products and Services   147
Distribution   148
Marketing Communications   150
   Communication Objectives   152
   Target Audience and Take-up Process   152
   Communication Channels and Promotion Mix 155
One-to-One Marketing   158
   Introduction   158
   Application of One-to-One Marketing   160
   Pricing and One-to-One Marketing   161
   Assessment of One-to-One Marketing   162
Summary   162

7 Roadmap for Business-to-Business Electronic Commerce **165**
Critical Assumptions and Strategy Development   165
   Quality of Market Research   165
   Dynamics of Technology and Growth of Electronic
      Commerce   168
   Towards a Global Legal Framework for the Digital
      Economy?   171
   Strategy Development—Strategic Fit   174
Scenarios for the Future of Business-to-Business Electronic
   Commerce   179
   Competing and Collaborating in Value Networks and
      Dynamic Markets   182
   Thriving on Information   211
   Converging B-to-B and B-to-C Electronic Commerce 227
   New Technologies, New Business Models, New Policies:
      New Rules?   238
Conclusions   244
   Hypotheses   244
   Summary of Main Conclusions   245

Bibliography   247

Endnotes   253

Subject Index   261

Foreword

Recently, the widespread adoption of intranets, extranets and the acceptance of the Internet as a business platform have created a foundation for business-to-business (B-to-B) electronic commerce that offers the potential for organizations to streamline complex processes, lower costs and improve productivity. Business-to-business e-commerce is poised for rapid growth and is expected to grow from $43 billion in 1998 to $1.3 trillion in 2003, accounting for more than 90% of the dollar value of e-commerce by 2003.

Business-to-business electronic commerce creates new dynamics that differ considerably from those of other e-commerce relationships. Business-to-business e-commerce solutions frequently automate or impact workflows or supply-chain processes that are fundamental to a business's operations. Also to have an impact, B-to-B e-commerce solutions must often be integrated with an enterprise's existing information systems, a process that can be complex, time consuming and expensive. Consequently, implementation of a B-to-B e-commerce solution represents a non-trivial commitment by the enterprise, and the costs of switching solutions are high.

However, while the technology side has evolved considerably, the business and marketing sides have not. For many companies, business-to-business electronic commerce seems like a confusing nightmare. Prices are under pressure. Channel behaviour and acceptance are hard to predict. Competitors are innovating at unexpected places. Organizations react sluggishly, even as some executives try to goad people into action. And, despite all the effort that is going into business-to-business electronic commerce, it's not always clear where the profits are.

In this book, Paul has done an excellent job of highlighting critical issues pertaining to business-to-business electronic commerce. Using case studies of companies such as Marshall Industries, FedEx, Industry.Net, Citius Belgium and Tradezone, he builds a clear picture of what the underlying structural issues are in business-to-business electronic commerce. He forces the reader to think about six critical questions:

- What is your next generation business-to-business trading relationship structure?
- What are your new economics?
- How is your channel structure changing?
- How do you reorganize your marketing strategy?
- How do you implement the necessary changes?
- Where's the value?

In this book, he will explain how to answer those six questions, so you can take advantage of the turbulence in today's business-to-business trading environment, rather than have some competitor take advantage of you.

Dr Ravi Kalakota
e-mail to: kalakota@gsu.edu

Dr Ravi Kalakota is a professor, strategist, speaker and author. He is the leading authority on e-commerce strategy and has written four books considered by Amazon.com to be "e-commerce classics". He has consulted extensively in the e-commerce area with Fortune 1000 companies. Ravi is the founder and CEO of e-Business Strategies in Atlanta, the Director of the Center for Digital Commerce and Chair Professor of Information Systems at Georgia State University, also in Atlanta.

Preface

Electronic commerce can be defined loosely as 'doing business electronically'. [1] Electronic commerce, or better electronic business, includes electronic trading of physical goods and of intangibles such as information. This encompasses all the trading steps such as online marketing, ordering, payment, and support for delivery. Electronic commerce includes the electronic provision of services, such as after-sales support or online legal advice, as well as electronic support for collaboration between companies, such as collaborative design.

Electronic commerce, in particular via the Internet, is developing rapidly. There is a great deal of speculation about potential opportunities. The most important part of electronic commerce is in business-to-business (B-to-B) trading, although business-to-consumer (B-to-C) electronic commerce receives most public attention. Electronic commerce over the Internet may be either complementary to traditional business or represent a completely new way of doing business. Little is known about successful approaches in business-to-business electronic commerce on the Net.

There is also much uncertainty about the development of electronic commerce. Business managers, researchers, MBA students, consultants and policy makers look for a better understanding of business-to-business electronic commerce in the Internet environment. They wish to learn from the experience of innovative companies involved in electronic commerce, in order to understand how they identified new business opportunities and developed key elements of their marketing strategy like competitive positioning and the building of networked partnerships. There is also a need for a systematic approach and a set of tools to develop successful Internet marketing strategies and business models. Finally, there is a need to 'imagine the future' through an in-depth analysis of possible scenarios for future business-to-business electronic commerce.

This book addresses those needs by analysing strategic marketing approaches on the basis of both marketing theory and international case studies. It sets out to answer four key questions:

- Which business models are relevant for the Internet?
- What are successful strategic approaches to marketing?
- What are appropriate related marketing programmes?
- How will B-to-B electronic commerce develop in the future?

After giving an overview of the opportunities and risks of the Internet for business, the book provides detailed case descriptions that give a real-life and in-depth account of how innovative companies today are developing competitive advantage from doing business using the Internet. Following this is a systematic classification of Internet electronic commerce business models. This shows how companies organize their business and where their sources of revenue come from. The case studies as well as other examples from current and experimental Internet business illustrate the most relevant business models. Subsequently, the marketing strategies of the companies in the case studies are analysed with the help of current marketing theory and economics, including some of the more novel marketing strategy and customer relationship concepts such as value configurations and one-to-one marketing. This analysis provides a range of tools for the development of Internet marketing strategies, in particular for business-to-business electronic commerce. The challenge of strategy development in the turbulent and fast-moving Internet business is addressed, leading finally to a vision of the future of B-to-B electronic commerce illustrated by four scenarios.

The application of several well-known concepts from standard marketing theory to this new environment turns out to be very fruitful in order to understand and classify marketing strategies. These concepts are also helpful in identifying potential future opportunities in B-to-B electronic commerce and the requirements for marketing strategies and programmes. Such concepts include value-chain analysis, competitive structure of industries, transaction-cost theory and benefits segmentation.

However, beyond applying strategic marketing 'as is', the book also identifies gaps in the current toolset for strategic marketing and marketing programme development. Therefore, a number of new marketing strategy tools are provided and the reader is invited to reflect on the validity of traditional marketing for the future ways of business-to-business trading and collaboration.

Although the number of books about electronic commerce is increasing rapidly, there are still very few books that address business-to-business electronic commerce, which is remarkable as the larger part of electronic commerce is predicted to be between businesses rather than with consumers.[2] Most publications are related to selling to consumers. In addition, there are relatively few textbooks that systematically apply strategic marketing. Quite a number of publications are largely anecdotal or incomplete in the sense that they give a set of rules without a systematic framework for strategic marketing. And the books that do provide strategic marketing frameworks are most often not written with a view to electronic commerce. With its focus on business-to-business electronic commerce and its systematic application of strategic marketing in the wide sense, this book therefore attempts to fill a gap in the market for serious textbooks about electronic commerce.

Opinions expressed in this book are the author's and do not necessarily represent the opinions of the European Commission.

About the Author

Paul H. Timmers is at the European Commission Information Society Directorate-General, Head of Sector for electronic commerce in the European Union's research and technology development and business pilot programme. He has also been Secretary to the G8 Global Marketplace for SMEs, a global collaboration to promote electronic commerce for small and medium-sized enterprises.

Before joining the European Commission, he was manager of a software development and product management department in a large multinational computer and telecommunications firm.

Paul Timmers is a frequent speaker at international conferences and has been lecturing electronic commerce and information economy at various business schools and universities. He holds a PhD in theoretical physics from the University of Nijmegen in the Netherlands and an MBA from Warwick Business School in the United Kingdom (email: paul.timmers@pandora.be).

For further information and updated links please refer to
http://users.pandora.be/paul.timmers

Acknowledgements

It has been a privilege for me to work with many inspiring colleagues and friends all over the world to collect the material for this book, to discuss trends in the exciting field of electronic commerce, to learn from their personal experiences, and to develop ideas.

The work on the case studies in this book has benefited tremendously from interviews with Ilse van Rijsbergen of Citius Belgium, Michael Jeffries of Tradezone UK, Ulrich Rethfeld of Globana Germany and Luc Schelfhout of SCS Belgium. I am grateful for their responsiveness and their openness in providing information during long-lasting interview sessions and far beyond. They provided me unique insights into their business and into marketing in practice.

Over the past few years I have been in contact with a very large number of people about electronic commerce. I thank them for their views and insights. Among them are the members of the G7 Global Marketplace Policy Group and others involved in this G7 Project. I want to mention in particular Jim Johnson of the GIIC and Patrizia Fariselli of Nomisma.

My colleagues at the European Commission have been a great sounding board and helped to shape my thinking for this book. Specifically, I want to express my thanks to Rosalie Zobel and George Metakides, for their interest and support. They were among the first to recognize the importance of Internet electronic commerce and have helped me to explore ideas and initiatives. Anne Troye, with great experience in electronic commerce, has made me appreciate the importance of the relationship between technology and legal issues. She has introduced me to the rich history of electronic commerce and electronic data interchange. I want to thank those who helped me to understand the business process and network dimensions, in particular Fieny Reimann-Pijls, Karl-Heinz Robrock and Ralf Hansen. Thanassis Chrissafis was helpful in reviewing the transaction cost section and actively contributed to ideas about future research. René van den Berg, Anestis Filopoulos and Paul Desruelle most kindly reviewed early versions of chapters. Discussions with Bror Salmelin helped me to clarify the value network and dynamic market concepts. Emmanuelle Minne has always been reliable in supporting me with the many contacts and the flood of information.

Sally Dibb, Senior Lecturer Marketing and Strategic Management at Warwick Business School, deserves special thanks. She has given me invaluable help in obtaining essential marketing material and has made marketing much clearer to me. Discussions with Bob Galliers at Warwick Business School and INSEAD, Georgios Doukidis of the Athens University of Economics and Business, Ravi Kalakota of Georgia State University, Rudi Hirschheim at the University of Houston, Brian Subirana at IESE Barcelona and Yelena Yesha at the University of Maryland at Baltimore County have given me the necessary encouragement to go ahead and write this book and provided valuable suggestions for improvement.

Finally, the work for this book would never have been completed without the loving and unfailing support and persistence of Kizito, my wife, the support of her mother and my parents, and the acceptance of Nyanza, Justus, Victor, Paul and Samuel that their dad could spend so little time with them for so long.

1
Introduction

OBJECTIVES

This book focuses on business strategies and models in business-to-business Internet electronic commerce. It analyses strategic marketing approaches on the basis of case studies, with a view to determining their key characteristics and providing a classification of Internet business-to-business (B-to-B) electronic commerce models. In view of the new features of the Internet, questions to be answered are:

- What are the (emerging) business models?
- Which business strategies are applied or emerging?
- What are the related marketing programmes?
- What are likely future scenarios for B-to-B electronic commerce?

The book sets out to investigate these questions. It is recognized that the area is still relatively unexplored. The intention is not always to provide complete answers—if any exist at all. Instead, the approach is to gain a better understanding of the issues at stake and arrive at partial answers to the questions formulated above, with the help of the insights from case-study analysis and marketing and economic theory. Two important hypotheses in this book are:

- Existing marketing theory and business economics are valid for the analysis of Internet electronic commerce.
- The business models, classification and terminology developed in Chapter 3 are applicable to actual business cases.

BOOK STRUCTURE

Following this introductory chapter, an overview is given in Chapter 2 of the specific characteristics of the Internet and their relevance for business-to-business electronic commerce. The focus is on showing how the Internet is different and what this can mean for building critical business assets to deliver customer value.

Chapter 3 provides a classification of the business models that are emerging in electronic commerce. A business model is defined as the organization of product, service and information flows, and the sources of revenues and benefits for suppliers and customers. The classification provides a common language for subsequent analysis, and has been developed and validated on the basis of the present book and earlier work by the author. In this classification, 11 business models, most of which are commercially being implemented, are included, although theoretically there is a far larger number of models that can be imagined.

Chapter 4 presents the case studies that form the core of this work. The case approach has been chosen to obtain a better understanding and illustration of the issues in business-to-business electronic commerce marketing, without attempting to be exhaustive. The cases illustrate most of the emerging Internet business models of Chapter 3. The case descriptions have been structured after marketing analysis frameworks as in Dibb *et al.* (1991) and Kotler (1991), as well as the marketing planning framework provided by McDonald (1997).[3]

Chapter 5 is the first part of the case-study analysis. It addresses the macro level, that is, the structure of industry and markets, and focuses on the new features that emerge when doing business electronically. Competitive structures, disintermediation, transaction costs and other much debated topics in Internet business are addressed.

Chapter 6 provides the second part of the case-study analysis, addressing approaches to marketing strategy, including segmentation and targeting, marketing communications and new approaches to customer interaction, like one-to-one marketing.

Chapter 7 consists of two related parts. In the first part, it puts the concept of strategy development into perspective. In a fast-changing environment like the Internet there are many uncertainties. Many assumptions have already proven to be wrong due to lack of market research, the unpredictability of technology development, or a lack of understanding of market and social mechanisms. Strategy development in such an environment is a challenge in itself. Taking into account this 'warning', the second part sets out to present a number of scenarios for the future of B-to-B electronic commerce. The chapter demonstrates why these futures may well become reality, and shows how business strategies can be developed for each of them.

Finally, an extensive bibliography, references and index complete the book.

2
Key Features of Internet Electronic Commerce

This chapter presents the key characteristics of the Internet and their relevance for business-to-business electronic commerce. After a brief introduction to Internet-based electronic commerce and its rapidly growing importance, it is demonstrated that doing business in the Internet environment can be quite different from 'traditional' business. It is also shown how these new ways of doing business help to build key assets and deliver benefits to customers.

ELECTRONIC COMMERCE—DEFINITION AND MARKET

Electronic commerce has already existed for over 20 years. In sectors such as retail and automotive, electronic data interchange (EDI) for application-to-application interaction is being used regularly. For defence and heavy manufacturing, electronic commerce lifecycle management concepts have been developed that aim to integrate information across larger parts of the value chain, from design to maintenance, such as CALS (Computer Assisted Lifecycle Support or Computer Aided Logistics Support).

These forms of electronic commerce have been fairly limited in their diffusion and take-up until now. For example, EDI is used by no more than about 50 000 enterprises in Europe and 44 000 in the USA, although it was intended to have wide applicability.[4] This represents not even 1% of the total number of companies. CALS is by design more suited for a limited number of industry sectors that have strong quality control and lifecycle management requirements.

Recently, however, we have seen explosive development in electronic commerce. The causes of that are, of course, the Internet and the World

Wide Web (WWW), which are making electronic commerce much more accessible. They promise easily usable and low-cost forms of electronic commerce. The Internet not only supports application-to-application electronic commerce similar to that already known from EDI, but also, and especially, person-to-person and person-to-application forms of electronic commerce.

Through the combination of interactivity, networking, multimedia and data processing, Internet electronic commerce offers a tremendously wide variety of electronic business opportunities, limited only by imagination. Electronic commerce on the basis of the Internet is set to become a very important way of doing business.

Internet electronic commerce includes electronic trading of physical goods and of intangibles such as information. This encompasses all the trading steps such as online marketing, ordering, payment, and support for delivery. Electronic commerce includes the electronic provision of services, such as after-sales support or online legal advice. It also includes electronic support for collaboration between companies, such as collaborative online design and engineering, or virtual business consultancy teams. This wide range of business activities illustrates that it makes little sense to come up with a restrictive definition of electronic commerce, but also that there is likely not to be a single unique definition (which creates problems, for example, for statisticians in measuring electronic commerce). For this book there is no need to restrict ourselves and we will work with a broad understanding of what electronic commerce is about, namely 'doing business electronically'.

Forrester Research (1997) forecast was that business-to-business (B-to-B) electronic commerce would grow to $327 billion in the year 2002—that is, the value of goods and services traded via the Internet. This excludes the value of the hardware, software and services that are needed to perform electronic commerce, whose value is likewise estimated at several hundred billions of dollars. It also excludes the value of other forms of electronic commerce mentioned before, such as collaborative design and engineering or electronic trading in financial markets. While this is only 1% of the forecast total world economy of $30 trillion in 2002, the growth is predicted to be exponential. Forrester (1998a) expected B-to-B electronic commerce to jump to $1.3 trillion in the US by 2003, which already amounts to 4% of the world economy. Others predict that the figure will grow further to 30% of the world economy in 2010. While such high growth rates will not be sustained, it is clear that electronic commerce will become pervasive: Datamonitor (1997) expected 630 000 US companies and 245 000 European companies to be involved in fully fledged integrated B-to-B electronic commerce in five years' time. The EITO'99 survey expected 47% of European companies to be using some form of electronic commerce in 1999. In March 1999 IBM claimed to be selling $1 billion online, out of total monthly revenues of $3.3 billion.[5] According to a survey by Grainger, a US-based MRO distributor, in 1998 only 8% of companies interviewed were using the Internet to order maintenance, repair and operations (MRO) supplies. However, of these, 85% intended to increase their online MRO ordering significantly. One out of four purchasing managers expect to use the Internet for MRO purchases in the future[6]. For 49% of those who were not using online purchasing, the main barrier was lack of access to the Internet[7]. This can be contrasted with data from *The Report on Electronic Commerce* (1998), which expects that Internet connectivity in business will grow from 10% in 1997 to an impressive 90% in 2001. IDC has estimated that in 2002, of the B-to-B electronic commerce in France, 43% will be MRO products, 30% will be primary goods including raw materials as well as intermediate (semi-finished) products, 25% will be purchases by distributors for reselling, and 2% will be personal purchases. Figure 2.1 illustrates the predictions for the growth of B-to-B electronic commerce. It also shows that the forecasts of the market research firms are quite different, indicating that there is still a great deal of uncertainty about the future development of electronic commerce. This phenomenon and other uncertainties that characterize this emerging area are addressed in more detail in Chapter 7.

The number of individuals connected to the Internet is expected to continue to grow explosively. Likewise, the tremendous growth of the number of Internet host computers (see Figure 2.2) will not abate for the next few years. However, business-to-consumer (B-to-C) electronic commerce, although also growing fast, is not expected to reach such

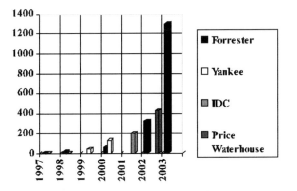

Figure 2.1   *Business-to-business electronic commerce market*

Sources: Forrester (1997), Forrester (1998), Yankee (1996), Price Waterhouse (1998), IDC (1998).[8]

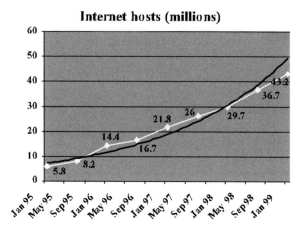

Internet hosts (millions)

Figure 2.2   *Internet host count (millions) with exponential trend line*

Source: Network Wizards (http://www.nw.com)

high levels within the next few years: most market researchers (1997) expect B-to-C to be about 10–20% of total electronic commerce. Business-to-business electronic commerce is therefore accounting for the larger part of the business.

With the new medium of the Internet, new ways of doing business are also developing. Most of those that capture the public attention are consumer oriented (such as Amazon.com, Tesco). Less publicity is given to the way that the Internet can be used for business-to-business electronic commerce, although such commerce is a reality today (e.g. Cisco, General Electronic procurement etc.). New forms of B-to-B electronic commerce are being piloted in many sectors of industry. Advanced pilot experiments are also being supported by the European Commission in the ESPRIT, ACTS and Telematics Applications European research, technology development and demonstration programmes (European Commission, 1998b) and in their successor, the Information Society Technologies Programme.[9] This work is part of a more general framework of policy making and programmes for global electronic commerce, which also addresses the legal and regulatory framework and other factors in the business environment.

The state of the market differs greatly around the world, with the USA being in the lead in most—but not all—areas of electronic commerce. The European market is estimated to be between one and three years behind, although it is catching up, with growth rates in business-to-business electronic commerce in 1998 that were higher than in the USA. Europe is more advanced in some electronic commerce-related services such as in electronic payments and in smart-card usage. The Asia-Pacific market is predicted by some to be developing even more rapidly and to overtake the European market in a few years' time (IDC, 1998).

THE INTERNET FOR BUSINESS

Internet commerce is growing so fast for the following reasons:

- Internet commerce has a *low entry cost* compared to other solutions such as EDI. An example calculation shows that the difference can be as large as a factor of 25.[10] A Web presence does not need to cost more than a few hundred dollars per year.[11] For that amount one can have a Web page hosted on a server and online access for maintenance. Of course, a Web presence on its own does not deliver much competitive advantage when a massive presence of companies on the Web becomes a reality in the next few years.
- With low entry cost, a *fast return on investment* is also possible. IMRG quotes a return on investment of weeks, where previously business used to think of several years, although clearly this depends on the kind of application.[12] A supplier who puts a catalogue online can build in direct support for regular customers with electronic ordering. Eliminating paper in the ordering and delivery process can lead to enormous savings, of a factor of 10 to 100. Therefore Internet commerce can offer immediate cost savings. Internet electronic commerce start-ups can also reach break-even quickly. Several of the new Internet companies presented during an Internet electronic commerce contest in France early 1999, eLectrophées, were already profitable within a year. On average, they expected to break even in two years' time.[13]
- Internet commerce has the promise of *protecting investment*. Whereas EDI-based systems have a tendency to be specific to the trading or supply-chain relationship, it is the hope that Web-based systems will be interoperable among suppliers. In this way switching costs are low and there is no need to buy multiple systems. A single PC can support trading relationships with a multitude of business partners. Internet commerce is based on *open networks and standards*, thereby helping to avoid lock-in.
- Internet commerce offers *connectivity and communication*. Getting access to the Internet usually means having an e-mail account and being able to browse the WWW. E-mail can bring immediate benefits in business-to-business commerce. Time can be saved by sending (simple) advertisements, order and delivery confirmations and enquiries via e-mail rather than by normal mail or even fax.

- Internet commerce *meets information needs*. To meet information needs it is sufficient to have a browser and surf the Web. It is not necessary to create a presence on the Web for the company itself. Information can be collected about offers, opportunities, competition, market trends etc.
- Internet commerce has already built up a *critical mass*, which attracts even more users and providers of the technology and of business solutions. In addition, governments and public authorities worldwide actively promote the use of the Internet for business. This creates confidence that electronic commerce over the Internet is a viable proposition.
- Last but not least, Internet commerce is in a *technology-driven 'virtuous innovation cycle'* of constant opportunity creation as a consequence of the very rapid progress of electronic commerce technologies. Many technology start-ups as well as established companies such as IBM and Microsoft continually create fresh opportunities through new Internet and electronic commerce technologies. These opportunities in their turn attract even more entrepreneurs, further fuelling the virtuous cycle.

Internet commerce offers a range of advantages that collectively have been shown to be important enough to attract massive interest on the part of businesses, both as users of the technology and as providers of technology and solutions.

However, there is still hesitation among many companies about committing any major effort to electronic commerce, let alone about fundamentally rethinking their business strategy in line with the new opportunities. The reasons for this hesitation are summarized below.[14]

- Lack of *awareness* and understanding of the opportunities and implications and uncertainty about the appropriate *business model*.
- Concerns about *total costs*, including the costs of retraining and the telecommunications (in particular in Europe).
- Concerns about *security* of sensitive data, such as credit-card numbers, personal data and business confidential data.
- Concerns about *interoperability* and the risk that competition between major suppliers (e.g. Microsoft and Netscape) will lead to incompatible sets of standards.
- Uncertainty about *applicable law* and the appropriateness of the *legal framework*.
- Lack of *usability* of the technology, difficulties in performing slightly more complicated electronic commerce than merely being present with a Web page.

That these barriers exist has been well researched. For example, the European Commission performed numerous consultations with businesses from 1995 to 1997, which enabled an inventory of barriers for electronic commerce and allowed policy measures to be addressed.[15] KPMG researched the 1997 e-Christmas experiment, which aimed to bring many merchants online in a third-party marketplace environment where the Web, payment and logistics services were provided by large companies such as Microsoft, HP, Visa, and UPS. While this failed from a short-term commercial perspective, it was an important learning experience in offering better understanding of the barriers to electronic commerce.[16] The previously cited 1998 Grainger survey found that lack of access to the Internet in companies was the main reason for not doing online MRO purchasing. Other barriers included lack of convenience (15%) and the current inability to fit with (company) polices and processes (9%).

CommerceNet performs a yearly survey in the USA and Europe into barriers to electronic commerce. In 1998 it found that the main barriers differed between large and small companies, but also that there are quite significant differences between the USA and Europe. In the USA, the most important barriers for corporations were integration with legacy systems and executive awareness. For large corporations in Europe, the most important barriers were about trust and security, as well as international trade barriers. Small companies in both the USA and Europe did seem to agree about the lack of business models for making money. US SMEs were also concerned about the lack of qualified personnel, while European SMEs were worried about the complexity of electronic commerce. Andersen Consulting, in a 1998 European survey, also found that the lack of clear regulation formed a particular barrier to electronic commerce development[17] and that executives believe that governments should do more to develop a global legal framework. The cost of telecommunications and Internet service provider costs and their relative weight vary greatly across countries. The difference between the highest and lowest charges (for six hours' usage per month) is as much as $46 for Russia versus $7 for Malaysia, for example. In some countries local phone calls are not charged for at all and only Internet access has to be paid, such as in the USA and Mexico.[18]

The following sections analyse some of the key characteristics of the Internet and the WWW and their significance for business-to-business commerce. Those key features are summarized in Table 2.1.

Online/Immediate/24-Hour Availability

A Web server is usually online 24 hours per day, and virtually immediately accessible (depending on line speed and network traffic, of course). This

Table 2.1   *Key features of the Internet for business*

Key feature	Implication
Availability	'Normal' business hours time constraints do not exist any more with online, 24-hours per day and immediate access.
Ubiquity	For most companies and customers there is no reason not to have Internet access—so assume that in the near future most will have it, just as we now assume that they have a phone and a fax.
Global	With no physical borders for access (but not always for delivery), our mental map of what is 'near' and 'far' will radically change.[19]
Local	Paradoxically, the Internet not only enables global commerce, but is also a perfect vehicle to reinforce local physical presence and local person-to-person business relationships.
Digitization	The real business will increasingly be happening in information space, even for physical products. Convergence is leading to the shake-up of major industries like telecommunications and broadcasting, as well as different thinking about the 'natural' laws of economics, like increasing rather than decreasing returns to scale.
Multimedia	A long-awaited combination of technologies is finally coming to business, not only to gain a competitive edge in information provision during buying and selling but also to provide completely new opportunities in consultancy, design and entertainment in combination with interactivity and networking.
Interactivity	Interactivity is a challenge, namely to overcome the virtuality of the business relationship, as well as an opportunity for greatly improving traditional customer service at an affordable price.
One-to-one	Based on data processing and customer profiling, possibly based on enriched interactivity, one-to-one marketing is a natural companion of doing business on the Internet. It may also be a necessity to overcome the anonymity of Internet business relationships.
Network effects and network externalities	Low cost and fast growth in the number of relationships enable business models that require a significant number of parties in the network and whose benefits increase faster with a growing number of parties. That is, these business models exhibit network effects and/or network externalities. Examples are implementations of open market concepts such as virtual communities and third-party marketplaces.
Integration	It has long been argued and to some extent demonstrated that the value of combined information across steps of the value chain is more than the sum of its parts. The Internet now provides at least part of the technology for value-chain functional and information integration. Advanced electronic commerce companies show how to exploit the added value.

creates time independence and enables customer service to be decoupled from supplier availability. Such 24-hour availability is a strong facilitator of a global presence, overcoming time differences. As the customer is in the first instance interacting with an automated system, there is a set of service requests that can become 'self-service'. However, automated systems can only handle fairly routine and simple requests. Technology (e.g. intelligent agents) is being developed to deal with the non-standard customer or with more complex inquiries. Alternatively, a Web presence can be combined with the option of contact with a call centre, or deferring answering by posting the request and waiting for a later e-mail or personal call in response.

Business-to-business commerce is a mix of standard and non-standard interactions. Automated interaction is applicable to:

- repeat orders;
- repeat information updating, e.g. a regular company newsletter or market survey;
- first customer contact (as an add-on to other forms of customer contact, see below);
- standard pre- and post-sales enquiries (e.g. using frequently asked questions—FAQ);
- order and delivery tracking;
- complementing other channels, e.g. as contact point for responding to customer enquiries generated by magazine advertising.

Combining automated and non-automated interaction can be critical. Chapter 6 addresses the appropriate channel mix (Internet and other channels).

Ubiquity

Global information networks (fixed and mobile, cable, satellite) promise to offer worldwide, large-scale and low-cost access to electronic commerce. For B-to-B electronic commerce the consequences are:

- *enabling global reach*: companies all over the world up to the smallest and in the remotest corner can be accessed electronically, resulting in access to new markets but also the entrance of new competitors into the home market;
- *changing role of gatekeepers*: the privileged points of contact, the gatekeepers, in companies that previously had to be dealt with in order to do business can be by-passed by providing information directly to the desktops of individual employees in the company. As a consequence,

the sales process can change dramatically. To indicate the scale of changes, some claim that the procurement function, previously located with specialists in the company, will become part of the task of every manager, and that specialist purchasing departments will virtually disappear.[20]

Global

It is often claimed that one of the largest changes brought about by the Internet is that it is global: companies get access to customers globally, customers get access to suppliers globally. Let's assume that this is true. The consequences could be:

- whole new markets opening up at low cost, especially for small companies that previously could not afford to build up global marketing— therefore size matters less;
- companies that previously divided the local market up among them find themselves confronted with new competition in their own backyard.

At the same time, one could reason that there is not going to be much competitive advantage in having global reach, as this holds equally for every company. Alternatively, one could suggest that large companies with an established brand and reputation will particularly benefit from easier access to a global customer base, as they are the ones that can distinguish themselves in the global cacophony through brand recognition. Finally, some claim that the cultural, language and trust barriers to going global are such that the dominant use of electronic commerce (for small companies) will be in local trading networks (e.g. Fariselli *et al.* 1997). The case studies also include an analysis of the strategic approach to exploiting the global nature of today's electronic commerce for B-to-B marketing.

Some of the approaches to exploiting the global nature of the Internet are detailed below.

- *Global product-market*: for example in the technical domain, or in software for the professional user, where it is often possible to market the product through an English-only Web site. NanoTechnologies, which specializes in technology for very small (nano-scale) material structures, is an example.
- *Global supply chain*: in this case the emphasis is on using globally standardized interfacing to link in suppliers or customers globally, as well as simplified trading procedures. EDI was expected to deliver such a global standard, but the diversity and cost of implementation

prevented it from becoming the easily available hook for globally connecting suppliers and customers. Integrating the Web with new forms of application-to-application data exchange, such as XML/EDI or BSR-Beacon, is now expected to fulfil that promise. Experiments like RosettaNet seek to demonstrate the feasibility of Internet-based supply chains that are open to many partners. However, simplification of trading procedures is still not achieved, despite liberalization of trade.

- *Multiple language support*: a costly approach that can only be performed either by major players or where a very limited amount of translation is required. Search engines like Yahoo and AltaVista take such an approach.
- *Franchising*: split the presentation of the product (front end) from other parts of the business, such as the logistics or catalogues (back end), and apply franchising to the front end. This is the approach of the Amazon Associates programme and of Tradezone. CitiusNet France licenses its concept to Citius companies in other countries with a view to becoming a global company. These companies are subsidiaries or joint undertakings with local operators, or independently established and owned companies such as Citius Belgium. CitiusNet in France is responsible for setting the overall business strategy, coordinating R&D activities worldwide and ensuring the interoperability of country-specific servers. The international subsidiaries are in charge of local marketing and sales as well as customer service.
- *Internet presence to complement physical global presence*: use Internet commerce as a complement to a worldwide physical sales and support presence, an approach for large companies such as Digital Equipment Corporation (now part of Compaq).

Almost opposite to the last approach is a phenomenon that has been increasing in importance since 1998, namely to establish a local Internet presence in major countries, setting up country Web sites complementary to the homebase Web site. It is interesting to note that even companies like Amazon.com consider it necessary to establish a local presence in this way (initially in the UK and Germany). Evidently it is not adequate to ship books from the USA using a global package-delivery company and/or to rely on local Associates to have sufficient market access in major countries. Likewise, Internet auctioneer eBay has decided to set up a presence in the UK and Canada. Although it is possible to buy and sell globally through eBay's homebase US Web site, a local presence and therefore physical nearness will significantly reduce shipping and customs costs and increase confidence in the fulfilment of a deal made in the virtual world.[21]

Local

Seemingly in contradiction to what has been said in the preceding section, the Internet also has strong possibilities for local exploitation. First, let's not forget that most buying—at least on the part of consumers—happens locally. It would not be reasonable to assume that this will change much even if these consumers get online access as an additional means of shopping. Here we are clearly talking about the mass of consumers that still has to go online, not about the select group of early adopters, who generally are better equipped financially and in their command of English—the language of the Internet—to shop globally. The same focus on the local market is true for many of the goods and services purchased and sold by businesses. This certainly holds for the mass of small businesses that still have to go online and for many of the services that will continue to have a strong local dimension (restaurants and catering, legal services, housing and construction, repairs and installation etc).

Secondly, the larger part of those businesses that will use electronic commerce in the near future will not be companies with a virtual presence only. They will seek to reinforce their local physical presence by means of a presence in cyberspace. Thus, the Internet needs to be in support of that local presence. The first examples are emerging of the Internet taking on that role. The Internet can be used as an information and marketing resource such that the customer is better prepared for the physical delivery of the product or service. The retail chain Mitsukoshi in Japan is using this approach, where its extremely dense network of convenience stores, open 24 hours a day, doubles as a delivery and pick-up point for any retail goods ordered via the Internet.[22] The local physical presence can be focused on improved service rather than on basic marketing or sales information provision. An example in retail chains with small retailers is the ESPRIT Internet Megastore project. Alternatively, the Internet can be following a local physical marketing presence, to implement and automate the routine (re)ordering that follows initial sales. This approach will be especially relevant where small companies in the same region are already working together. Moreover, in all these examples local exploitation of the Internet is not hampered by the difficulties created by differences in language, culture, payment and delivery methods. Finally, local exploitation can be made even more relevant by using information about local events and conditions such as traffic or geographic information, local complementary services, local public services.

It may well be that after the wave of enthusiasm—and hype—about the global opportunities of the Internet, the next phase will instead be a wave of locally oriented initiatives to exploit it for local business (Steinfeld and Klein, 1999; Timmers, 1999b).

Digitization

The Internet and the communication and computer systems connected to it are all processing digital and digitized information. Digital information can be easily stored, transmitted, processed, mixed, transformed, in short manipulated in many ways, independent of its source or carrier. This has two important consequences that are only briefly touched on here:

- *convergence* of communications, information processing and media. Convergence creates opportunities for new products and services (e.g. phone over the Internet, WebTV, Netcasting). It also implies the emergence of a new 'convergence' industry accompanied by large-scale industry restructuring among communications businesses such as telecommunications companies, IT industry and media/publishing;
- *increasing returns to scale*, for products and services that can be reproduced digitally and can be delivered electronically, such as software, information services, customer self-service over the Internet etc. The cost of dealing with an additional customer or making an additional product is virtually zero. Therefore, contrary to traditional economic logic, returns are not decreasing when numbers increase, but rather they continue to increase as the fixed costs are shared among more customers while the marginal costs do not increase. Chapter 6 addresses the relationship between increasing returns and one-to-one marketing, another aspect that can be greatly enabled by the Internet.

Multimedia

Closely related to digitization is the aspect of multimedia, referring to the capability to deal with and deliver information in several ways: text, graphics, sound, video, eventually tactile. The Internet currently supports text, low-resolution still graphics, simple animation and sound in a fairly effective manner. With on-going information technology and network advances, it is also likely that within the next few years real-time video and 3D animation will be able to be delivered at relatively low cost for mass-market use. Tactile interaction may be limited more to very specific application areas (such as design or 3D modelling). It is not impossible, however, that this will also find a mass market also.

Multimedia considerably enriches the opportunities for the promotion of goods and services, for the provision of in-depth information, as well as for person-to-person interaction. It was the standard multimedia (text + graphics + animation + audio + video) browser interface to the Internet that turned out to be the 'killer application' that managed to unlock the potential of this worldwide network of information resources.

For business-to-business commerce, multimedia may be essential. While repeat sales from an electronic catalogue can be performed with text support only (as in EDI systems), it is evident from physical B-to-B marketing that multimedia presentation is essential if such marketing is to be done electronically. This pertains to:

- multimedia product catalogues, showing the physical product;
- application examples or application notes, which can be as simple as diagrams, or range from animations to fully fledged online videos;
- interactive training or simulation, in order to explain product usage, as well as to resolve customer problems;
- audio or video-conferencing for personal support (pre- or post-sales).

Beyond marketing, there are other business processes that may require intense multimedia support in electronic commerce, such as collaborative design and engineering.

Interactivity

As opposed to EDI, which is for application-to-application data exchange, the Internet offers person-to-person and person-to-application interactivity. Even if one side of the interaction is automated, through a Web-server program, the interaction possibilities are wide ranging and can be extremely varied and engaging. In fact, even those who see the Web as no more than an extension of physical world advertising cannot ignore the opportunities that interaction brings. It can deliver:

- retention of customer attention, which translates into increased sales opportunities;
- more knowledge about the customer profile (demo/sociographics, preferences), providing opportunities for better targeting (including one-to-one marketing) and repeat sales;
- customer feedback, for example to improve product design and presentation and increase customer involvement and loyalty;
- customer self-navigation, where customers guide themselves to what is most relevant and interesting, saving sales costs;
- customer self-selection, enabling the interaction offer to be tuned to the type of customer (from unassisted to full personal assistance), again saving sales costs and increasing chances for customer retention.

In physical B-to-B marketing, a high level of person-to-person interaction is often normal, for example where the salesperson visits the corporate procurer. In that respect, Internet marketing may be perceived to be less effective. Interactivity is a way of making up for the loss of this type of personal contact. In addition, it is likely that in many cases such personal contact is only for repeat sales, and that it is not felt as a loss when this is being substituted by an automated Web site.

One-to-one

The Internet makes customer profiling fairly easy, by capturing and analysing customer characteristics. Technically, this can consist of storing some information about the customer on the customer's computer (e.g. a 'cookie'), which is retrieved when the customer returns to the site. This can be combined with more detailed information, partially solicited from the customer and partially collected by the merchant, e.g. the pattern of purchases. Many sites encourage potential customers to provide an e-mail address, personal data etc. Customer profiling technology can be complemented by 'intelligent agents' that assist in the sales process.

Recently, one-to-one marketing has become in vogue, championed by Peppers and Rogers (1997a,b) and supported by software from a growing range of companies like Broadvision (USA), Intracom (Greece), Etnoteam (Italy), and others. Internet one-to-one marketing is applicable for B-to-C as well as for B-to-B. In the traditional AIDA (Awareness–Interest–Desire–Action) model of customer communications,[23] one-to-one marketing focuses primarily on enhancing the Interest phase. One-to-one means are used to engage in a personalized dialogue, with the intention of soliciting a positive purchase action. However, we will see in chapter 6 that one-to-one marketing is also particularly interesting when used to support an additional step in customer communications, namely customer loyalty.

Network Effects and Network Externalities

Network externalities are external benefits or losses of the presence of products in the market that are *not* reflected in the market price, that is, for which there is no compensation through the price—these are therefore market inefficiencies (Choi, Stahl and Whinston, 1997). Network effects, on the other hand, are positive or negative influences of the networked market that *are* reflected in the market price. In Internet commerce there are numerous examples of positive feedback loops that create increased benefits for increasing numbers of users in the network. Low cost and fast extension of the number of relationships enable business models whose benefits grow faster than linearly in the number of participants (usually after a certain threshold number of parties in the network has been passed).

Often users are not charged for these benefits and thus these business models exhibit network externalities. Examples are implementations of open-market concepts such as virtual communities, Internet auctions and third-party marketplaces with shared catalogues. In all of these, as more information providers and information consumers or buyers and sellers join in, it becomes even more attractive to become a member. The amount of information and choice per user rises at least linearly, whereas the price per user remains constant. Total benefits thus grow faster than the number of users.

The acceptance by the market of a single standard for a product where relations between users matter is another example that brings increased benefits to all users, such that it is often a condition for a viable market being established at all. Examples are the WWW protocols and Java, but also a *de facto* standard such as Microsoft Word. This can even lead to the company that owns the standard achieving market dominance, with possible negative monopolistic effects. 'Network' is used in this context in a loose sense: rather than the physical network it refers to the community of users, a virtual network.

Integration

The Internet and notably the WWW, with its extensions to run Java or Active-X, make it possible to deliver at a single user interface and point of access a wide variety of functionality. 'Integration at the desktop' can now become more than a slogan. For example, when today a consumer orders a book from Amazon.com, he or she not only uses the Web browser, but also transparently accesses the book catalogue held at a back-end server system. In the near future, with the implementation of the SET standard, the buyer will transparently invoke credit-card authorization. And finally she or he obtains details about shipment status without being aware that yet another back-end system—this time for logistics—is being interrogated. In this case at least four parties are involved: the customer, the online bookshop, the credit-card company and the shipping company. Several data elements are exchanged between them, such as transaction identification and customer details. In order to make this exchange possible, public or proprietary standards are required such as the WWW, SET and logistics data interchange.

Customer service is greatly enhanced by integrating the functionalities of the transaction parties on the basis of standardized information flows. The single point of entry, the online bookshop, becomes a full service centre, where the customer can handle almost all operations involved in purchasing a book, from browsing, selecting, ordering and paying to arranging for shipping. Not included, however, is the payment of customs or VAT charges that are due on importing into the country of destination. Offering a single full service point is an important means of capturing and binding the customer.

One-stop integration of functions—that is, integrating all the necessary functions for a transaction at a single point of access and with seamless flow of information between them, as illustrated by this example—is, however, only one aspect of integration. *Information integration* is another opportunity to extract additional value by analysing data from various steps of the transaction or across transactions. An online bookshop can use this to automatically replenish the stocks of books that are in highest demand. A business-to-business procurement intermediary like Tradezone or Citius (a third-party marketplace provider, see Chapter 3) can use information integration to bundle products from different suppliers if it turns out that these are frequently ordered together. This form of integration can be realized within one company or across companies, in value networks or other forms of business relationships, as will be addressed in detail in later chapters.

Intranets, Extranets and the Public Internet

Internet technologies provide internal and external remote access to business information. Information related to business is recorded and stored electronically. Low-cost and easy access to this information is now possible via open network protocols, often combined with the integration of legacy systems. This allows for completely new forms of business organization. Reengineering of business processes can happen within the company with access provided via the internal Internet, that is, intranet. It can also happen between businesses by giving preferred business partners partial access to internal company information using an extranet, which is a partial opening up of the intranet. The Marshall case in Chapter 4 provides a good illustration of using the public Internet as well as extranets and intranets to create new ways of doing business. New players in the market also create new forms of business organization. Examples of these are trusted third-party service providers or market brokers, who use the public Internet to collect and access business information. Generally, the introduction of the Internet (whether in the form of intranets, extranets or the public Internet) challenges the existing business organization.

BUILDING ASSETS TO CREATE CUSTOMER BENEFITS

In business-to-business applications the use of the Internet is argued to enhance business value,[24] bringing benefits to customers and improving suppliers' capabilities and asset base. The key assets are also the basis for creating sustainable competitive advantage. In other words, wherever key assets are described below, these should at the same time be seen as essential ingredients of the competitive strategy of a company. The next sections address the key assets and benefits in detail, with a summary provided in Table 2.2.

Table 2.2   *Supplier assets and customer benefits*

Lower cost base enables suppliers to price more competitively and customers to purchase at lower prices and/or reduce their internal transaction costs

Time-to-market reduction enables suppliers to compete in just-in-time markets or have fast product roll-out to capture market share, while customers can meet increasingly tighter time constraints, accelerate their learning curve or obtain benefits earlier for early exploitation in their own markets

Brand image of suppliers increases customer awareness and loyalty, while the customer will have more confidence in purchasing online and can reduce search and evaluation costs

Market share and access to markets for suppliers enables economies of scale and gives customers global sourcing and a standard reference point for connecting their business systems

Customer orientation, to enhance the product offering, generates new sources of revenue, captures proprietary information from customers, reduces service costs while increasing customer satisfaction through higher service levels, greater service availability with self-service and automated service, and more convenience and choice for customers

Quality, because suppliers can obtain more specific and supplier-owned customer information for customized products, increasing customer lock-in and loyalty, providing customers with enhanced 'fitness for *their* use'

Customer loyalty, since suppliers are able to have a captive customer base through new types of switching costs based on increased customer involvement such as one-to-one customer relationships, self-service and partnerships, while customers gain benefits such as a more complete and customized product/service offering

Functional integration, as a supplier capability, leads to reduced cost for customers and new services such as automatic upgrading and maintenance of equipment and supplier-managed inventory

Network integration—that is being the 'spider in the Web' based on business relationships, technology and the setting of standards—leads to lower transaction costs for customers, as search and interconnection costs are reduced, and higher value, as there are more parties that are interoperable and thus accessible to business

Innovation orientation for new products and services, based on close interaction with customers and competition monitoring to distinguish a supplier from the competition or at least stay equally competitive, while providing customers with new features according to their specific requirements or those of their peers

Innovation orientation to create new business models allows suppliers to obtain new sources of revenue, to change the 'rules of the game', to reposition relative to competition. Customers benefits depend on the business model and can include lower prices and reduced transaction costs, less time lost, more accurate information and new services and products.

Improvements in suppliers' asset base may not always be sustainable. The primary reason is that entry barriers are generally lower on the Internet than in traditional business and competitors may relatively easily gain similar benefits. The analysis of sustainability of competitive advantage is subject of the industry structure analysis, Chapter 5.

In many cases, delivering benefits to buyers can be used in a strategic way to strengthen key supplier assets. For example, reduced transaction costs for the customer can be expected to lead to an increase in market share for the supplier. However, some customer benefits will work against strengthening supplier assets. For example, increased customer choice will lead to customers switching suppliers or negotiating a better deal. Hagel and Armstrong (1997) argue that the combined effect will still be a win–win for both buyers and suppliers overall. Their argument is that reduced total transaction costs will make buyers purchase more of the same or lead to more buyers purchasing the good, whereas more sales will lead to better margins for the suppliers. Therefore, both the demand curve and the supply curve will shift to larger volumes. From the relevant case studies here (i.e. CitiusNet, Tradezone, Marshall, FedEx, where there are competitors providing the same good or service in a traditional, non-electronic way), it is not yet clear whether such a win–win is indeed the overall outcome. A more integrated study, also involving traditional suppliers, would be needed to answer this question.

Often business-to-business relationships are not purely of the seller–buyer nature, but may be more of a partnership. The benefits listed below are also applicable to such partnerships. The trends in industrial buying are towards more sophistication of the customer, a reduction of the number of suppliers and a stronger orientation towards supplier partnerships. Internet business-to-business commerce might reinforce this latter trend in industrial buying, namely that it is becoming more and more strategic and integrated into business processes (Egan, 1995). However, at the same time it could be argued that the Internet enables buyers to maintain many more relationships with suppliers and to engage increasingly in *ad hoc* relationships. Moreover, such relationships can more easily go beyond mere purchasing and also involve collaboration in design, R&D, product specification, marketing and other business functions.

Cost Base: Lower Transaction Costs and Better Prices

The costs of production and sales can decrease substantially. Cost reductions of a factor of 100 in certain process steps at the supplier end have been reported.[25] The ANX Internet-based automotive network that went into production in 1998 is expected to lead to a $70 cost saving on every car produced (Mace, 1997). Another form of cost reduction is in the provision of customer service. Fedex saved more than $10 million by allowing people to track packages themselves via the Internet rather than a service representative answering customer enquiries about the shipping of packages.[26] Sun Microsystems offers online customer support that has led to savings of over $4 million (Neece, 1995). Cisco's CEO Chambers commented at CEBIT'98 that his company is annually saving $400 million by selling its networking equipment via the Internet (at a total sales volume over the Internet of $3.6 billion, which was 41% of Cisco's total turnover at that time)[27]. Cost reduction in service is largely achieved by moving towards customer self-service, with the help of technology. Part of the cost reduction can be passed on to the customer.

Customers can significantly reduce transaction costs. Jelassi and Lai (1996) report that Texas Instruments, using CitiusNet, could reduce procurement costs for low-value non-strategic items from $200 to $5. CitiusNet itself calculated that a purchase order of $1000 traditionally carried an additional cost of $725 (in ordering, logistics and storage, sourcing and referencing, and accounting and finance). This cost was reduced to $180 through electronic purchasing. Savings were in all categories and were largest in ordering, logistics and inventory storage. Reduced inventory levels imply more inventory turns per year. They reduce the need for working capital that is locked up in goods in storage, as well as inventory interest, warehouse space cost and materials handling costs. With more inventory turns, delivery times from stock to customers also improve.

More choice should lead to more competition. With lower supplier costs, this should lead to lower prices. The extent to which this is already happening in business-to-business is not yet clear. It is even possible that total costs increase in B-to-C electronic commerce (taking into account the full cost, including shipping and customs).

Time to Market

The ability to distribute a product as soon as it has been created or with a tightly controlled timespan between order and delivery is important in many markets. Just-in-time delivery has been for years the hallmark of 'traditional' electronic commerce, e.g. in the automotive industry. The electronic delivery of designs or manufacturing instructions (numeric control) has enabled time delays to be reduced from days to minutes (for instance in the aerospace industry, see the Aerotech example in Upton and McAfee 1996).

The Internet can also enable companies to outpace competitors by being first to market. A strong example was the online distribution of pre-versions of the browser software as Netscape's competitive weapon to quickly capture a dominant market share in an emerging market.

Brand Image

Many industries use the Web to affirm or build their corporate identity and brand image. In business-to-business this is actively used by:

- established technology suppliers. Many 'old' computer companies like IBM, Digital, and HP have been using the Web in order to create the image of being a knowledgeable provider of this new kind of Internet hardware, software and business solutions. Deutsche Telekom/Globana considered to aim at a specific part of the market: to promote global engineering as an umbrella concept, a new way of thinking. By pushing this concept in association with its products, it tries to build a name as being a knowledgeable and advanced provider of collaborative engineering platforms;
- technology-oriented firms in order to raise their profile in a basically rather undifferentiated business among a technology-minded customer base (such as Marshall Industries, in electronic components);
- established providers of business information and services that see the Web making significant inroads into their existing business, such as Dun & Bradstreet or Gartner;
- newcomers, to build an image and establish a name through the Web (Peter Doyle, a business consultant, runs an Internet marketing discussion list and provides a Web newsletter on business-to-business Internet business solutions;[28] NanoTechnologies, in the high-tech field of advanced materials technologies where customers are likely to use the Internet, has a similar approach).[29]

Market Share and Market Access

The Internet allows companies to increase or build market share. CitiusNet's competitors include traditional industry catalogue sellers, which are competing in a rather undifferentiated business. CitiusNet is now taking market share away from them by proposing a new mode of industrial buying through its electronic catalogues. Marshall Industries is attempting to increase its share of the electronic components distribution market at the expense of its paper-based competitors. It can also profit from the 'back to core business' trend among large component manufacturers, which are willing to outsource part of their distribution and will look for an innovative, competitive distributor to take over this activity.

For new services, the name of the game is usually to establish and then maintain dominance in the market. An example is in support for online collaborative design and engineering, as considered to be offered by Deutsche Telekom/Globana with its Industrial Cooperation Service (ICS). In this case, competition is from large software and solutions providers such as EDS, who are building up experience in the US automotive industry with the ANX collaboration platform (Automotive Network Exchange). This will be an extranet solution involving 8000 suppliers and, eventually, 20 000 dealers—a development that is being closely watched by financial and healthcare industries and by the government and the automotive industry outside the USA (Mace, 1997).

Tradezone sees itself as being in competition with electronic catalogue providers rather than with the traditional paper-based cataloguers. It seeks to build market share rapidly knowing that market dominance will help to achieve economies of scale and thereby leverage the investment in technology. Its franchising approach is based on this reasoning.

ICS and Tradezone marketing goes hand in hand with attempting to set standards. The leadership role in controlling and/or being the first to implement and further develop a standard is expected to help in maintaining and reinforcing market share as a sustainable asset.

Potentially the Internet can help companies to make inroads into untapped or competitor-dominated markets. Such markets can exist all over the world, as the Internet has—in principle—global reach. However, as argued before, not many companies are yet able truly to exploit the global nature of the Internet in business-to-business commerce.

Customer Orientation

Internet and electronic commerce technologies help companies to build a strong asset in customer orientation, which brings benefits for customers in the form of improved service, convenience and choice.

Online technologies are developing rapidly to enhance customer service significantly, as well as to improve products, in terms of functionality and quality. Interactivity is key for:

- customer feedback on products and services;
- customer self-service facilities.

FedEx offers customers the possibility of tracking package deliveries online, as an adjunct to existing phone enquiries, thereby enhancing customer service. Marshall offers online self-training about the use of electronic components. Many companies in the software business notify their customers of software updates and patches, which they can subsequently download.

The Internet can greatly enhance customer convenience in purchasing or obtaining access to product-related information. Customer appreciation will be especially high if the non-Internet way is tedious and time consuming for the type of purchase that is considered to be a nuisance or an unavoidable 'must'. In B-to-C the standard example is groceries shopping. Examples in business-to-business are the ordering of routine supplies (e.g. components for car repairs or office supplies), or the booking of business flights and hotels. Other examples that lend themselves to building a competitive advantage by providing convenience are in offering access to basic market research data, company data and fact sheets. Specialized Web sites are starting to appear that aim to collect all conceivable information about a focused area, for example electronic components. Their business model may include charging for the information as well as generating income on the basis of their large Web traffic (e.g. from advertising).

Another example where convenience is the critical element is in the online auctioning of surplus stocks. Whereas it would otherwise be too much effort and too costly to announce that surplus stock is available for sale and to negotiate a price, this can now be done on the Internet in a matter of minutes. In this case, transaction costs are lowered to the extent that a market is created where before none existed, leading to a more efficient use of resources and less waste.

Customer choice increases, as much more information is readily available. In fact, a query about any product is likely to give many more 'hits' than one can handle, as well as interpretation problems as product description are usually not harmonized and easily comparable. It also leaves the impression that there might be important information missing. The opportunity, therefore, is to provide customers with much more targeted, relevant and complete information in a shorter time. Search engines and intelligent agents are individual technologies to perform this on an *ad hoc* basis. Shopping malls, industry marketplaces and collaborative environments seek to collect and structure information in advance of queries (e.g. Industry.Net or Global Engineering Network; see Chapter 4).

Quality

Can Internet electronic commerce be a tool for building a key asset in delivering quality or in other words, for enhancing 'fitness for use'? Some examples seem to indicate that this is indeed possible. In business-to-consumer electronic commerce, Levi's provides custom-made jeans, fitting exactly the measurements of the individual customer that have been transmitted over the Internet. At the same time, a customer profile is built that serves to provide perfectly fitting pair of jeans even faster the next time round.

In some process-flow industries, customers can follow online the quality of the bulk products that are going to be delivered to them for further processing. Monitoring their supplier's production process over the Internet enables them to tune their part of the production process optimally. The resulting closer integration between supplier and customer production processes provides a competitive advantage to the supplier.

Customer Loyalty and Switching Costs

Building and maintaining customer loyalty are particularly important issues in Internet commerce as customers get more and global choice and generally reduced switching costs, and because the customer is often not in personal contact with the supplier any more, or might even be anonymous. Personal relationships, so important in business-to-business marketing to build loyalty, have to be reassessed. However, the Internet also offers new ways of building customer loyalty, in particular through support for one-to-one marketing and brand image, working actively with customer feedback, as discussed above, by sharing cost benefits with the customer, rewarding the most valued customers,[30] by providing uniquely valued services, and through partnership building. Other forms of building customer loyalty come through providing special software and user interfaces that require an investment from the customer's side in training time, information supply and/or fees, and through contractual arrangements. All of these raise switching costs for the customer. An increasingly popular approach is to engage the customer in 'self-service', that is, offer the customer the possibility of navigating, searching, specifying preferences, finding solutions to problems etc., all within a workspace defined by the supplier. This brings multiple benefits, such as reducing work for the supplier, providing the customer with a customized solution and, above all, offering a way for the supplier to lock in the customer (as the customer may invest a considerable amount of time and effort in this self-service). Dolfsma (1999), who analysed this in the context of B-to-C electronic commerce, even sees consumers becoming 'subcontractors' to suppliers. In *Enterprise One to One* (Peppers and Rogers, 1997a), it is argued that an investment from the customer's side in building up an information base that is held at the supplier makes switching particularly difficult.

The companies studied, like Marshall and Tradezone, build customer loyalty through partnership schemes, which require significant personal investment, contractual arrangements, special software and customer-built information bases.

FedEx maintains customer-provided shipping lists of addresses and preferences. This type of customer profile is proprietary information, which, although provided by the customer, is in the hands of FedEx and would not be given to any competitor (not to mention the problem of lack of interoperability of customer-profiling systems).

Functional Integration

A supplier that has mastered the Internet and electronic commerce technologies in such a way that it can interconnect information systems across multiple parties in the value chain and let information flow across functional boundaries has many opportunities to deliver new benefits to customers. This is also a key asset for providing completely new products and services. Examples are in supplier-managed inventory, where the customer's and supplier's stock-management systems are tightly interconnected, or in customer-driven design.

Network Integration

A supplier that manages to be tightly connected to business partners, or who possesses a key facility with a network effect such as a *de facto* standard interconnection technology, is like a spider in a web. This supplier is in control and will be involved in some way or another in the business that is happening in the network. New market mediators, such as third-party marketplaces (see Chapter 3) or catalogue hosts, seek to obtain such a position. Platform providers like Microsoft and Cisco have obtained it already. Being in this pivotal position might be exploited monopolistically and can lead to customer lock-in with correspondingly reduced choice and increased switching costs, but can also be applied to bring important benefits to customers. Customers will lose less time in searching for partners or products, as they will orient themselves to the central reference point provided by the supplier. They are also more likely to find compatible products, services or partners, as the supplier provides interoperability with a positive network externality. Network integration, which is not a new kind of asset but certainly far less common outside Internet electronic commerce, thus is probably one of the most important ingredients for obtaining a sustainable competitive advantage.

Innovation Orientation—New Products and Services

Innovation is claimed to originate two-thirds from customers and one-third from within the company itself.[31] Listening to customers and, beyond that, engaging in a dialogue with the customer *and* listening to the comments that customers have to make to one another about the products, are important means of obtaining input for sustained innovation. To that end, companies are now regularly using, next to traditional means, e-mail response addresses, FAQ lists, discussion forums and online questionnaires. It is reported that in consumer-oriented virtual shopping malls, customer feedback is often implemented within a matter of hours. Seeing the result of their input additionally motivates customers. However, innovation at the user interface level is often difficult to protect. The top virtual shopping malls are constantly monitoring each other and rapidly copying improvements in their visual presentation on the Web.[32]

Virtual community facilities focus on customer-generated content. Companies can gain significant information for innovation by participating in such communities, although competitors will then have access to the same information. They can also add such facilities to their own product/service offer. As virtual community operators know well, stimulating customer-provided information does not come for free, but once a critical mass has been built a virtuous cycle sets in (Hagel and Armstrong 1997). An information base provided by customers can become an important asset for the company, as the information can be kept private to the company. The companies studied here invest to a varying extent in stimulating customer feedback and interaction and build new services from customer information, as addressed in Chapter 6.

Information for innovation and for other purposes such as better-targeted marketing can also be obtained from online use in an indirect way, by monitoring customer behaviour. In principle, each customer click can be tracked and to some extent be connected to the customer identity. Through click-through analysis companies can find out about interest in new product features (of which a demo or simulation can be provided online) or in experimental information services (by tracking visits and downloads). It is even possible to get an indication of potential customer interest in a new feature by offering a link that, once selected, returns a message like 'under construction' or 'coming real soon now'.

Yet another example of new information-based services is being piloted in the ESPRIT project LOGSME.[33] One of the partners in the project is Kewill, originally an EDI supplier. Via the Internet it collects a lot of information on its manufacturing and logistics planning packages that are installed at the customer site. This information is analysed to provide advice to the client—again via the Internet—for fine-tuning production.

Innovation Orientation—New Business Models

Many companies seek competitive advantage through innovation in processes and organization, and thereby intend to build a unique asset. The Internet provides tremendous opportunities for this type of innovation, which is categorized in Chapter 3. All the companies studied here are trying out new business models. However, the Internet also makes copying an interesting business model rather easy, for the following reasons:

- Often large parts of the business model logic are fully visible, as they have to be presented online on the public Internet.
- Attractive user interface elements can be copied and modified with readily available tools, and copyright protection can be circumvented easily.
- Underpinning technologies are often available from several suppliers—proprietary technologies are becoming increasingly rare.

Therefore protecting a business model requires a marketing strategy built on other assets too, such as dominance in the market, a strong brand image, proprietary access to customer information, favoured links to partners or relentless innovation.

SUMMARY

The Internet possesses a combination of features that makes it radically different from any other sales channel: ubiquitous and global presence, multimedia and immediate interactivity, digitization and integration, yet individualized handling of information all come together. Moreover, it is much more than merely a sales channel. Rather, it is a versatile tool for building assets that companies can exploit to deliver new benefits to customers. It can be used to reduce the cost of transactions and the amount of investments; it can significantly reduce time to market; it is a means of building a brand globally; it provides access to new markets or a new inroad into existing markets. Customers can benefit from lower prices, better service, improved quality and a much wider choice with greater convenience.

Yet the Internet also poses threats, such as lower customer-switching costs and reduced loyalty. Competition increases for market share, customer attention and innovation in the search for new ways to create value as price pressure increases. To make effective use of the Internet, new business models may be required. However, many aspects of these new business models, such as the concept and the user interaction, are not easily protected. These aspects can be readily copied as they are exposed through the Internet and the technology to implement them is becoming widely available. These emerging business models are the subject of the next chapter.

3
Business Models for Electronic Commerce

This chapter introduces a terminology and classification for business models in electronic commerce. A business model is defined as the organization (or 'architecture') of product, service and information flows, and the sources of revenues and benefits for suppliers and customers. This terminology will be applied in the subsequent case description in Chapter 4 and used for the analysis in Chapters 5 and 6, while Chapter 7 draws some conclusions about the applicability of the terminology and classification.

We present a systematic way of identifying architectures for business models, based on value-chain deconstruction and reconstruction, that is, identifying value-chain elements and identifying possible ways of integrating information along the chain. This also takes into account the possible creation of electronic markets. These can be fully open—that is, with an arbitrary number of buyers and sellers—or 'semi-open'—that is, with one buyer and multiple sellers, as in public procurement or vice versa.

While this systematic approach leads to a large number of potential business models, in practice only a small number of these can be observed being implemented. In the current classification, 11 such business models or generalizations of specific business models are included. Examples of all of these can be found on the Internet today. Some of these are still experimental, while others are in fully commercial operation. The selection of 11 has been made on the basis of background and case-study research.[34]

The chapter concludes with a qualitative mapping of the 11 business models along two dimensions. The first dimension is the extent of innovation of the business model, that is, whether the approach is essentially an electronic version of an existing 'physical world' business model or whether it is much more innovative. This dimension focuses attention on marketing approaches that have been translated from the physical world to cyberspace and actually calls for an assessment of the validity of this procedure. The second dimension is the extent of integration of information and functions along the value chain. It is along this dimension that we find that strategic choices are being made in a number of the cases studied in Chapter 4.

VALUE-CHAIN ANALYSIS AND BUSINESS MODEL ARCHITECTURES

The literature about Internet electronic commerce is not consistent in the usage of the term 'business model' and, moreover, often authors do not even provide a definition of the term. Therefore, before embarking on an approach to constructing business models, first a definition is given of a business model (see also Timmers 1997b, 1998b, 1998d).

Definition of 'Business Model'

- An architecture for product, service and information flows, including a description of the various business actors and their roles; and
- a description of the potential benefits for the various business actors; and
- a description of the sources of revenue.

A business model in itself does not yet provide understanding of how it will contribute to realizing the business mission and objectives of any of the companies that are actors within the model. We also need to know about the companies' marketing strategies in order to assess the commercial viability of the business model and to answer questions like how competitive advantage is being built, what the positioning is, what the marketing mix is, which product-market strategy is being followed. Therefore it is useful, beyond business models, also to define 'marketing models'.

Definition of 'Marketing Model'

- A business model; and
- the marketing strategy of the business actor under consideration.

The classification developed below is for business models only. Marketing models are analysed in the case studies. In reading this chapter, it is important to keep in mind that 'form follows function', that is, the business model should follow the marketing strategy; or at least the two cannot be seen as independent of each other. Indeed, there is likely to be only a limited number of possible combinations between business model and marketing strategy. To fully understand the business the marketing model should be analysed, rather than the business model on its own. The cases in Chapter 4 in fact illustrate some of the different marketing strategies for the same business model, namely that of third-party market-place provider. It is also shown what happens if a change of business model is not accompanied by an appropriate change of marketing strategy, in the case of an industrial mall operator that unsuccessfully attempted to become a third-party marketplace provider.

A systematic approach to identifying architectures for business models can be based on value-chain deconstruction and reconstruction—that is, identifying value-chain elements—and identifying possible ways of integrating information along the value chain. The framework is as follows:

- Value-chain deconstruction D means identifying the elements D_i of the value chain, for example as in Porter (1985), who distinguishes nine value-chain elements consisting of the primary elements of inbound logistics, operations, outbound logistics, marketing and sales, service; and as supporting elements technology development, procurement, human resource management and corporate infrastructure. A more detailed description can be obtained by using business processes instead of value-chain elements. However, there is not yet a standardized terminology for business processes.[35]

- Interaction patterns I, which can be for example 1:1, 1:many, many:1, many:many; these are identified with I_i, $i = 1..4$. In this context, '1:1' is to be understood in an enumerative sense rather than in the 'one-to-one marketing' sense. It is also understood that 'many' means integration or combination of information from several actors. This set of example interaction patterns simplifies the interaction description to a few macro-level types, which reduce the interaction in essence to the bilateral form. Alternatively, such a macro-level interaction could be broken down into a sequence or network description of multiple smaller bilateral interactions, or be extended with multilateral interactions, or be extended to a longer enumeration of the most important interaction types.

- Value-chain reconstruction $V(\{a\},\{b\})$, that is, integration of information processing across a number of steps of the value chain. $\{a\},\{b\}$ list the value chain elements involved in such integration of, respectively, party a and party b in the N:M relationship. If business processes are chosen as the unit of analysis, $\{a\},\{b\}$ would become a list of relevant business processes, either within each party or crossing the interaction between the parties (shared business processes).

Possible architectures for business models are then constructed by combining interaction patterns with value-chain integration. For example, an electronic shop is about single actor to single actor (1:1) marketing and sales. A basic electronic mall consists of N times an e-shop. An electronic mall built around a common brand offers many-to-1 marketing and sales (brand information is common across 'many' suppliers in the mall). An electronic auction where multiple buyers are bidding for the sales offer of one supplier brings together marketing and sales of one supplier with the procurement of multiple buyers, while combining the bid information from the multiple buyers.

The *a priori* feasibility of implementation of the architecture of any business model depends very much on the state of the art of the technology. This holds for the integration dimension, for the realization of the single functions and for the support for interaction patterns. The commercial viability of any business model is a different matter altogether.

The above approach stays within the concept of the value chain. However, the notion of 'chain', i.e. a linear sequence of activities, might no longer hold for certain types of electronic business (Bollier, 1996). For example, when inbound logistics is very tightly integrated with operations, just-in-time delivery of components for *individual steps* of the production (operations) process becomes possible. In that case, inbound logistics and operations are as much interlinked as are the individual steps of operations process. This can only be realized through intensive use of information and communications technology. Another example is in new forms of software distribution. When software under construction (a so-called β-version) is provided to customers in the way that companies like Netscape have done, this is accompanied by service support to customers, as they are essentially the ones doing the β-testing: operations and service become closely intertwined.

Value-chain elements are often associated with departments within companies. In electronic business, however, value-chain elements may come together in one person, rather than in one department. As an example, procurement will be revolutionized through information technology when this is brought to the desk of each and every manager. In this vision, the role of the central procurement department—if it remains—becomes much more one of policy setting and technology exploration, rather than provision of support activity to the primary activities. Likewise, in flexible work for a project, where human resources are contracted on an *ad hoc* basis, the key issue is to select the skills needed for the project at a particular moment, with the support of information technology. This is a human resource management function that is to be in the hands of the operational (project) manager, rather than the personnel department.

We observe, from actual business on the Internet and pilot projects, that:

- information and communications technology enables a wide range of business models;
- the capability of the state-of-the-art technology is just one criterion in model selection;
- guidance to technology development can come from the definition of new models;
- many of the conceivable models have not yet been experimented with commercially.

CURRENT BUSINESS MODELS

While the systematic approach of the previous section leads to a huge number of potential business models, we observe in practice only a small number of these being implemented. In this section, 11 such business models (or generalizations) are described in more detail. Examples of all of these can be found on the Internet today. Some are still experimental, while others are in fully commercial operation. The more general approach presented above remains useful in order to identify further business models.

E-shops

This is Web marketing of a company or a shop. In the first instance it is done to promote the company and its goods or services. Any company that creates a Web site just to have a Web presence can be considered to have created a very basic e-shop (even though the Web site may be quite sophisticated and artful in terms of the user interface). The possibility of ordering and possibly paying is increasingly added to this very basic e-shop, often combined with traditional marketing channels. Benefits sought for the company are increased demand, a low-cost route to global presence,[36] and cost reduction in promotion and sales. Benefits for the customer can be lower prices compared to the traditional offering, wider choice, better information and convenience in selecting, buying and delivery, including 24-hour availability. Where repeat visits to the e-shop are made, one-to-one marketing can increase those benefits for both seller and buyer. Seller revenues are from reduced cost, increased sales and possibly advertising.

Most commercial Web sites are business-to-consumer electronic shops, selling for example flowers (e.g. Fleurop, http://www.fleurop.com) or airline tickets (TISS, http://www.tiss.com; Travelocity, http://www.travelocity.com). An example of a business-to-business e-shop is Merck's (http://www.merck-ltd.co.uk), for laboratory equipment and products. It offers browsing through the company product catalogue for non-registered users, and extends this to online ordering and payment for existing (offline-registered and validated) Merck customers. Many ISPs are now becoming e-shop providers, that is, they are building and hosting e-shops for others.

E-procurement

This is electronic tendering and procurement of goods and services. Large companies or public authorities may implement some form of e-procurement on the Web. An example is Japan Airlines (http://www.jal.com). Benefits sought include having a wider choice of suppliers, which is expected to lead to lower cost, better quality, improved delivery, reduced cost of procurement (e.g. tendering specifications are downloaded by suppliers rather than mailed by post). Electronic negotiation and contracting and possibly collaborative work in specification can further enhance time and cost savings and convenience. For suppliers, the benefits are in more tendering opportunities, possibly on a global scale, lower cost of submitting a tender, and possibly tendering in parts that may be better suited for smaller enterprises, or collaborative tendering (if the e-procurement site supports forms of collaboration). The main source of income is reduction of cost (of tender processing, and getting more cost-effective offers).

E-malls

An electronic mall, in its basic form, consists of a collection of e-shops, usually enhanced by a common umbrella, for example of a well-known brand. It might be enriched by a common—guaranteed—payment method. An example is Electronic Mall Bodensee (http://www.emb.ch), giving entry to individual e-shops. When they specialize in a certain market segment, such malls become more of an industry marketplace, like Industry.Net (http://www.industry.net/), which can add further value by virtual community features (FAQ, discussion forums, closed user groups etc.). Industry.Net is discussed in detail in Chapter 4. The e-mall operator may not have an interest in an individual business that is being hosted. Instead, the operator may seek benefits in enhanced sales of the supporting technologies (e.g. IBM with World Avenue). Alternatively, benefits are sought in services (e.g. Barclays with BarclaySquare), or in advertising space and/or brand reinforcement or in collective benefits for the e-shops that are hosted such as increased traffic, with the expectation that visiting one shop on the e-mall will lead to visits to 'neighbouring' shops.

Benefits for the customer (real or hoped for) are the benefits for each individual e-shop (see above), with the additional convenience of easy access to other e-shops and ease of use through common user interface elements. When a brand name is used to host the e-mall, this is expected to enhance the trust and confidence of customers, and therefore increase readiness to buy.

Benefits for the e-mall members (the e-shops) are lower cost and complexity of being on the Web, with sophisticated hosting facilities such as electronic payments, and additional traffic generated from other e-shops on the mall, or from the attraction of the hosting brand.

Revenues are from membership fees (which can include a contribution to software/hardware and set-up cost as well as a service fee), advertising and possibly a fee on transactions (if the mall provider processes payments).

There are some indications that the e-mall model has certain flaws in its current implementation and in the current state of the market. IBM World Avenue, for example, has ceased operation. One of the reasons may be that the 'neighbour' concept does not translate into physical distance in cyberspace, where each location is only one click away. Therefore, not much additional convenience in finding shops is delivered. Furthermore, the sophisticated user (i.e. the majority of those on the Web today!) is able to handle a variety of seller–buyer user interfaces and therefore may be less attached to a uniform user interface. On the other hand, there are also indications that an increasing number of companies wish to outsource their Web operations,[37] which may increase the opportunity for e-malls or third-party marketplaces (see below). This possibly reflects a shift from early adopters to mass-market use of the Internet among businesses.

E-auctions

Electronic auctions (on the Internet) offer an electronic implementation of bidding mechanisms also known from traditional auctions. This can be accompanied by multimedia presentation of the goods. Usually they are not restricted to this single function. They may also offer integration of the bidding process with contracting, payments and delivery. The sources of income for the auction provider are in selling the technology platform, in transaction fees and in advertising. Benefits for suppliers and buyers are increased efficiency and time savings, no need for physical transport until the deal has been established, and global sourcing. Because of the lower cost, it becomes feasible to offer small quantities of low value, e.g. surplus goods for sale. Sources of income for suppliers are in reduced surplus stock, better utilization of production capacity, and lower sales overheads. Sources of income for buyers are in reduced purchasing overhead cost and reduced cost of goods or services purchased. Examples of business-to-business electronic auctions are Infomar,[38] which is discussed in more detail in Chapter 4, and FastParts (http://www.fastparts.com).

Virtual Communities

The ultimate value of virtual communities comes from the members (customers or partners), who add their information on to a basic environment provided by company operating the virtual community. Membership fees as well as advertising generate revenues. A virtual community can also be an important add-on to other marketing operations in order to build customer loyalty and receive customer feedback (see Hagel and Armstrong, 1997).

Virtual communities are already abundant within specific market sectors, for example in books such as Amazon.com (discussed in detail in Chapter 4), in apparel/garments (http://www.apparelex.com/bbs/index.htm), in the steel industry (http://www.indconnect.com/steelweb/), in nanotechnology (http://www.nanothinc.com/), and many others. Firefly provides an interesting case of virtual community building, adding value to the community by building customer profiles (http://www.firefly.net/). Virtual communities are also becoming an additional function to enhance the attractiveness and opportunities for new services of several of the other business models listed here (e.g. e-malls, collaborative platforms, or third-party marketplaces).

Collaboration Platforms

These provide a set of tools and an information environment for collaboration between enterprises. This can focus on specific functions, such as collaborative design and engineering, or on project support to a virtual team, for example a team of consultants. Business opportunities are in managing the platform (membership/usage fees) and in selling the

Table 3.1   *Internet business models (1)*

- *E-shop*: promotion, cost reduction, additional outset (seeking demand)
- *E-procurement*: cost reduction, additional outlet (seeking suppliers)
- *E-auction*: electronic bidding (no need for prior movement of goods or parties)
- *E-mall*: collection of e-shops, aggregators, industry sector marketplace
- *Third-party marketplace*: common marketing front end and transaction support to multiple businesses

specialist tools (e.g. for design, workflow, document management). Examples are in the products and projects spun off from the Global Engineering Network concept (Rethfeld, 1994), such as Deutsche Telekom/Globana's Industrial Cooperation System (GEN/ICS), discussed in detail in Chapter 4, the ESPRIT project GENIAL, and in experimental projects for 3D collaborative design and simulation.[39]

Third-party Marketplaces

This is an emerging model that is suitable if companies wish to leave Web marketing to a third party. Often, therefore, the third-party marketplace is an additional, online channel to other existing channels, including physical outlets. They all have in common that they offer at least a user interface to the suppliers' product catalogues. Several or all of the additional features, such as branding, payment, logistics, ordering and, ultimately, the full-scale implementation of secure transactions are added to third-party marketplaces. An example in business-to-consumer electronic commerce is providing common marketing around a special one-off event profiled by well-known brand names, such as the 1997 e-Christmas experiment.[40] ISPs may be interested in this model for business-to-business, using their Web builder expertise. However, it may equally appeal to banks or other value-chain service providers. Revenues can be generated on the basis of a one-off membership fee, service fees or a percentage of transaction values. Examples of third-party marketplace providers in MRO products are Citius[41] and Tradezone (http://tradezone. onyx.net/), which are analysed as case studies in Chapter 4. An interesting third-party marketplace in retail is the Internet Megastore project, which is being piloted in food/groceries and furniture retail chains and as an enhancement of physical shopping malls. The chain or mall manager sets up an online version of the set of shops, with support for online ordering and payment where appropriate. Each shop owner can enhance the basic Web site and product offer with his or her own promotions and brand enhancement. The concept accommodates the virtual as well as the physical world, for example delivery and additional services are still assumed to be happening in the physical stores. It thus strengthens local presence and geographic concentration, which can especially benefit small retailers. An example implementation in local communities such as small cities is LocalEurope.com.

Value-chain Integrators

These focus on integrating multiple steps of the value chain, with potential to exploit the information flow between those steps as further added value. Revenues come from consultancy fees or possibly transaction fees. An example value chain integrator is TRANS2000 in the area of multi-modal transport.[42] Marshall offers its customers added value from transaction information, which is provided through extranet solutions like PartnerNet and MarshallNet, discussed in detail in Chapter 4. Some of the third-party marketplace providers are moving in the direction of value-chain integration.

Value-chain Service Providers

These specialize in a specific function for the value chain, such as electronic payments or logistics, with the intention of making that into their distinct competitive advantage. Banks, for example, have been positioning themselves in this way for a long time and may now find fresh opportunities using the open Internet network. New approaches are also emerging in production/stock management, where the specialized expertise needed to analyse and fine-tune production is offered by new intermediaries. A fee- or percentage-based scheme is the basis of revenues.

Examples of value-chain service providers are FedEx (http://www. fedex.com; see also the FedEx case study in Chapter 4) or UPS (http:// www.ups.com), who provide Web-based logistics support.

Information Brokerage, Trust and Other Services

A whole range of new information services are emerging, to add value to the huge amounts of data available on the open networks or coming from integrated business operations, such as information search, e.g. Yahoo (http://www.yahoo.com), customer profiling, business opportunities brokerage, investment advice etc. Information and consultancy may have to be paid for either through subscription or on a pay-per-use basis, although advertising schemes are also common. For example, Excite, an information portal, relies 75% on income from advertising.

A special category is trust services, as provided by certification authorities and electronic notaries and other trusted third parties. These services charge subscription fees combined with one-off service fees, with software sales and consultancy as additional sources of revenue. Example of trust service providers are Verisign (http://www.verisign.com), Belsign (http:// www.belsign.be) and many others.

Many consultancy and market research companies are now offering commercial business information services via the Internet. Search engines are a special category of information services, with the public Internet facility (rather than intranet versions) usually based on advertising as a source of revenue. Advanced information brokerage to support negotiation between businesses is being developed by the **ESPRIT CASBA** and MEMO projects (http://www.cordis.lu/esprit/src/home.htm).

Table 3.2 *Internet business models (2)*

- *Virtual community*: focuses on added value of communication between members
- *Value-chain service provider*: supports part of value chain, e.g. logistics, payments
- *Value-chain integrator*: adds value by integrating multiple steps of the value chain
- *Collaboration platforms*: business process cooperation, e.g. collaborative design
- *Information brokers/trust providers*: business information and consultancy, trusted third-party services

CLASSIFICATION

A qualitative mapping of these 11 business models on two dimensions is shown in Figure 3.1. The first dimension is the degree of innovation. This ranges from essentially an electronic version of a traditional way of doing business to more innovative ways, for example by externalizing via the Internet functions that previously were performed within a company or by offering functions that did not exist before. The second dimension is the extent of integration of functions, ranging from single-function business models (e.g. e-shops that only provide the marketing function over the Internet) to fully integrated functionality (e.g. value-chain integration).

In the lower left-hand corner of Figure 3.1 are basic e-shops, which are merely electronic versions of traditional ways of selling. At the other extreme, in the upper right-hand corner, is value-chain integration, which cannot be done at all in a traditional form, as it is critically dependent on

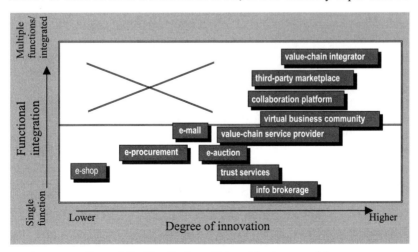

Figure 3.1 *Classification of Internet business models*

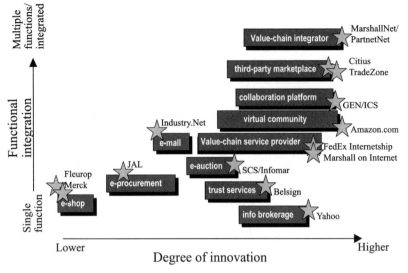

Figure 3.2 *Examples of Internet business models*

information technology for letting information flow across networks and creating added value from integrating these information flows. In between are business models that often find some degree of analogy in non-electronic business. For example, trust services have been provided for years by public notaries or by industry bodies. Their functionality is being reimplemented by electronic trust services. However, at the same time new trust functionality is being added that intrinsically requires IT support, such as encryption and public and private key management. The same holds for value-chain service provision, such as electronic payments support. This is partly a matter of offering by electronic means the same as what is already being offered non-electronically, such as account management. At the same time, new functionality is being provided such as Internet smart-card support, e.g. for purchase cards in business-to-business trading.

Figure 3.2 maps a number of the examples mentioned in this chapter on the business models classification. Some companies run several business models at the same time, as will be illustrated for Marshall and Amazon in the next chapter.

TRENDS AND EVOLUTION

At least two trends can be observed in business models (see Figure 3.3):

1. A move towards increased integration of information flows.
2. The development of specialized, highly innovative services.

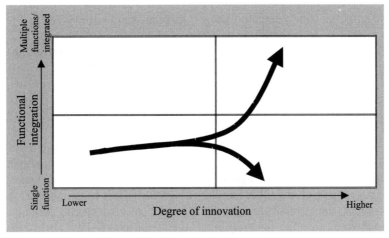

Figure 3.3   *Trends in business models*

An example of the first trend is the integration of transaction-handling functions into industry malls. Examples of the second trend are the specialization in information brokerage or trusted-third party services. These two trends are obviously related to the marketing strategy of the companies involved and the competitive pressures in their markets.

Some companies seek to generate additional value or increase their grip on the market by offering related products and services. For example, Amazon.com has expanded its offer with CDs and gifts, and might consider offering a range of other off-the-shelf consumer items such as magazine subscriptions, software, apparel and others.[43] Many e-shops are upgrading their services by adding online payment support. Such added functionality very often goes together with increased integration, where customer data from one part of the online application are reused in another part, e.g. to smooth the payment process by avoiding reentering customer data, or in order to do cross-sales. Such integration is also demonstrated by a number of the cases described in Chapter 4.[44]

Other companies seek to profile themselves as specialists in a specific service, e.g. as a search agent (cf. AltaVista or Acses) or trust provider. Again, this is related to their marketing strategy and competitive pressures.

Trust provision, for example, can be expected to become increasingly important as a global service. A trust service company may well believe that its market is a truly global one (e.g. to provide certificates for national as well as international business). For such a company it makes sense to pursue a global presence and thereby capture market share and increase value for customers that need trust guarantees across borders, rather than investing in additional trading services such as payment support etc.

Typically, the newly created trust service companies such as Verisign tend to pursue such a globalization strategy. The other example mentioned before, Belsign, is now expanding under the name GlobalSign in Europe, where the cross-border provision of certificates is expected to become very important as a consequence of the importance of trade within the European Single Market. These companies also attempt to piggyback on the global roll-out of browsers, by being packaged into the default browser configuration.

A question that naturally arises is whether there will be sufficient added value from a 'pure' trust or 'trust-only' service. Or are such companies ultimately only viable in a partnership with 'richer' service providers?

Considering on the other hand the long-established trust providers such as banks, the tendency seems to be to pursue a marketing strategy of added value through integration, cf. the evolution of the Isabel banking association in Belgium (see also Chapter 4). However, the globalization of the banking world and of its customers may well lead the banks to increase the emphasis on globalization of their specialized trust or financial services. An example is the announcement by a group of banks and financial companies of a global certificate service.[45] Whether they can and indeed intend to maintain a high level of integration remains to be seen.

Several of the business models rely heavily on advertising for their revenue (e-malls, search engines as information brokers). The expectation has been that a significant part of corporate non-Internet advertising would move to the Internet. The early exponential growth of ad revenue did seem to confirm this. However, there are indications that the growth will be slowing down. More and more advertising-oriented Web sites are entering the market. The effectiveness of Webvertising is dropping, reflecting the fact that the simple transposition of advertising on non-interactive media such as TV, newspapers, magazines, billboards to the Net isn't going to be realized. Therefore, if ad revenues do not grow as fast as expected, the Web companies relying on them will be forced to look for other sources of revenue, such as information subscription fees or transaction fees. Pursuing the latter, they will move in the direction of third-party marketplace providers (see also Chapter 5).

The business models are not always mutually exclusive. For example, virtual communities lend themselves to being combined with almost any of the other models. Often virtual community facilities (discussion lists, FAQs, user forums) are added without charge to the participants, with a view to enhancing customer loyalty, e.g. with British Telecom's privilege site, which itself is essentially a marketing front end for BT (http://www.infoexchange.bt.com/public/ohome.cfm). The virtual community facility can also be considered as a separate source of income coming from advertising. Membership fees are another possible source of income, although a prospective member would expect a clear list of products/ services to be provided, rather than paying for the somewhat uncertain value coming from the other members.[46] Another example of combining business models is the partnership between ONSALE Inc. and VerticalNet, which provides auctions for business-to-business, industry-sector-specific e-malls. From each of VerticalNet's 20 'vertical trade' communities, where regular catalogue-based purchases can be made, one is able also to access an e-auction operated by ONSALE. The e-auction part takes care of buying/selling excess stock and capacity.[47] Clearly, the two business models complement each other.

SUMMARY

This chapter provides a classification of 11 business models that are currently found in Internet electronic commerce (business-to-business as well as business-to-consumer). Some of these models are essentially an electronic reimplementation of traditional forms of doing business, such as e-shops. Many others go far beyond traditional business, such as value-chain integration, and seek innovative ways to add value through information management and a rich functionality. Creating these new business models is feasible only because of the openness and connectivity of the Internet. A consequence of the same open nature of the Internet is that it may be rather difficult to keep the details of a business model hidden. The possibility is not excluded, however, of protecting the intellectual property of a business model by legal means. For instance, Priceline.com acquired a US patent in August 1998 for its reverse auction business model.

The terminology and classification developed in this chapter are used in the subsequent chapters to describe and analyse a number of cases.

4
Business-to-Business Electronic Commerce Cases

INTRODUCTION AND OVERVIEW OF SELECTED CASES

This chapter presents eight cases in business-to-business electronic commerce. The case approach has been chosen to obtain a better understanding and illustration of the issues in business-to-business electronic commerce marketing, without attempting to be exhaustive. The first four cases all happen to be from the USA and have been investigated on the basis of literature surveys, Web research (including the Web sites of the companies concerned and their customers where possible), online discussion lists, personal communications and conference presentations. The second set of four cases, from Europe, have also been investigated by all those means, with in addition structured interviews with company CEOs.

These cases illustrate most of the emerging Internet business models of Chapter 3. They include technology users as well as providers. They represent add-ons to existing business, as well as new companies that are creating a completely new business (see Table 4.1). Some of the businesses analysed are operating in a highly specialized niche, while others are oriented towards mass-market commodity products or services. The case interviews and descriptions have been structured after marketing analysis frameworks as in Dibb *et al.* (1991) and Kotler (1991), as well as the marketing planning framework provided by McDonald (1997).

The cases are the following:

- *Marshall Industries* is probably one of the most-studied companies in business-to-business marketing. Ample description is available. NetMarketing selected Marshall as the best example of B-to-B marketing in 1997.[48] Marshall has added electronic commerce, centred around electronic catalogues, to its existing business in electronic components distribution.

Table 4.1 *Overview of cases*

Case	Business	Add-on (A) or new (N) business	Niche (N) or mass-market commodity (C)	User (U) or provider (P) of technology
Marshall	Electronic components distribution	A	N	U
Fedex	Shipping/logistics	A	C	U + P
Industry.Net	Industry marketplace	N	C	U
Amazon	Book distribution	N	C	U
CitiusNet	Electronic catalogues/ third-party marketplace	N	C	P
Tradezone	Electronic catalogues/ third-party marketplace	N	C	P
GEN/ICS	Collaborative design and engineering/catalogues	A	N	P
Infomar	Fisheries auction	A	N	U + P

- FedEx is using electronic commerce as an enhancement of its existing business. The focus is on logistics, a specific business service, to which FedEx is adding further value through electronic means. FedEx is fairly well known from the literature. Use was also made of its contribution to the *Business on the Web* conference in Paris in May 1996, organized by the European Commission and the W3C Consortium.[49]

- *Industry.Net* (Nets Inc) is one of the first examples of an industrial virtual marketplace, and started as a completely new venture, rather than as an add-on to an existing business. It is interesting to study as it has been pioneering a new business model and has already gone through various phases in its lifecycle, including bankruptcy and resurrection.

- *Amazon.com*'s Associates and Advantage programmes are addressed as they provide important examples of industry-sector-oriented global marketing in business-to-business electronic commerce. In this book the emphasis is less on the business-to-consumer aspects of Amazon, although its importance in building a virtual community of consumers and in creating a strong Internet brand is clearly recognized.

- *CitiusNet or Citius* is in the third-party marketplace business, in a generic, non-sector-specific way, with its origins in pre-Internet elec-tronic commerce (EDI) and now moving into the Internet environment. Similarities and differences can be found in relation to catalogue-based forms of electronic commerce (e.g. Marshall), as well as to new business operations like Industry.Net, GEN and Tradezone.

- *Tradezone*, a recent Internet business venture, has a strong component in electronic catalogues. As with CitiusNet, this is provided as a generic solution, while adding other technologies such as Internet payments and security. Its focus is on acting as a third-party marketplace. The comparison of business models and marketing strategies between Tradezone and Citius is of particular interest.
- *Global Engineering Network/ICS* goes beyond an engineering-oriented collection of product catalogues to propose a new business venture, namely collaborative design and engineering. This is a completely different kind of electronic commerce.
- *Infomar* is an extension of an existing business, providing an electronic auction while addressing in an integral way the associated business processes and industry sector organization (fisheries). Of interest in this case are the new business model and the marketing strategy that has to address a conservative market in which the way of doing business has been established over many years.

MARSHALL INDUSTRIES: A NEW CHANNEL WITH ADDED VALUE

Business

Marshall[50] is an electronic components distributor, a 'junction box' between 100 major US and Japanese manufacturers and 30 000 customers worldwide (from very small, one-off customers to very large and long-term ones), distributing 125 000 different products. Marshall employs 2280 people and had 1998 sales of nearly $1.5 billion.

Customers

Customers of electronics distributors value product availability, competitive pricing, customer service, and technical expertise and distribution coverage. In addition to the physical distribution of components, distributors have increasingly taken on tasks such as technical support, processing payments and accounts receivable, offering credit and inventory, personnel and IT investment. The semiconductor industry is cyclical, causing major delivery and inventory problems. Large customers are global, requiring global sourcing. Time-based/time-to-market competition and mass customization at the customer end require a fast and flexible response from distributors (product lifecycles can be as short as three months). Just-in-time and supplier-managed inventory are increasingly required from the distributors. These demands require tight integration of information along the value chain (Young *et al.*, 1996).

Products and Services

Marshall has been pioneering the use of the Internet and IT applications, with a view to reengineering its business and creating new competitive strengths. Current Internet-related products and services as well as others form an impressive range, from very simple product information to sophisticated support integrating information from sales and marketing with manufacturing. Internet-based services include:

- *MarshallNet intranet*: to support its 400 field sales employees, who are equipped with laptops and have access to a 'marketing encyclopaedia' of details about component suppliers and their product lines. This enables staff, in real-time, to check inventory and product specifications, quote orders, communicate with other employees, collaborate on projects and make presentations. This intranet is integrated with PartnerNet, the extranet.
- *Marshall on the Internet*: through the Web customers can get information about products, prices and availability; order parts; request samples; do online order tracking (with UPS); find electronics industry news in text, pictures, audio. Online, real-time, 24-hour discussion with Marshall engineers for sales assistance, trouble shooting and product design expertise is offered as direct support by a separate company called @ONCE. A special service, @ONCE/VAR, targets value-added resellers, e.g. companies that buy a selection of components and assemble these as a new product, such as a customized PC.
- Internet access is complemented by a *telephone system* to meet customers' need to speak to a real person, and which like the Internet is available 24 hours a day, seven days a week.
- *SEI on the Internet*: SEI is a strategic European partner to Marshall, offering MarshallNet features in 17 languages, with additional information about local events and specials.
- *MarshallNet PartnerNet*: allows registered customers and suppliers to access parts of the intranet, where they find customized Web pages, their purchase history and customer-specific prices. In addition it offers electronic payments. For components manufacturers this offers insight into product and customer sales patterns. A Manufacturing Account Profile Planner profiles customer projects and Internet visits, to allow a manufacturer to do its own planning.
- *Electronic Design Center*: provides customers with technical specs and download simulation software, making available inexpensive 'virtual

components' testing and saving customers' time. This can go as far as Marshall having sample components produced at customers' request.

- *NetSeminar*: provides real-time audio and video seminars over the Internet, bringing together potential customers and suppliers who design new products. Presentations are archived for future look-up. Participants have live interaction.
- *ENEN*: Education News and Entertainment Network is a separate consulting activity that has grown out of the NetSeminar concept of live Internet. It has broad application, such as interactive public product announcements, sales training etc.

Competition

Distribution of components is characterized by fierce competition and thin margins (in the case of Marshall, income/netsales = 3% in 1998 and 4.4% in 1996). Consolidation has been happening aiming at economies of scale. Major manufacturers tend to require exclusivity from distributors, which also have to compete against direct distribution by manufacturers. Distributors are also threatened by disintermediation through direct electronic distribution, which Marshall set out to counter. Marshall argues that its competition in the future is no longer a given entity, as the industry is fluid, with continually shifting boundaries between organizations and strategic alliances. Benchmarking against the competition is not relevant instead its measure is customer value.

Marketing Strategy

Marshall has followed a comprehensive strategy since 1991, its mission being to realize 'Free, Perfect, Now' for its customers (which includes suppliers), while providing constant value innovation (Young *et al.*, 1996). Having analysed the electronics distribution business environment and trends as well as its internal organization, Marshall set out to make radical changes inside the organization and in its support of customers. The aim was to improve its short-term performance, as well as continuously provide new opportunities by creating new customer value. The option that this would ultimately lead to redefining the business scope is not excluded (viz ENEN) (Venkatraman, 1994).

The changes addressed the following:

- the company value system based on continuous improvement and innovation with partners, and 'customer intimacy';

- the organizational set-up based on teams, flat hierarchy, with decision making by those closest to the decision, and a compensation scheme based on common profit sharing, no commissions (to get rid of one-person sales acts and unproductive internal bonus competition);
- information technology being applied pervasively, with the internal and external systems described before.

Marshall's marketing strategy can be characterized as being:

- customer centric rather than competition focused;
- positioning itself as an enabler of value creation in a dynamic 'value constellation' of customers and suppliers; its presence on the Internet is a part of that approach;
- competing on value innovation, allowing for any new products, services and relationships that can exploit the intellectual asset (which is seen as the most important asset);
- using IT as an enabler to create value between customers and suppliers;
- willingness to adapt the organization to this strategy.

Summary—Marketing Model

Marshall's business model began with being a value-chain service provider in a particular industry sector. The basic service is access to catalogues of electronic components. Beyond that service, Marshall has enriched the intermediation function (to better guide the customer in the selection of components) and integrated additional-value chain functions (such as payments). Therefore, Marshall has moved more towards value-chain integration. In addition, new business has been created, such as online training (another value-chain service provision). While it is hotly debated whether electronic commerce is leading to disintermediation, one can see that Marshall is an example that negates the disintermediation hypothesis.

FEDEX: FROM LOGISTICS TO GENERIC ELECTRONIC BUSINESS SERVICES

Business

Federal Express (Goldhoff and Skoog, 1996) is best known for its world-wide express shipping of packages. It has operations in 211 countries, with more than 500 cargo aircraft, and employs 122 000 people, delivering more than 2.5 million packages every working day.

Products and Services

FedEx started to offer Internet services in 1995, namely allowing customers to obtain the status of their shipments with the help of a reference number that the customer types into the Web front end of the online tracking system. FedEx InternetShip now offers additional customer services, including onscreen preparation of air-shipment documents and printing by the customer, storage of address books at the FedEx server and management of shipping history information. InternetShip functions to:

- enhance customer service and save cost for the customer in preparing shipments;
- save cost for FedEx in answering customer calls;
- generate additional shipments from its hook into online sales sites (see e.g. Virtual Vineyards).

FexEx VirtualOrder is an expansion from shipping into helping businesses to get online. A business (merchant) gets software to set up an online catalogue that resides on a FedEx secure server. This user interface hooks into a FedEx order-handling system, which registers online customer orders and assigns confirmation numbers, passes the order to software at the merchant, who packs the order, possibly with automatic inventory updating. The merchant software generates shipping labels for shipment by FedEx. The online tracking system allows both customer and merchant to track orders online. Peppers and Rogers quote the system as a success story of one-to-one marketing[51] (for an assessment of this claim see the analysis in Chapter 6). VirtualOrder creates two sources of revenues, as it:

- extends FedEx business into order-handling services;
- generates additional shipping business.

FedEx Learning Lab is a service that is 'dedicated to helping companies maximize their use of distribution as a strategic weapon'. FedEx provides training about logistics in general. The Learning Lab can contribute to:

- an additional source of revenues, in training and consultancy;
- building the image of Fedex as *the* logistics company (i.e. more than just worldwide shipments).

Customers

FexEx is not very specific about the customers it targets with VirtualOrder. Essentially any business with a catalogue that wants to go on to the Internet is being addressed. The only requirement is that the business will ship orders via FedEx. However, the VirtualOrder service is currently only being offered in the USA and for US exports. One reason for that may be that the sales process of the VirtualOrder service itself is only performed in a limited way via the Internet. As soon as a potential customer has gone through the basic information about the service that is available on the Internet, a sales representative needs to be contacted for further steps (contrary to, for example, Amazon.com Associates, where the full sales process is being done online). Possibly FedEx cannot offer that type of sales support internationally.

Competition

FedEx competitors are primarily other express package companies like UPS, DHL and TNT, which have essentially the same profile, as well as more locally oriented fast-delivery companies which might compete on speed and customer service and the postal services in general (who usually already have a specialized package-shipping business unit). InternetShip exploits shipping as a generic global business service, and as such is in competition with similar facilities from UPS and others. The same holds for VirtualOrder when positioned as an easier way to integrate a generic, critical worldwide business service. However, VirtualOrder's catalogue facility competes with many others offering such *front-end* services (e.g. CitiusNet, Tradezone, as well as large platform providers such as Microsoft with Merchant Server etc). Finally, the Learning Lab, if intended as a commercial service, competes with many others who provide such logistics consultancy and training to corporate clients as well as to small companies (in Europe, for example, Logica or CMG).

Although FedEx does not yet offer VirtualOrder outside the USA, it might be well placed to do so. Its direct competitor in the shipping business, UPS, demonstrated that international shipping companies might have a key asset, namely their knowledge of the complexities of international shipments with respect to customs and taxation. In the UPS case this became clear from its central and critical role in the business-to-consumer e-Christmas experiment referred to before.

Some of FedEx's large competitors, building on their shipping experience, are starting to go into more integrated logistics *back-end* services, in particular stock management combined with shipping. For example, UPS provides this as the basis for shipping the several million titles in Amazon's online bookstore. Other value-chain services such as digital certification are also a logical extension of the shipping business, as being explored for example by UPS and some postal operators such as the UK Royal Mail.

FedEx, and the other large express package companies, are also being challenged by small companies, which combine low investment and tight integration of customer service with a dispatch service for efficient scheduling and knowledge of the individual customer (e.g. usual shipping addresses, most frequently used delivery service) for one-to-one marketing.[52] Such services beat the competition by being faster for local deliveries, with a better-quality response to individual customers delivery needs.

Marketing Strategy

FedEx's mission for the WWW is to 'leverage its global brand name while enabling locally relevant activities' (Goldhoff and Skoog, 1996). Its Internet business model is focused on being the best in providing online use of fast and worldwide shipping of packages: a single critical generic global business service. Its entry point for business is InternetShip and it is actively building awareness of this service among online businesses through banner advertising, always in combination with its logo for brand building.

Summary—Marketing Model

FedEx's entry into Internet business-to-business electronic commerce is through offering Internet access to its global logistics service. This can be used either on its own with online preparation of shipping documents and tracking of packages, or it can be integrated into another electronic commerce system. FedEx logistics can therefore be classified as value-chain service provision (according to the classification in Chapter 3). Beyond this basic form of electronic commerce, FedEx is also offering VirtualOrder, built around its strength in global package shipping, as it tightly integrates its logistics service with Web catalogues provided by suppliers. FedEx VirtualOrder can therefore be classified as third-party marketplace provision.

INDUSTRY.NET: PIONEERING AN INTERNET INDUSTRY MARKETPLACE

Business

The story of Industry.Net, the pioneer of industrial marketplaces on the Net, reads like an industrial saga of which the ending is still inconclusive.

Industry.Net was formed in 1990 as an electronic 'industry marketplace', providing information about products, services and suppliers for manufacturing and engineering professionals. Such products and services are part of the maintenance, repairs and operations (MRO) market, estimated to be worth between $60 and $300 billion annually in the USA.

Bill Gates, CEO of Microsoft, was an early investor in Industry.Net. Former Lotus president and CEO Jim Manzi became its CEO in January 1996. He set out to move Industry.Net from information provision to full electronic support for all stages of the transaction cycle. In July 1996 Industry.Net merged with AT&T New Media, to become Nets Inc. The intention was to extend the service with business news. With the high-profile personality of Manzi, Industry.Net received a great deal of publicity as a model for doing business on the Internet (among others in *Fortune* and *Business Week*). However, early in 1997 Nets Inc. filed for bankruptcy under Chapter 11. According to some, the reasons included 'monumental mismanagement' and 'only halfway support for transactions'.[53] Manzi stated that the company never got a financial foothold and was hurt by investors' jitters about Internet companies.[54]

Next in turn was Perot Systems, buying Industry.Net out of bankruptcy. Perot provided the technical expertise to develop further the full trading system concept. Less than six months later, Industry.Net was sold again, this time to Information Handling Systems Group. IHS Group is a $360 million professional database-publishing company, with industry information in engineering, oil and gas, chemical, publishing and regulatory. It announced that it would take Industry.Net back to its information roots, rather than extending into full transaction support. Perot System's electronic commerce group (Timeq) will continue to host and develop the Industry.Net Web site. Industry.Net is intended to become the basis for a new IHS Group company, which will provide both free and pay-per-use information on industrial products and services over the Internet.

Industry.Net generates its revenues from supplier membership fees, as well as from Web advertising. 'Selling members' post their catalogues, paying anywhere from $1000 to $200 000. All information is free and much of it is available without becoming a registered 'buying member'. A simple online registration process provides additional access to the Business Centres. During the brief alliance with AT&T, subscription fees for business information were also considered.

Products and Services

To any registered and non-registered visitor, Industry.Net offers:

- searchable catalogues of products, services and suppliers;
- business and manufacturing news by region and industry;

- online events covering major trade shows and conferences;
- trade association information.

To buying members (registration is free), Industry.Net offers in addition:

- access to Business Centres for detailed information about products/ services from individual companies;
- interactive forums organized on topics of professional interest.

To suppliers, Industry.Net offers:

- support to bring their catalogues online;
- advertising space on Industry.Net's Web pages.

Customers and Benefits

Industry.Net addresses the engineering and manufacturing community, that is, suppliers on the one hand and purchasing or engineering professionals on the other hand. First, it offers:

- buyers easy access to a large amount of information about products and services;
- suppliers exposure to a large number of potential buyers.

Industry.Net had 600 000 registered buyers in 1999 and featured over 20 000 companies in its directories, of which 3000 offered a Business Centre, with 10 million products in 9500 categories. The Business Centres range from single-person machine shops to huge international companies like HP, Sun and Honeywell. For the latter, Industry.Net offers an additional online access point to the potential buyer, next to Web sites maintained by these companies themselves.

Secondly, by enabling low-cost access to products, services, suppliers and buyers, Industry.Net reduces the costs of purchasing. The objective was to take cost reduction even further by supporting transactions electronically.

Competition

In its original concept Industry.Net offered breadth of information through a very large number of members, buyers and suppliers, with a large number of products and services in a wide range of industrial areas.

Breadth in terms of covering vertical markets has to be traded off against focus on expertise in a single vertical market and the associated opportunity for community building. In addition, information provision is only one step in the buyer–supplier relationship. Other steps consist of ordering, paying, delivering, in short full transaction handling. Product specification, design, after-sales support, training etc. are still other aspects that can be considered for an electronic marketplace. Breadth of functionality is therefore another dimension on which to compete. These are two of the competitive dimensions mentioned in Chapter 5 on industry internal competition. Figure 4.1 below shows these two dimensions.

The figure also shows the positioning of some potential competitors to Industry.Net. The analysis of this is as follows. PlasticsNet provides information about purchasing and application of plastics in industry. It aims at building a focused plastics industry community. GEN/ICS is more focused too, in this case on the engineering world, but also considerably richer in functionality than Industry.Net. CitiusNet, Tradezone and GEIS TPN Register are all rich in (catalogue and transaction) functionality, although they are currently less wide in industry coverage than Industry.Net. GEIS TPN is a combination between the online transaction capabilities of General Electric Information Services and the product and suppliers' catalogues of Thomas Register. Grainger's site Grainger.com has a history in large catalogues, originally on paper and on CD-ROM, combined with proprietary legacy transaction systems. This combination is now being moved towards the Web.

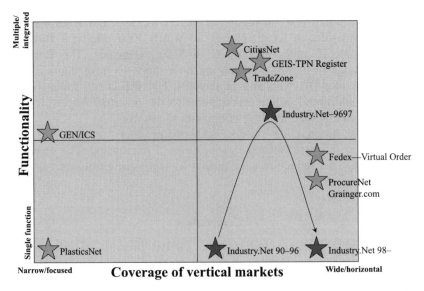

Figure 4.1   *Competitive positions in electronic trading (dimensions and positions of competitors based on the case analysis in Chapter 4)*

Fedex VirtualOrder has support to bring catalogues online just like Industry.Net and in addition offers transaction and shipping support. However, it is not a single point of access to a multiplicity of sellers, organized in categories (i.e. a marketplace). In that sense it is still no outright competitor but might well become so.

Marketing Strategy

Industry.Net's marketing strategy initially was to become the largest online marketplace. It played out its first-comer advantage, being the innovator that developed the industry marketplace concept on the Web. This attracted a lot of media attention in the general business press, which fitted well with the objective. However, Industry.Net still stayed US oriented and never became truly global.

Having built a large base of members up to 1996, it then wished to create new sources of revenue, beyond membership fees. It decided to add transaction capabilities. Its marketing strategy was built around emphasizing the cost-reduction potential. However, it failed in the implementation and credibility compared to other large players who started to copy the industry marketplace model. Figure 4.1 shows that Industry.Net could also have chosen to add value by increasing content for specific markets (moving to the left instead of upwards). It only partially pursued a content-oriented approach through its short-lived alliance with AT&T.

When the bankruptcy crisis was over, it turned out that Industry.Net did not have a captive membership, seeing its number of Business Centres shrink from 4500 to 3000.[55] This is understandable, as there was no proprietary element in the technology, or exclusive access to content, or an intimate customer relationship that could have kept the customer loyal to Industry.Net. The company did build up a brand name, however, and a large membership, sufficient reasons for a takeover by IHS with its considerable content assets.

IHS now has the task of getting the business model right for this combination of assets. It states that it will offer customized links to manufacturers, distributors and other service providers (i.e. Industry.Net as it is, plus access to existing IHS catalogues), as well as the services of the advanced electronic database and catalogue publishing bureau of Dataware Technologies, which is part of the IHS Group. It states that it sees Industry.Net as another distribution channel for its own products.

Summary—Marketing Model

Industry.Net's concept is that of an electronic industry mall (e-mall) for a wide range of industry sectors including MRO products. It is seeking dominance by providing access to a very large number of products and suppliers, building on the assets of its parent company, and by brand building.

AMAZON ASSOCIATES AND ADVANTAGE: OPENING UP THE VALUE CHAIN

Amazon.com claims to be the largest online bookstore in the world. At the end of 1998 it featured a catalogue of three million titles, compared to a few hundred thousand for the largest physical bookstores. It offers book search, ordering and payment by credit card, international shipping of books by normal mail or express delivery and online checking of order and shipment status. The multimedia catalogue information service is enriched by author-supplied information, readers' opinions, reviews and statistics prepared by Amazon staff. Customers can request to stay informed about new editions related to their interest profile. In this way, Amazon builds an online community whose value is continuously increased by the customers themselves. Amazon is growing very fast, although it is still not making a profit. Net sales were $540 million in 1998, up from $148 million the year before. Its customer base grew from 0.34 million early in 1997, to 1.5 million at the end of 1997, exploding to 4.5 million by the end of 1998 and surpassing the 10 million mark by June 1999. Amazon added CD and video sales in 1998 and launched business-to-consumer and person-to-person auctions at the beginning of 1999.

The primary customers are the readers who order books. Secondary customer groups are publishers which are supported by the Amazon Advantage service and resellers which are serviced by Amazon Associates. It is on those two business-to-business services that this section focuses.

Business

With Advantage and Associates Amazon has two services that radically break up the traditional book-publishing value chain (see Figure 4.2).

Amazon enables a value network/dynamic market configuration (see Figure 4.3) in which the actors can assume multiple roles, depending on the value functionality that they wish to offer. In this configuration, important functionality stays with Amazon:

1. Community building: author- and customer-supplied information related to specific books.

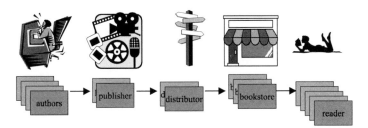

Figure 4.2   *Traditional book-publishing value chain*

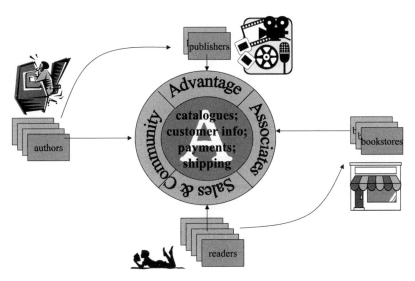

Figure 4.3   *Amazon book sales and publishing as a value network/dynamic market configuration*

2. Sales interface:
   - *direct* customer order intake, shopping registration of individual readers; and
   - *indirect* via Associates.
3. Core information management:
   - building and providing access to a very large catalogue, linked to Advantage;
   - building up a huge customer database and deriving added-value information.
4. Core handling and processing:
   - payment processing between readers, authors, publishers, resellers and Amazon;
   - shipping and delivery administration.

In fact, Amazon is the central information store in a hub-and-spoke system. This again is very similar to what other electronic trading systems aim for.

Products and Services

The Advantage service is a catalogue service for publishers, of the centralizing kind, that is, the publisher's catalogue information is absorbed into Amazon's catalogue. The Advantage service, for which registration is done over the Internet, therefore offers to publishers:

- inclusion of their books in the Amazon online catalogue—Amazon adds cover pictures to the online info and search facilities;
- an (additional) outlet towards Amazon's large customer base;
- inventory control (Amazon signals out-of-stock and performs automatic reordering);
- sharing of revenues (45% to the publisher, 55% to Amazon);
- no set-up or service fee.

The Amazon Associates programme is for online bookstores, or in fact for anyone who wishes to sell books online. It is essentially a referral service, in the sense that an online bookstore refers to the books in Amazon's catalogue and leaves all of the handling of ordering, payment and shipment to Amazon.

Therefore it offers:

- easy set-up, via the Internet itself, of online sales of books;
- no hassle with ordering, payments, delivery ('we take care of the hard part');
- revenue sharing (up to 15% to the online bookstore);
- no set-up or service fee.

Customers

Publishers

Amazon estimates that there are between 10 000 and 50 000 independent publishers in the USA alone. It has set out to be the largest online bookstore in the world and started by bringing a few large catalogues online. By offering an easy, low-cost way to absorb the book offer of any publisher into its online system, it aims to continue to extend its catalogue. It is not known how many publishers are customers of the Advantage program.

Online Bookstores

The Associates program is an innovative way to extend end-customer reach. In principle, anyone who may have an interest in selling books online can become a customer of the Associates programme. The set-up effort is indeed so low that it is a matter of a few hours to set up an online bookstore, or to add online book sales to an existing site. For Amazon, any site that generates Web traffic is of interest, as ultimately a part of that traffic will be ending up at Amazon's site through the referral mechanism. Moreover, Amazon's brand is made accessible from many more points on the Web while it is impossible for an online bookstore to completely hide Amazon's brand (as a customer who buys a book ultimately has to end up at Amazon's own site). Amazon thereby gets a hook into the thousands of Web sites of online communities and interest groups, as well as into other online bookstores.

Also interesting is that a referral site can be any local site, which is maintained in the local language. Therefore, at least for the marketing front end towards the customer, Amazon can get global, multilingual reach, with minimal investment. This is one of the few examples of a strategy that may be able to exploit the global reach of the Internet for language/culture-dependent products. To fully support this Amazon will have to absorb non-English books into its catalogues. In principle, the Advantage programme is a complementary piece in the puzzle to achieve global presence. However, there are also missing pieces in the puzzle, notably a global distribution system that supports decentralized inventory and a decentralized shipping system with guaranteed delivery quality.[56]

In September 1997, Amazon.com, Inc. announced that enrolment in its Associates programme had reached 15 000 online booksellers. In February 1998, the number was 30 000; in June 1998, this was 60 000; and in September 1998, there were 150 000 associated online booksellers, growth of a factor of 10 in one year (see Figure 4.4)! Sites with hundreds of referrals are rare, however. Most list a very small number of books, fewer than 30. One reason for this might be that many sites are only starting with the referral service and will gradually expand their offer. In addition, many Associates are likely to be individuals, having created a microcommunity.

Amazon.com distinguishes the following groups of Associates:

1. *Publishers*: this is an interesting example, as publishers have put their books in Amazon's catalogue, possibly with the Advantage programme, and also sell these books online through Amazon's service.[57]
2. *Authors*: again, this is an interesting example of how easy access to functionality gives the possibility of assuming multiple roles, namely being an author as well as a bookstore.

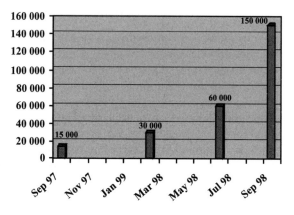

Figure 4.4   *Number of Amazon Associates*

3. *Familiar Web sites*: these are the sites that generate a lot of traffic, like Netscape or Motley Fool.
4. *Print publications online*: these enhance their online publications by referrals to books, which is a natural extension of any online publication that references book, e.g. for any academic article published online.
5. *Special-interest Web sites*: these are virtual communities around a shared and focused interest. Their advantage to Amazon is that they have the in-depth expertise to make a meaningful sub-category of books. Amazon could ultimately build such categories by itself, by analysing purchasing patterns. However, the virtual communities also add recommendations by the peer group of specific books. A specific virtual community is being created through an educational programme at the Spanish business school IESE together with Harvard Business School. They use the Amazon.com case to let students very quickly create their own online bookstore and analyse it from a marketing perspective, with the help of a CD-ROM-based template and course module.[58]

Competition

Amazon's business-to-business services face competition from the following:

*   Other large online bookstores that carry a well-known brand, such as the Internet Bookshop, Barnes & Noble, Waterstone. Amazon has a very low barrier for publishers and online booksellers to integrate catalogues or to provide an access point to its catalogues. The

Internet Bookshop offers online registration for affiliates/associates but not for publishers. Barnes & Noble only has contact addresses for affiliates and publishers. Waterstone does not offer any of these services.

- Publishers/distributors that keep their catalogues and logistics under their own control and go online either directly or through other online bookstores than Amazon.
- Distribution centres in other countries that exploit the opportunity to offer lower shipping costs.
- Potentially any distributor that can handle shipping and payments better than Amazon (e.g. that supports electronic bank transfers).
- Popular sites that can leave more of the value of a book purchase to the small publisher, which makes use of (upcoming) standards for low-cost connection to logistics management and payment services.

Marketing Strategy

Amazon has set out to be the largest online bookstore in the world, that is, having the largest share of the online book sales market. This is built on several aspects:

- having the largest catalogue;
- having the largest distribution, that is, access to customers;
- being the best-known brand.

Amazon's business-to-business Advantage and Associates programmes have been designed to have a very low set-up cost and to bring immediate and visible financial benefits. They offer to publishers a share in Amazon's large customer base and information about customers, and to online booksellers a share in Amazon's large catalogue and information related to books. Amazon's strength is in the management of the combination of catalogue information and customer information with fast and well-known delivery and payment systems from third parties such as DHL, UPS and VISA, Mastercard.

Although the two programmes have the potential to make Amazon global in terms of both catalogue and customer interface, there are still missing links, notably in local distribution and in multilingual support.

With its B-to-B programmes Amazon goes far beyond being an electronic bookshop, although it also continues to pursue being a generic e-shop for books (while in the meantime CDs have also been added). It is an e-shop as well as two value-chain service providers, namely for customer access to customers for publishers and for fulfilment to bookstores.

This multifaceted presence is still coherent, as Figure 4.3 above shows: the core information systems are solidly in Amazon's hands. They are Amazon's natural resource for one-to-one marketing-based added value.

Summary—Marketing Model

Amazon Associates is a programme that allows online booksellers or virtual communities to become a value-chain service provider to Amazon. The service they provide is marketing, including marketing for Amazon itself, by providing access to the books in their catalogue and adding value on the basis of their knowledge of specific communities of interest.

Amazon Advantage makes Amazon into a third-party marketplace provider for publishers, according to the classification developed in Chapter 3.

While in this book the focus is on business-to-business electronic commerce, it is noted that Amazon also operates a virtual community for its consumer-customers, that is, book buyers. Book buyers/readers add their book reviews and recommendations to the Amazon Web site, and Amazon uses customer analysis to construct interest profiles and thereby provide book recommendations to any potential buyer.

CITIUS BELGIUM: FROM EDI TO INTERNET MARKETPLACE

The Citius story[59] started in 1978 when Jean-Philippe Passot, in his father's office supplies and computer products company in France, decided to implement electronic links between its warehouses and headquarters and subsequently added tele-purchasing capabilities for its customers, on Minitel terminals. This system gradually evolved to support EDI and PCs. When Mr Passot realized that customers actually wanted a system connecting multiple suppliers to purchasers, the idea of the electronic marketplace was born (Figure 4.5). In 1992 the company that was later named CitiusNet was created and by 1997 the company was well

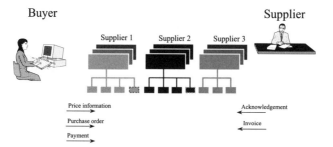

Figure 4.5 *Purchasing information, traditionally based on documents*

on its way to establishing global presence, with subsidiaries or partners in the USA, Canada, Switzerland, Austria, the Netherlands, Belgium, Luxembourg, Germany and the UK.

Citius Belgium, the focus of this case study, was established in 1997.[60]

Business—Customers—Competition

Business

Citius Belgium (http://www.citius.be) licenses the marketing concept, the technology and the brand from CitiusNet France. In October 1997, CitiusNet France and its subsidiaries were acquired by Electronic Data Systems (EDS), the world's largest software company, with more than US$15 billion turnover and 110 000 employees.

Citius Belgium (Citius for short) stayed outside this acquisition. Founded by a group of entrepreneurs in 1997, the main shareholder Belgacom (the incumbent telecommunications operator of Belgium) exercised its buy-out option at the end of 1998 and took over all minority shares. Citius focuses on facilitating the purchase and supply of 'non-productive' or 'logistics' materials, e.g. office supplies such as paper, printer toner, pens or chairs, drinks, food etc., that is, goods that support the production and administrative processes but are not core to it.

Citius provides a third-party electronic trading system consisting of the following (see also Figure 4.6):

- *Online catalogues*: support to suppliers for bringing catalogues on the Web with the Altius module; catalogues are maintained by the supplier and Citius maintains an identical copy; item prices can be

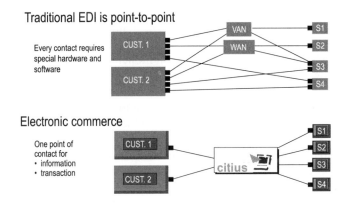

Figure 4.6   *Citius's approach compared to traditional EDI*

made dependent on the purchaser; catalogues are accessible via the Internet or via a VAN.

- *Selecting and ordering*: software and support for purchasers to select and to order; with a proprietary Citius user interface or via the Web and a standard browser; budget authorization controls can be specified, such that persons in any level of the purchasing organization can order up to their allowed limit without need for authorization intervention.
- *Order processing*: electronic transmission of orders and related confirmations between purchasers and suppliers; involves EDI, where Citius takes care of translating between different EDI implementations that might exist between (various) suppliers and the purchaser.
- *Invoice handling*: electronic transmission of invoices; again based on EDI with an audit trail.
- *Electronic payments*: optional support for electronic payments, based on electronic funds transfer; this involves a link from the Fortius module to supplier and purchaser banks.

The central Citius server stores copies of catalogues, customer-specific data like authorization levels, and transaction records. It also provides transparent access to catalogues on other Citius servers worldwide. Collectively these servers are called the 'Citius network'.

An agreement is signed between the purchaser and suppliers in advance of getting involved in transactions. The agreement provides proof of identity and mutual guarantees for delivery and payment. *Ad hoc* relations between purchasers and suppliers can be supported but are currently not being marketed.

Benefits

The main benefit of the Citius system is in significantly reducing the cost of purchasing those non-productive materials. These materials typically take up 15% of total purchase volume in monetary terms, while requiring 50% of the total personnel cost involved in purchasing. An economic study[61] has shown that Citius reduces ordering costs by 20–60%. Internal stock costs such as value of stock and warehouse personnel are reduced by 30–40%. Total cost savings are then in the order of 20–45%. This corresponds to the cost savings reported by Jelassi and Lai (1996) at Texas Instruments, as quoted in Chapter 2. Citius also reports a reduction in order-processing time from an average of eight days with the traditional paper-based method to virtually zero. As a consequence, purchasing productivity has increased significantly, in some cases by more than a factor of five. Moreover, electronic purchasing significantly reduces the order error rate (traditionally in the order of 2.5%). Savings come about not only because paperwork is greatly reduced, but also because the built-in budget authorization facility allows purchasing to be delegated to a much lower level in the organization, reducing the overhead at central purchasing in dealing with authorization and small-item purchases.

Other benefits come from the control that the electronic system gives. All transactions are logged and can easily be analysed for the potential for cost reduction, for instance by choosing a cheaper supplier. Equipped with more information, purchasers are in a better position to negotiate. Previously, in many cases purchasers even had so little insight in their own inventory that they were dependent on action by their routine suppliers to restock materials.

Customers

There are two types of markets for the Citius system:

- *Market Type A*   Large purchaser market: large organizations that do a lot of purchasing and have to deal with many suppliers, in a hub-and-spoke configuration. Typically this includes the top 500 companies and public organizations in each country (e.g. Belgacom Belgium), as well as multinational companies (e.g. Texas Instruments, Alcatel, Solvay).
- *Market Type B*   Small suppliers market: whole sectors at a time in which there are many small and medium-sized enterprises (SMEs) that would benefit from exposure through a central, up-to-date and accurate aggregrate electronic catalogue. There are many such sectors. Citius-France has been introduced in this way in the wine sector (CEDIVIN) and in the Rhône-Alpes construction sector. Citius-Belgium is running pilot installations in hospital supplies and in the construction sector.

While the two markets may seem to overlap, they in fact require very different marketing approaches (see below). And while the basic product offering is essentially the same for both types of markets, each has specific service requirements. Current and potential size and growth in those markets have not been quantified, however.

The trends influencing customers are:

- *fierce competition on price*, therefore seeking cost reduction in purchasing and better control of the purchasing process and of stocks;
- *time-based competition*, such that time to market and just in time require faster response from suppliers;

- *more customization*, larger variety of goods in use, therefore more suppliers need to offer a larger variation;
- *consolidating on fewer partners* (concentration of supply), therefore with fewer suppliers these need to be able to supply a larger set of related products.

Citius addresses these customer needs for cost reduction, time reduction, customization and concentration by means of integrated purchase/supply of all materials through its electronic support system.

A purchasing support system such as Citius is capable of reversing certain trends that over the past few years have been considered as wise for business to follow:

- *From reduction to broadening of the supplier base*: while the trend among purchasers has been to limit the number of their suppliers, the Citius system would in principle allow for a much wider choice of suppliers. Comparing multiple offers would then be supported at the point where all catalogues are held, namely the Citius system. Although some of the (potential) purchasers are starting to consider this option and Citius itself is quite aware of it, the possibility of reorganizing the supply network is not yet being implemented.
- *From centralized to decentralized purchasing*: while the trend has been to centralize purchasing information at one point of control, the Citius system at the same time decentralizes the purchasing activity, as ordering capability can easily be made available at each employee's PC in a company.

Competition

Mrs van Rijsbergen, co-founder of Citius Belgium and marketing manager until the end of 1998, states that, in order to have a chance to win as an electronic commerce provider, you need to have '3 Cs', namely Community, Content, Control. All of these three help to add value for the customer (choice, trust, quality etc.). This means:

- community building around your product;
- providing rich trading content such as catalogues;
- being in control of the system and the process.

Citius's potential competitors score quite differently on the 3 Cs:

- B-to-C service providers with ambitions in B-to-B, such as Internet Shopping Network or Yahoo, have a very different approach to the customer and address different needs that does not provide the control required for B-to-B. For example, they do not use price differentiation (individual pricing) or authorization control.

- Traditional paper or CD-ROM catalogue providers, who acquire or build an online electronic trading platform, are probably too limited in terms of the range of different catalogues that they offer. They do not provide enough content.
- EDI providers, while they might consider becoming Internet-based third-party marketplaces, tend to concentrate on integrating EDI with the Internet (lite EDI or XML/EDI, of which a variety of approaches exist).
- Generic service providers, from financial services (banks) or logistics as well as ISPs, need to build up the content, in order to build a strong community. It is not evident how they would do this and thereby prevent customers from switching.
- Telecommunications operators tend not to be very strong in Internet and EDI and generally need partners (the control issue).
- Computing platform providers like Netscape, Microsoft, Hewlett-Packard or Internet trading software providers like Intershop[62] or OpenMarket are either too much oriented to B-to-C, or too much technology-focused and missing content for this type of B-to-B.
- Value-added network service providers like EDS and GEIS could well be in a good position. They tend to understand the importance of community building and of control, as this corresponds more closely to their VANS business. Acquisitions like EDS-Citius help them to move faster in a business that they already understand. They may have to acquire content, however, or deliver this through partnerships.

Competitive Advantages

The 3 Cs are the assets that provide key competitive advantages, as explained by Mrs van Rijsbergen.

Community can be one of the strongest assets in this business. This is how it works in the large purchaser–many suppliers market (type A). Once the hurdle of the initial investment and effort of introducing Citius has been taken by the large purchaser, cost savings are enormous. To avoid running paper and electronic systems in parallel, the purchaser will now push more and more of its suppliers to be part of the Citius network. As suppliers go online they also realize cost benefits. In addition, they now start to receive new business opportunities, as their catalogues are online in any case. At relatively low additional cost they can attract new customers. Once a few large purchasers are using the system with a range of 'non-productive parts' suppliers, it becomes valuable for other large companies to use the same system, as they will often be purchasing the same kind of goods.

Once the system is in regular use, the full impact will become visible, namely, that much more can be gained by redesigning business processes at purchasers and suppliers. An example of business process reengineering (Coulson-Thomas, 1997) is that the central purchasing department gets a more strategic role by analysing the data from the Citius system (e.g. pre-defining preferred suppliers in the system on the basis of their cost and delivery speed). At the same time, new value-added services will be offered by either Citius or its financial partners, again on the basis of analysing the transaction data. Examples are one-to-one marketing support to suppliers, additional Web customer-information services, catalogue packaging or advance credits. All of these reinforce relationships between the parties: purchasers, suppliers and Citius as a third-party marketplace provider with its associated service providers such as banks. The critical issue here is, of course, to get the first large purchasers using the system.

Community building is equally important for sector-based markets (type B), but seems to have been less successful up to now. The high fragmentation and lack of organization in these markets are likely to play a role in this.

Content can become a key asset too. While the community is growing, the set of catalogues will become increasingly rich. However, this in itself does not provide a defendable strength unless there is exclusivity in bringing the catalogues online and making them available within the full trading system. Such exclusivity is, in the case of Citius, achieved by contractual arrangements rather than through proprietary software, as it was common in pre-Internet EDI times. Today there are such strong concerns about interoperability from the user side that it is virtually impossible to achieve customer 'lock-in' by means of proprietary software. Therefore, customer 'lock-in' is no longer through specific software.

Control means the extent to which the purchase/supply process (including the system, contractual arrangements, link to additional services) is overseen by and managed by the third-party marketplace provider. The key assets related to control are twofold: first, the understanding of the business requirements and business processes; and, second, access to the transaction data. The first of these is the tool to build a customer base. The second is the tool to continue bringing new value to customers and thereby defend the customer base.

Building assets in community, content and control at the same time is core to the competitive advantage of the Citius concept.

The competitive advantage of Citius's implementation of the third-party marketplace concept is based on the combination of assets in Community, Content and Control. Once a community of networked customers has been established, it will be very difficult to make them switch to another provider.

Structure of the Industry of Third-party Marketplace Providers

In summer 1997, one could say that the business was still in its early days, with competition being beneficial as it helps to develop the market. By the beginning of 1998 it was evident that the critical issue had become building global market share before very large operators moved in, taking over the market and enabling price/brand competition to set in. At the same time, the first signs were appearing of the formation of isolated niches in the market, in which small players could find a place. Mrs van Rijsbergen believes that ultimately the market will be sliced up between a few large, consolidated players. This process is not only a matter of large suppliers gobbling up smaller ones, but is also influenced by the decision making of large users once they move to electronic purchasing. With several competing systems, it is likely to be the choice of the large multinational purchasers that will determine who will be the winner.

It is noteworthy that EDS has in the meantime acquired Citius. The reason for the acquisition is stated by J.-P. Passot, the founder of Citius, as follows:

> The e-commerce market development needed for Citius a reinforced partnership. [...] We are expecting a complete synergy, with the EDS experience in manufacturing processes and cost reduction efforts.[63]

This acquisition is fully in line with the analysis of competition in the business of third-party marketplace providers in general.

Given the strong position of EDS and the marketing arrangement with Citius Belgium, Mrs van Rijsbergen believed that there were no major threats to Citius in the Belgian market in early 1999. However, at the same time she observed that investment in electronic purchasing was being delayed by the introduction of the euro and the millennium bug problem. Consequently, on the one hand there is an opportunity for newcomers to enter the market. Internet access providers (ISPs), catalogue-building Web houses or Internet shopping technology companies like Intershop are attempting this. On the other hand, once large companies are past the year 2000, it is expected that their decisions about electronic purchasing will follow rapidly, reducing the duration of the window of opportunity.

Newcomers need rapidly to build up knowledge of the complexities of large-scale purchasing and of the integration with back-end and order-processing systems. Experience with application-to-application communication (as known from the EDI world) and a profound understanding of security are also considered to be critical.

Marketing Strategy

Opportunity, Segmentation and Targeting

Citius focuses on the supply chain of 'non-productive goods and services'. Therefore, the underlying product-market segmentation is on the basis of the critical importance/value of a good to the actual production at the purchaser and degree of structuring in the market in terms of organization around large purchasers (Figure 4.7). Citius targets product-markets A and B.

Customers in product-market A are typically in concentrated businesses such as chemicals or consumer electronics, as well as in monopolistic or oligopolistic public services such as the post or police, or they can be governments and public administrations.

Customers in product-market B are sector organizations in highly fragmented, relatively unstructured sectors of industry, such as construction, publishing or agriculture.

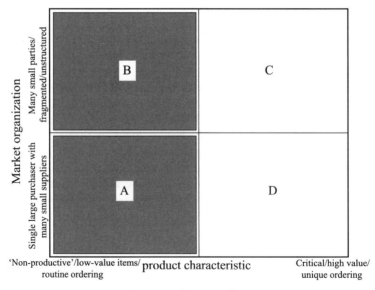

Figure 4.7   *Citius's purchasing market segmentation*

Product-market C would consist of critical production goods (e.g. machinery) in fragmented or unorganized sectors. An example might be tractors for farmers, or trucks for the transport sector. Trading systems for these heavily rely on extensive and detailed but to a large extent standardized and reusable product information, complemented by personal advice and service. They are likely to be strongly sector oriented.

Product-market D consists of large companies and high-value, one-off purchases, possibly with multiple suppliers. An example is the contracting of a complex project. The 'trading system' in that case is likely to consist of a multidisciplinary team doing person-to-person negotiation and following a case-by-case approach.

Using the benefits segmentation developed in Chapter 6, Citius's offering can be positioned as in Figure 4.8.

For large corporate purchasers and their suppliers (target market type A), Citius positions itself as the cost-reduction leader. It will bring the largest benefits in reducing the cost of purchasing and supply. In addition to that, Citius is emphasizing global presence, notably through EDS but also through partnerships with other large companies like telecoms operators. Global presence is important as it corresponds to a customer need at the purchasing end for global sourcing, that is, the lowest cost globally, or availability of new products needed related to expansion in global markets. Therefore global presence not only means offering the same

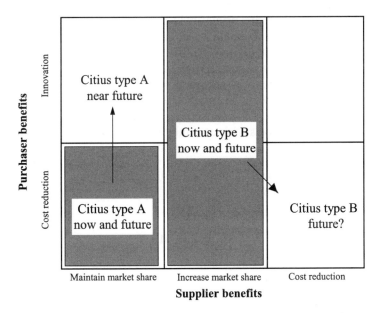

Figure 4.8 *Position of Citius in a benefits segmentation approach*

product categories worldwide, but also extending the set of catalogues with suppliers from other countries. This again has important consequences in being able to set up contracts and ship and handle financial transactions across country borders.

For the sector markets (type B), the main benefit sought by suppliers is in obtaining access to new customers, that is, to increase market share. Those new customers (i.e. purchasers) would be seeking new, better (innovative) or cheaper products from the sector.

Mrs van Rijsbergen believes that the current product is well positioned in what are potentially high-growth markets.

Strategic Objectives

Citius Belgium's strategic objective for the next few years is to become firmly established in the market, that is, to become the dominant third-party marketplace provider with a number of leading industrial and service firms in the country, and to make a start in the sector organization market. While Belgacom has several interests in the Internet, multimedia and electronic commerce, it is not clear if a long-term position in this specific type of electronic commerce business is part of its strategic objectives.

The product-market strategy to achieve these objectives is twofold:

1. Focus on current sales opportunities on the basis of the argument of cost-reduction benefits, primarily in the large purchaser market, with the objective of establishing a firm market presence among opinion leaders in the country.
2. Introduce product and service improvements and innovations through the Internet or new types of services, to sell to new customers who value the benefits of Internet access (low cost, multimedia) or additional services like financial management. Alliances with EDS and banks or associations of banks like ISABEL[64] should help to create such improvements and innovations.

Originally Citius followed a franchising/licensing approach for its geographical expansion. Since the takeover EDS has become responsible for this.

Marketing Mix

Product Customization and Development

Of Citius's set of products and services, only the central module (called Citius) is mandatory. Customization is not required, but is recommended since it increases the value for the customer. Standard Citius allows, at the suppliers' end, integration of catalogues and inclusion of purchaser-dependent pricing; and at the purchasers' end, inclusion of authorization control. Thus Citius can also offer an off-the-shelf product. The central server requires no adaptation by the customer.

Product development, now undertaken by EDS, is shaped by:

- analysis of trends in market and technology;
- competition watch;
- sales feedback;
- requirements of large customers.

A Citius user group has been established, driven by EDS, to guide product development. It is not felt that the product itself is especially innovative, nor can it be protected by patents or proprietary technology. Instead, the strength is in the concept and in market presence.

Promotion, Branding and Sales Process

As Mrs van Rijsbergen says, in this business not only the 3 Cs are required but also the B of branding. Branding is concentrated around the name Citius, which has already been well established in France, Canada and Belgium. Establishing a liaison with large partners (in the past this has included Bell Canada, France Telecom and Belgacom) is another element in branding. Now that EDS has moved in, its name will be used, in addition to Citius, to convince potential customers that they can trust the technical quality, support and long-term maintenance of the product. Citius considers it essential that the brand is established worldwide. This is especially important for large purchasers, who themselves operate or wish to source globally.

However, the branding strategy has not yet been explicitly formulated. Branding is gradually realized as becoming more important. The consolidation that is expected in third-party trading systems will require a stronger focus on branding.

Citius Belgium uses all the usual means for promotion: brochures, journals, print catalogues, TV/infomercials, Internet, CD-ROM, trade shows, personal contact/word of mouth. Promotional material is always centred on the name Citius and the key message in all of these is that Citius will bring large cost savings.

Currently, the sales process is considerably personalized and requires extensive sales effort, especially to convince large purchasers. The market is still very much in an information and awareness stage, with large purchasers taking a lot of time for their decision making.

Interestingly, there is an educational influence from the business-to-consumer market: decision makers in large companies who have seen that electronic commerce is real because they are Internet shoppers themselves (as consumers) are more easily convinced of the parallel value of B-to-B electronic commerce.

Customer Loyalty

Customer loyalty is, as discussed before, likely to be strong, because the implementation of the concept leads to a profound integration of a network of business relationships with the Citius system. The integration is in terms of:

- organization of the way of working;
- investment in putting customer information in the system (e.g. catalogues, authorization);
- being used to certain types of applications;
- installed software and possibly hardware.

Switching systems would only be possible at considerable cost, not so much in terms of equipment but rather in terms of having to convince a large number of people within the company and among trading partners to switch too. Switching to another provider would require the whole community to switch over or to run similar chains of purchase/supply business processes and systems in parallel, which is not desirable.

The value of the Citius system is larger than the cost saving on each transaction. In a sense, Citius intimately captures customers' way of working and helps them, combined with transaction records, to improve on it. This form of 'customer intimacy' meets one of the conditions of one-to-one marketing as described by Rogers and Peppers (see Chapter 6).

Further exploitation of one-to-one marketing, based on analysis of customers' actual use of the Citius system, is an option that is currently being considered. This might include customer profiling in order to invite selected groups of customers to promotional and educational events.

Pricing

The (early Internet) pricing model is detailed in Table 4.2.

Assuming a purchaser with 10 workplaces (PCs) and 100 transactions per month, this works out in the first month to a total cost of about €4300 for the purchaser and €2100 for the supplier.

With this build-up of fees, the turnover of Citius Belgium in the first year of operation comes mainly from consultancy, in the second year

Table 4.2   *Citius's pricing scheme*

Fees	Purchaser	Supplier
Installation fee (one-off)	€375 per workplace	€375 (normally one workplace)
Catalogue set-up (one-off)	–	€750–2500
Monthly maintenance	€12.5–75 per PC	€12.5–75
Transaction fee	€0.75 per transaction	€0.75 per transaction

mainly from service fees, and in the third year and beyond mainly from transaction fees.

Mrs van Rijsbergen observes that this pricing model leads to a rather uniform total price among competitors. Nevertheless, this is more or less by chance as currently the pricing strategy is not really competitor based. Instead it is market based, in the sense that pricing is determined by assessing the value of the customer benefits. However, Mrs van Rijsbergen expects that price will increasingly become a competitive factor. The reasons are that as usage of the system increases customers become more aware of the burden of the transaction fees (which are already considered to be relatively high, although a comparison to a paper environment would justify even higher transaction fees), and that the market becomes more saturated.

The pricing strategy leads to a moderate initial cost for the purchaser, where the cost savings—as calculated on paper—are soon larger than the initial investment. As an example, a calculation from Texas Instruments shows a cost reduction in purchasing from $200 to $5 per line item, a reduction in throughput time from about eight days to virtually zero, and an increase in productivity in purchasing of more than a factor of five. However, such a calculation only addresses the 'hard' costs and savings such as the fees mentioned above and the reduction in effort for purchasing a single 'non-productive' item, and does not take into account the effort for introducing the system (training, reorganization).

Summary—Marketing Model

The Citius Belgium business model is that of a third-party marketplace provider. Its marketing model is to combine this business model with a marketing strategy aimed at establishing a dominant position among the opinion-leader large purchasers. It does this in the first instance by offering them compelling cost-reduction benefits. Sustainable competitive advantage is to be based on building strong assets in Community, Content and Control at the same time.

The main benefits for Citius's customers are in significantly reducing purchasing and supply costs. All transactions have to go through the Citius server, with the main income for Citius coming from transaction fees, as well as maintenance fees. In the future the model could be significantly enhanced and move more towards value-chain integration, with revenues from new services. Such services would be based on integrating information from various parts of the value chain, such as:

- new financial services, e.g. credit arrangements based on analysing the ordering and financial flows between several partners and consolidating such information;
- new catalogue services, e.g. grouping products from several suppliers together into a virtual catalogue for one-stop ordering, based on the analysis of purchasing correlations;
- new delivery services, e.g. supplier-managed inventory, by analysing information from the order and delivery cycle.

TRADEZONE: INTERNET FOR THIRD-PARTY MARKET ACCESS

Tradezone provides third-party marketplace services on a franchising basis. The information in this section is based on company information,[65] publications from related ESPRIT projects,[66] and discussions with Mr Michael Jeffries, CEO of Tradezone International and of Onyx Internet.[67] It describes the situation until the end of 1998.

Business—Customers—Competition

Business

Onyx Internet, a UK-based company, has developed and tested Tradezone over the past few years together with partners such as Hewlett-Packard and NatWest Bank. Tradezone is now marketed by an independent company, Tradezone International, as an international franchising concept for operating a secure third-party transaction-management service over the Internet for non-critical purchases. Onyx Internet has itself become the first operator of the Tradezone service. Tradezone's service components are the following:

- *Catalogue access*: a directory of supplier catalogues, with a global cross-catalogue search facility, based on a proprietary product-classification scheme.
- *Order processing*: selection of items, calculation of total order cost, including VAT and delivery cost, presentation of a signed quotation,

intake of signed orders and transmission of these to the supplier for fulfilment with reporting to the purchaser on fulfilment status, all with an audit trail.

- *Payments processing*: selection of payment method, payment authorization and reporting; Tradezone supports purchase cards where a franchisee can act on behalf of a partner bank as a card guarantor towards the supplier.
- *Access control*: known purchasers, and all suppliers, use certified public and private keys on smart cards for authentication and digital signatures, with rights specific to the user (e.g. to update catalogue, make customer-specific price lists; or to perform certain types of purchases only); anonymous purchasers have access limitations.
- *Site security*: all parts of the system, such as catalogue, sales order, administration servers, are secured.

Tradezone expects the online B-to-B market to be worth $370 billion by 2002 (cf. the Forrester estimates in Chapter 2). It concentrates on the online MRO (maintenance, repairs, operations) market, defined as consumables, non-strategic supplies and time-critical sundries, which it estimates to be 60% of the total market, that is $220 billion, in the year 2002.

Tradezone's strategic objective is to become a major player in the global online MRO market: the target is to process 17.5% of world-wide MRO purchases by 2002.

Customers

Tradezone has several types of customer:

1. *Tradezone service operators*, which are franchisees for the Tradezone service across the world. These could be banks that are seeking to add value to their financial services because they perceive that otherwise their core business would be threatened or eroded by emerging alternative financial providers. Other Tradezone service operations could be telecom operators who want to exploit their basic communications network through added-value services, or Internet service providers needing to upgrade their access services, which is increasingly becoming a commodity causing their revenues to be under pressure through price competition.

2. Tradezone users: *purchasers and suppliers of MRO products*. Purchasers are under pressure to reduce purchasing cost (selection, payment, administration), need to shorten time to market and require global choice with easy extension to new suppliers, as well as 24-hour

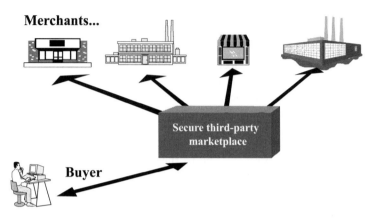

Figure 4.9   *Tradezone as a secure multivendor/single-service interface third-party marketplace. (Reproduced by permission of Tradezone International Ltd)*

availability and traceability. The main driver for purchasers, at least for the large ones, is to reduce purchasing cost for business sundries. As in the case of other third-party marketplaces such as Citius, cost reduction in the order of 40–50% is considered achievable. Purchasers wish to get rid of approved-supplier lists, recognizing the opportunities of flexibility of choice, that is, multivendor support. At the same time, they need to reduce administration costs and empower individual buyers in the company, with a simple single purchasing interface (Figure 4.9). Suppliers, following the purchasers or expanding proactively, are seeking access to the global marketplace, which requires 24-hour order intake. They aim to reduce marketing costs. They demand better cash-flow control with guaranteed national and international payments.

Competition

As Tradezone deals with the MRO market and intends to become a major player, it has many potential competitors and the number is still increasing. Traditional catalogue providers, technology platform providers and global business service providers are all interested in having a share of the huge MRO market. Some competitors have been listed before: GEIS TPN, IHS Industry.Net, EDS Citius, Grainger, FedEx Virtual Order, Reed/Elsevier Business Services etc. All of these provide a generic solution, in the sense that they are not limited to a single industry sector. Some provide an integrated range of functions, beyond catalogue management. Some are associated with a strong global brand. Mr Jeffries himself mentioned as potential competitors among others GEIS TPN, Intershop, TradeWave, E-FACT, ECAT and OpenMarket.

Mr Jeffries considers that it is beneficial in the short term for competition to come in. This will help customers to make comparisons and better understand third-party marketplace benefits.

Structure of the Industry of Third-party Marketplace Providers

Competition among the current providers is expected to heat up considerably over the next few years. In addition, Tradezone is well aware that the service providers of the system could well become providers themselves and pose a threat. This holds for technology, financial services, logistics, business consultants, and system solution and communications/telecom companies. Tradezone International, itself still a small company, aims to overcome this threat by building strategic partnerships with a number of those providers. HP will provide a turnkey UNIX-based Tradezone system to Tradezone service operators (franchisees). Arthur Andersen will market the concept to service operators worldwide; NatWest and possibly other banks will provide financial services, including purchase cards, and will potentially act as Tradezone service operators themselves (although this may lead to a conflict of interest *vis-à-vis* other franchisees). Discussions have started with the major logistics companies. Some of the partners could become financial shareholders as well.

Loyalty on the part of Tradezone's direct customers, the franchisees or service operators, is created through an interesting co-ownership arrangement: together with Tradezone International, the franchisees own the further extension of the product-classification scheme. On the one hand, this extension critically depends on them, as they need to bring the new catalogues in. On the other hand, the use of the same product classification across all Tradezone nodes will realize the global network that is essential for the operation of any franchisee. In this way, the risk is reduced that they might be tempted to become an independent competing third-party marketplace provider.

Tradezone is aware that third-party marketplace systems may be introduced within a sector as a whole, e.g. automotive components, and that this would effectively block it out of such a sector.

Being at the forefront of information and communications technology, Tradezone/Onyx is confident that it can integrate and exploit new emerging technologies.

Main Difficulties

Since Tradezone went into operation it has encountered, according to Dr David Horne, Business Development Director, three main problems in the implementation of the service:

1. *Confidence of customers*: reluctance to accept technical or functional assurances.
2. *Generating critical mass*: acceptance of the benefits of this third-party trading service approach and correspondingly the evolution of the marketing programme.
3. *Technical*: principally the development of adequate end-user tools and global classification issues.

These problems have had to be addressed through an appropriate marketing and product-development strategy, as addressed below.

Marketing Strategy

Opportunity, Segmentation and Targeting

Onyx Internet contributes profound knowledge of Internet technologies and of the business of Internet service provision. Onyx has been able to perform advanced R&D in secure Internet commerce together with partners like HP in European ESPRIT projects. Nevertheless, it does not consider that it has a distinctive advantage in Internet technology. Rather, it believes that the global technology and interconnection of the Internet provided the opportunity to implement the franchising concept, which *is* the key to its strategy.

Tradezone has decided that its strategic objective—to become a very large player worldwide—is best achieved by targeting a small number of large companies as franchisees, rather than a very large number of smaller ones. From a technical point of view, any small technical company such as a local ISP could operate a third-party marketplace system like Tradezone. However, Tradezone believes that a few very large intermediaries will dominate each regional market. This is not an unreasonable expectation: business-to-business electronic transactions require a strong trust relationship and it is almost a tautology to associate this with a well-established large brand. Furthermore, in business-to-business there is a significant added value in reducing payment delays. One way to achieve this is to buffer outstanding payments. This requires a financial strength that only a large intermediary can provide.

This choice of a small number of large 'routes to market' (whether franchisees or subsidiaries or strategic partners, including large purchasers) seems to be shared by most of Tradezone's competitors.

To find large potential Tradezone service operators, Tradezone International segments the market on a geographic basis, where each region or country represents a GDP of at least $160 billion. There can be only one franchisee for such an area. For example, this means that there will be about 50 franchisees/service operators in the USA, roughly one per state. The transparent worldwide interoperability of franchisees ensures that each franchisee can still look like a global service offering. Sector-based segmentation is not pursued, although the possibility is not excluded that a sector-specific channel partner could operate a franchisee focused on a sector, e.g. automotive.

The primary target customers (franchisees) are banks, as these are under pressure to change their business. Many banks are worried about their traditional retail banking business, which is under attack from Internet/home banking and retail banking services delivered by large retailers such as Tesco in the UK and Albert Heijn in the Netherlands. The retailers realize that one of their main assets is to have direct 'physical' access to consumers and are expanding from pure retailing into a variety of new services.[68] Banks therefore seek new ways to add value to their core financial services, notably for business. Transaction processing as offered by Tradezone might be a logical extension. A bank adds financial expertise and its licence for banking services, e.g. purchase card support or bank account management, as well as its trusted party image and brand.

Other target customers have been mentioned before, such as telecom operators and ISPs. Clearly, the small ISPs will not be targeted.

As for secondary customers, the users of the Tradezone services, the expectation is that the most important target groups will be large purchasers and channel partners such as trade organizations. The latter could help to get better market reach and even become a virtual Tradezone franchise and receive commission. However, segmentation and targeting per region of the end users of the Tradezone system is left to each franchisee.

To generate confidence among the target customers in such a novel third-party solution, Tradezone conducted a series of pilots with a small number of individuals from large purchasing organizations that already had a level of 'belief' in electronic commerce.

Competitive Advantages

Despite a long list of potential competitors, no one else currently offers a service like Tradezone, according to Mr Jeffries. He believes that most solutions are either stand alone, or working with proprietary catalogues, or oriented to a single supplier. Even GEIS TPN, perceived by him as the closest competitor, has against it that it seems to be for a closed group only (which might have been true early in 1998, as at that moment only General Electric companies and a few other large purchasers were supported).

Tradezone's key competitive advantage is in the combination of:

- an ambitious, purposeful franchising scheme with co-ownership elements;
- knowledge of technology to provide transparency of access and search in multiple catalogues and fair settlements between franchisees;
- strategic partnerships with HP as global technology platform provider, Arthur Andersen as global consultant for prospective customers, and NatWest and others in the future as large financial service providers.

Tradezone is also different in that it integrates content (catalogue), supply (contracting) and transaction management.

Mr Jeffries believes that the true subject of competition is global market share. Therefore it is essential to realize critical mass quickly, which will form the main barrier to entry and protect market share. Tradezone will build this through a global network of catalogues and a fast global roll-out. The window of opportunity is about three years. The Tradezone business plan aims at signing up 200 franchisees in that timeframe.

The Tradezone service is to be offered through franchisees that serve a given region (see below). The multiple catalogue facility is key in the globalization of the Tradezone concept: all catalogues hosted by different franchisees are accessible to any purchaser, with support from the multiple catalogue search facility. This requires a 'deep' product-classification scheme, which is based on the combination of a number of industrial classifications. Tradezone registers the fact that two franchisees are involved in a transaction. The franchise formula ensures that revenues are shared between them.

In addition, Tradezone is interesting for partners, which bring Tradezone to the franchisees or complement the franchisee's operation. These include technology platform providers, such as HP, banks such as NatWest in the case of Onyx, or consultants who help to find Tradezone franchisees and develop their business, such as Arthur Andersen.

Positioning

Tradezone International uses the following as unique selling propositions towards potential franchisees:

- provision of a turnkey system;
- global scale as part of a worldwide network;
- benefits from cross-zone commissions.

The franchisees use the following as unique selling propositions for MRO buyers (purchasers):

- one interface with access to many catalogues;
- support of three types of buyers and three methods of payment:
  1. anonymous buyers who are not known to Tradezone (guests)— they would pay with credit/debit card secured with secure sockets layer encryption (SSL) or with credit/debit/corporate purchase card secured by the secure electronic trading (SET) standard;
  2. registered buyers, who have registered their details with Tradezone but not yet obtained their digital ID from Tradezone; they would pay by the same means as anonymous buyers;
  3. authenticated buyers, who have a digital ID; they may also payout of band by cheque or bank transfer, as they can be authenticated as being who they say they are, and as such forms of payment are quite common in business.
- minimal administration;
- audit trails and archiving of transactions;
- support for purchase authorization and control;
- customer-differentiated price lists.

For suppliers, the unique selling propositions are:

- ease of entry and low entry cost, if desired via the 'bureau service' (hosting of catalogues and subscription to purchase card);
- commission paid is nearly the same as for purchase card-support only;
- immediate global presence.

Marketing Mix

Product Customization and Development

A Tradezone node is delivered as a turnkey system. It requires only a limited amount of customization to support franchisee identity and brand. A franchisee may wish to set up own Web-pages, but this is relatively straightforward.

Previously development was technology driven, aimed at concept exploration (e.g. the European E2S project with HP and Visa). Now that the product is being rolled-out commercially, further developments will be customer driven as well as depending on the competition, and will be more strongly based on market research. Future directions are to cover supply-chain integration, the handling of critical or non-catalogue purchases next to standard items, and possibly support for auctions and tendering. In all of these areas Tradezone would clearly run into new competition. Technical difficulties have been experienced in particular in maintaining a truly global product classification and trading service reach, which were being addressed by a dedicated team at the company that

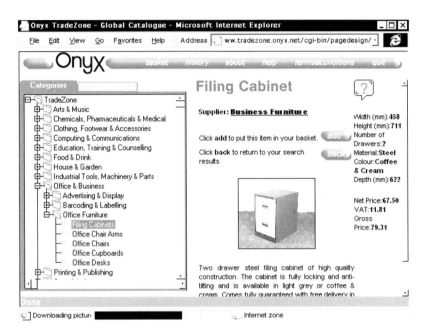

Figure 4.10   *Screenshot of Tradezone's Web user interface. (Reproduced by permission of Tradezone International Ltd)*

worked together closely with catalogue producers. An example of the global catalogue, expanded into sub-catalogues, leading to the selection of a specific item, is given in the screenshot, in Figure 4.10.

Distribution and Fulfilment

Distribution of Tradezone to the franchisees is largely outsourced. Most of the sales are foreseen as happening via Arthur Andersen. The delivery and installation of supporting hardware and software are the task of HP (turnkey systems approach). Only after-sales support will be direct from Tradezone to its franchisees. Regional support centres are expected to be set up.

Franchisees might work directly with their customers, although they can also engage channel partners, as mentioned before, to have a wider reach, leading to a second level of 'virtual' Tradezone nodes.

Promotion

Brand building is key for Tradezone International in achieving customer confidence and generating critical mass. The larger part of the initial venture capital investment in Tradezone International will be used for brand promotion, for which a global PR company is contracted. In addition, Tradezone uses exhibitions and special events.

Franchisees can determine their own promotion, for which Tradezone International will provide copy. However, in order to achieve wide brand recognition, it will also be necessary for the franchisees to contribute significantly to Tradezone brand promotion. The total promotion budget was estimated to be $5 million per month, shared between Tradezone International and the franchisees.

Some of the franchisees may have a strong brand themselves, e.g. banks or telecom operators. However, Mr Jeffries believes that it is better for them to make use of a new brand, Tradezone, rather than use their own brand as the primary one. An existing brand may have unwanted connotations and implications, for example suppliers may not want to deal with a specific bank that also happens to be the Tradezone franchisee.

Pricing

Franchisees have to invest about £250 000 in the hardware and software. In addition, they have to contribute upwards of £1 million in marketing and working capital.

The turnover is to be generated from transaction fees as follows (all figures are indicative). Each transaction is charged at 2%, of which 0.5% goes to Tradezone International and 1.5% to the franchisee. If an inter-franchise transaction is done, the purchasing franchisee gets 0.5% of the 1.5% and the supplying franchisee gets 1%. If the market-share objectives materialize, this would make Tradezone International into a $200 million company by the year 2002.

A franchisee can also generate turnover from the bureau service, which provides income from bringing catalogues online and updating them and from fees for purchase card-support. Franchisee service fees might be controlled by the franchise agreement in order to avoid price competition at the expense of quality among franchisees.

Tradezone International charges a $10 000 annual fee (to prevent would-be franchisees taking out non-used franchisee licenses). Suppliers can go online at very low cost, e.g. a 1000-item catalogue costs only £2000.

It is expected that by 2003 price pressure will emerge, with suppliers and purchasers starting to complain about the transaction fees.

Process and People

The franchisee plays a key role in delivering the service. Franchisee staff are actively involved in bringing the catalogues online, in identifying and certifying suppliers and purchasers and in integrating their own other services. Tradezone International will conduct quality and security audits.

Summary—Marketing Model

Tradezone's strategic approach is to build global market share rapidly as a third-party marketplace provider in the emerging global online MRO market through a well-designed franchising programme and strategic partnerships. This approach makes franchisees co-owners, while the partners ensure critical functions such as platform delivery, financial services, acquisition and consultancy. The basis is a technology platform, which Tradezone considers to be the best in the market for the suppliers and purchasers in its support for transparent global trading and the best for the franchisees in its support for co-ownership, fair sharing of commissions, security and turnkey installation.

Tradezone International might take its partnership-cum-outsourcing approach even further, such that a core company results whose only roles are product and process IPR ownership, brand ownership and R&D.

Postscript

The description above reflected the situation at about mid/end 1998. By that time Tradezone had decided to differentiate its offering further and package it into seven different types of licences. These include the franchising/Tradezone service operator scheme, as well as a scheme in which the purchaser would operate its own electronic trading system based on Tradezone's technology. The latter is most relevant for large purchasers who wish to trade directly with their suppliers, rather than through a third-party-operated marketplace. This purchaser-operated procurement option was starting to generate more sales than the third-party marketplace franchising approach. This development has parallels in the evolution of Citius. The reader is also referred to the analysis of industry competition in Chapter 5, which addresses the power of large customers and identifies purchaser-operated trading systems as a possible development.

GLOBAL ENGINEERING NETWORK/INDUSTRIAL COOPERATION SYSTEM: COLLABORATION AND TRADING IN DESIGN AND MANUFACTURING

Business—Customers—Competition

Global Engineering Network (GEN) is a concept, rather than a product: the idea is to enable collaboration in distributed design and engineering projects using the Internet to share data and designs, manage a project and perform ordering, payment and delivery. The GEN concept, first presented by Rethfeld in 1994, fits closely with the emergence of new paradigms in manufacturing and business process organization, such as agile enterprises, non-linear production chains and self-organizing systems, which are all important areas of research.[69]

Radeke (1997) gives an example of how a GEN-like system works in mechanical engineering: a designer, using a computer-aided design package (CAD), needs a motor for a robotic arm. He/she searches with the same search engine both internal and external databases on the intranet/extranet or public Internet. Suppose an external supplier has a suitable drive. CAD data are transmitted to the designer and integrated into the design. When the design is completed and production is planned, a production engineer can order the motor within the same environment.

The GEN concept thus utilises both company internal data and external data, which can be accessed transparently with appropriate access permissions via the intranet, extranet or the public Internet. These data are accessed and manipulated on the basis of domain-specific semantics, a meta-level description that is shared across the GEN environment. Companies can also put their data on the intranet of a value-added service provider, e.g. a branch organization or an ISP, which is particularly relevant for SMEs within an industry sector.

Business

An association of companies and universities, GLENnet has been created to promote the GEN concept. Some of the members provide products that implement the concept, one of which is Globana Online. Another implementation of the concept is Procat-GEN, oriented towards collaborative publishing of engineering catalogues.[70] The description below is based on interviews with Mr Rethfeld, VP of Globana Online GmbH[71] who is at the origin of the GEN concept, and literature surveys.[72] Deutsche Telekom (DT) supports Globana's implementation of the GEN concept, named Industrial Co-operation System (ICS). The collaboration between Deutsche Telekom and Globana, called DT/Globana below, was being reviewed for DT's strategic involvement in the GEN concept by the end of 1998. The description below largely reflects the thinking before this time.

DT/Globana aims to provide complete supply-chain support, including production-capacity management and trading, as well as the core functionality of the original GEN concept, collaborative design and engineering. A system like ICS can potentially involve an industry sector as a whole.

Globana's business is in product development, services and special project engineering for industrial cooperation. While DT's core business is in telecommunications, it has recently created an electronic commerce business unit to deal with 'Web-oriented industrial electronic commerce', which is a completely new business segment for DT. Deutsche Telekom is to provide the ICS product, telecommunications and related services, while both Globana and Deutsche Telekom are to offer engineering support. Although DT is to host the ICS system, i.e. provide the communications support, the information built up in the system is not to be managed or held by Deutsche Telekom.

Data from the Yankee group, provided by Globana, illustrate the attractiveness of the emerging business-to-business electronic commerce market. These show that industry was moving towards Internet technology for intranets during 1997 and from 1998 onwards will use the same technology for interenterprise business relationships at increasingly larger scales in extranet configurations that will replace expensive and proprietary communication facilities such as SNA from IBM. Once the open, interoperable, interindustry communication infrastructure is in place, the B-to-B electronic commerce market is expected to grow exponentially, from DM6–7 billion in 1998, to DM100 billion in 1999 and DM250 billion in 2000 (worldwide).

DT/Globana market research indicates that there are 10 000 potential customers for ICS-like products in Germany, and that companies are willing to invest DM500 000 to 1 000 000 to be enabled to go on to Internet technology-based communication by means of an ICS-like system. Therefore, the German first installation market can be estimated to be DM5–10 billion. While this first market will exist during first four to five years, it is believed that the services and communication revenues that will be generated later on will be considerably larger in turnover. Services, for example, could have a value of DM60–100 billion yearly. Turnover contributions thus consist of:

- first installation;
- upgrading;
- services;
- telecommunications.

Benefits

The benefits that ICS sets out to deliver are multiple:

- reduced time to market;
- reduced design cost through reuse of designs and other information;

- reduced production cost through cheaper sourcing;
- reduced overall transaction costs:
  - by concentrating company resources on its core competencies;
  - by working together with other companies who provide their core competencies;
- improved product quality, through knowledge pooling and collaborative communication;
- improved product lifecycle management, including after-sales management;
- increased customer orientation through supplier-managed 'information stock';
- product innovation;
- industrial services innovation.

GEN's overall goal is to make structured engineering information and knowledge easily accessible in all business processes.

The GEN concept not only enables faster access to information, but also leads to better management of information. Customers can search for specific components, designs or services. The supplier administers data related to a customer in the supplier's information store. This may include product specifications such as design diagrams. In this way, the customer is relieved of this type of data management. Data can be pulled together to build up a complete project involving multiple partners. Cooperation functions are added to this, enabling the company to take a step towards the virtual enterprise. Furthermore, a wide range of additional consultancy services is conceivable around the core concept.

The example given above illustrates some of these benefits. The robotics arm designer has first of all fast access to a worldwide pool of component designs in the GEN network, reusing design knowledge through external sourcing. He/she can thus concentrate on core tasks, losing less time in finding components and avoiding reinventing the wheel. By integrating the ordering process a further reduction of time to market is achieved, while the maintenance of customer-specific information, at the supplier's site, allows for better management of changes or reordering after production. New service providers can take part in the network, for example those who pool information and make this accessible such as industry sector organizations, or those who provide online robotics design assistance or run a robotics designer virtual community.

Customers

In principle, any production-related (industrial) company is a customer. This includes designers, manufacturers that perform the ultimate assembly or construction, subassemblers, suppliers, distributors, consultants etc. Typical sectors are construction, mechanical engineering and electrical engineering, which have rather complex requirements.

The primary driver in such sectors is reduction of time to market. Customers are well aware that information and communications technology can be a means to speed up the search for information and that collaboration can help to reduce design and construction time. The main gain is expected to be in greater and faster reuse of internal as well as external knowledge. For example, in a process plant realization project, 70–95% of the design work could consist of the reusing, configuring and assembling of existing components, solutions and knowledge.

In these sectors a new 'post-mass-production' paradigm is emerging, which takes into account the global dimension, provides more customized products with higher value added, and has the capability of reconfiguring the products for different purposes and produce and reproducing a single product in various facilities. To implement such a paradigm, knowledge must be systematized and navigation and retrieval systems are needed to make external and internal knowledge available for each business process (Salminen *et al.*, 1997).

Customers in these sectors may already be working with business partners, but are seeking ways to overcome the limitations of cost and lack of compatibility that have until now been barriers to wide industrial collaboration.

Competition

Globana considers as its main competitors EDS and GEIS and other large companies that are system integrators and solution providers at the same time. In 1996 GEIS created a joint venture with Netscape, called Actra, to develop Web-enabled solutions for (partial) value-chain management. In 1997 Actra became a fully owned development company of Netscape. Netscape is now owned by AOL in a strong partnership with Sun. An example of what could ultimately evolve into a GEN-like system is ANX in the US automotive sector, in which both EDS and GEIS are involved. Currently, ANX is still more about interconnection of suppliers and manufacturers than about collaboration. Mr Rethfeld believes that EDS and other system integrators aim to be the dominant player in all industry sectors, very similar to Deutsche Telekom's broad approach, which is not limited to a single sector.

An important difference between DT/Globana and EDS or GEIS is that the latter two are global whereas the former is focused on the German market only. This might become an important disadvantage for DT/Globana, as the supply chain extends across several countries in many industrial sectors.

In the same category as EDS and GEIS, but not (yet) having a product offering, are large system integrators like Debis. Another company that has been active in developing the GEN concept from its inception is Siemens, which has created a business services division that is expected to move into this area based on GENIAL, Siemens/C-Lab implementation of GEN.

The GEN literature also identifies industrial engineering marketplaces like CompoNet, PartNet,[73] Transtec and EMV-Online as potential competitors. However, the disadvantage of these systems is perceived to be their centralizing approach. In the GEN concept, the end-user engineer at the individual company level maintains the information, supported by common engineering semantics.

The GEN products do not aim at routine, repetitive purchases. Engineering is much more specific, project oriented, has a high technical content and delivers non-routine solutions. Therefore third-party electronic marketplace systems like Citius, or shopping malls like Industry.Net for routine, non-critical or standard, off-the-shelf products, are not perceived as outright competition.

One might object that companies will have both routine and non-routine purchases, but would prefer to have an integrated purchasing system. For example, their financial system needs to consolidate the two modes of purchasing. Technically there are various ways to combine or integrate the two modes of purchasing (ranging from desktop integration to back-end order processing). From the marketing point of view, the logic is compelling of being able to offer at least both routine and non-routine electronic purchasing, let alone being able to offer an integrated solution.

In this respect, it is interesting that EDS is capable of offering both, having purchased Citius. However, there is no integrated solution as of today. GEIS is potentially in a similar position through its alliance with Thomas Register, offering GEIS TPN Register. It is not known if Deutsche Telekom has similar plans to offer an electronic trading system, or in other words to become a third-party marketplace provider (cf. Belgacom with Citius). For a telecommunications provider to offer such a system will also depend on pure telecommunications revenues that can be generated, in addition to its interest in revenues from a new area of business of third-party marketplace services. It must be said that the volume of data involved in individual transactions in routine purchasing is far less than in an online design and engineering collaboration.

Table 4.3 provides an assessment of the competitive strengths and weaknesses of DT/Globana and its major competitors.

Table 4.3   *Assessment of Deutsche Telekom/Globana's ICS and competitors*

	Key Assets	Key Weaknesses
Deutsche Telekom AG/Globana	Strong sales network in Germany Strong telecommunications presence in customer base Technological base in telecoms Advanced and comprehensive concept and initial implementation	National orientation Telecommunications rather than than industrial engineering culture New business services division still in start-up phase Management commitment not clear
EDS	Systems integrator and solutions culture Involved in ANX Complementary global trading system Global presence	Not yet an industrial solution
GEIS	Systems integrator and solutions culture Involved in ANX Complementary trading system (although US focused)	Centralising approach may be perceived as not customer friendly
Siemens	Strong presence in Germany and in many other countries Strong information technology base Near to implementation of GEN-like system	Relatively strong national orientation Management commitment not clear Relatively new electronic commerce services division
IBM	Strong global presence Large system services and not solutions division Strong technology base	Not (yet?) a product offer Not an industrial engineering culture in the services division

Competitive Advantages

DT/Globana considers that it would have the following competitive advantages:

- comprehensive 'benefits to all parties' concept and vision and early innovation;
- broad technological capabilities, from basic telecommunications to distributed database systems and Internet multimedia interfaces;
- brand name of Deutsche Telekom (primarily in Germany);
- pervasive DT-operated data communications infrastructure;[74]
- large existing DT customer base of industrial telecommunications users;
- tight relationships with all industrial parties;

- involved in ENX, (http://www.enx.de) the European counterpart to the US ANX network.

Mr Rethfeld emphasizes the difference between two ways of thinking about industrial cooperation. The first is the '1:N Business Net', the hub–spoke approach in which smaller suppliers have to follow standards and possibly several implementations of major manufacturers. This approach may be fast to implement, being driven by the market power of the large actors. However, Mr Rethfeld believes that the '1:N Business Net' will deliver benefits mainly to the large manufacturers.

The alternative way is the 'M:N Business Net', a network defined by a 'co-opetition' of members of the supply chain, with a neutral organization being responsible for common standards and possibly the operation. This will ensure maximum compatibility, with an arbitration function. ICS is along the second line of thinking, aiming to deliver benefits to all parties involved.

Structure of the Market of Collaboration Platform Providers

The collaborative platform market remains in its infancy. The GEN concept still needs to be explained and actual sales are only just starting. Mr Rethfeld believes that competition is needed to develop the market. At the same time, he foresees that the market will ultimately develop towards a situation in which there will be one dominant player for each industry sector. This is understandable, as the new networked collaboration systems are of an infrastructural nature, involving a sector as a whole rather than an individual company. Equally, the market is expected to grow rapidly and become very large, as stated before.

The 'big three' of ANX (Ford, GM, Chrysler) presented their vision of future communication strategy at an ANX conference (in Detroit, 1998), as explained in Figure 4.11. A company will install and operate its fully controlled intranet (even in worldwide distributed locations). For any communications with the outside world there will be two controlled connections. One is to the public Internet for the following applications:

- worldwide e-mail communication;
- presenting the company image;
- business-to-consumer solutions for information and selling;
- business-to-business solutions in selling and purchasing for non-production-related goods and services.

The second connection is to a closed 'sectornet' (like ANX, ENX). Applications are:

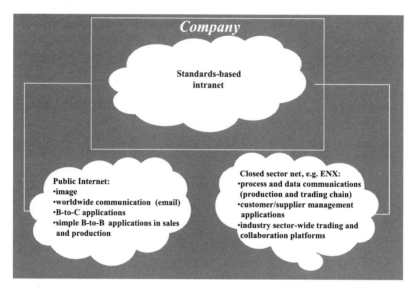

Figure 4.11   *Use of intranet/extranet/public Internet*

- direct program-to-program and data-exchange communication via Virtual Private Networks (VPN);
- customer/supplier management solutions for interactive collaboration between one enterprise and its customers or suppliers (1:N Business Net);
- industrial sector-wide trade and collaboration marketplaces.

Although initiatives like ANX and ENX are prerequisites for GEN-like platforms such as ICS, they are in no way in competition.

Early adopters and innovators, regardless of the industrial sector, may not be willing to wait until the complete industrial sector, possibly driven by their associations, will take the initiative to set up a sector net. For these a 1:N business net solution will offer enough benefit to start their own investment to connect their existing suppliers and/or customers. These solutions typically run in an extranet configuration. They should later be gathered into a M:N business net. Therefore DT/Globana would concentrate its marketing effort first on 1:N business net solutions and monitor and support any initiatives at sectorial level, even outside of the industry.

Consequently, it is understandable that Globana, as a small company, is not considered to have the resources needed to become the dominant provider of such collaboration platforms, and instead requires a strong partner. Deutsche Telekom is such a partner because of its underpinning communications technology, its financial strength and its extensive marketing infrastructure, in Germany at least. Globana's strength is largely complementary to DT's, providing concept development and technical implementation, based on a strong knowledge of the business of industrial intercompany collaboration. In this partnership arrangement DT has little influence on product development. It does, however, fill in market research gaps at Globana. There is some concern at Globana that DT is still in the early days of developing its new electronic commerce business. Coming from the phone business ('counting ticks'), the software and service business is not readily accepted and still has to prove itself.

Global presence is not considered to be a high priority at this stage, although DT's partnerships with other telecom companies such as France Telecom are expected to help in getting access to other geographic markets. The lack of emphasis on global marketing presence is somewhat surprising, in view of the global thinking behind the original GEN concept, driven by the trends in the customer base (as described above).

The competitors for collaborative platforms thus consist of large companies, some of them in partnership with smaller specialist companies (e.g. DT/Globana, GEIS-Thomas Register, EDS-Citius).

At the supply side of collaboration platforms are telecommunications providers or Internet service providers (in the case of ICS, the supplier is DT itself). Most ISPs are too small to be a threat, and it is expected that large ISPs such as Deutsche Telekom itself will swallow many of them. Furthermore, ISPs generally do not have the capability to run large projects. Other suppliers include hardware and software companies, like IBM, HP and Microsoft. Mr Rethfeld believes that Microsoft will not pose a competitive threat as a supplier, as it aims at a lower level of business support than collaboration platforms. IBM, with a large services division, could move into this area, but does not yet have a product offer. Yet another technology supplier is Intershop, whose technology is part of ICS but is also used by DT for business-to-consumer electronic commerce.

Some of the potential customers might be in a strong position towards the collaboration platform providers, depending on the sector. The automotive sector, for example, is well organized and has strong companies. As it is in a position to define its own sector-wide solution, DT/Globana has a large interest in working closely with them. One potential threat is the close relationships of the automotive industry with system integrators (e.g. Debis is owned by Daimler; EDS's former link to GM, GEDAS, is owned by VW). They could decide to have their own system developed instead of using a customized version of ICS. DT/Globana's neutral position could then be an advantage.

Marketing Strategy

Segmentation and Targeting

DT/Globana aims at the largest industrial companies in Germany, without differentiation among sectors. In the first phase of the introduction of ICS, only potential early adopter/early innovator companies are contacted, as this is a new way of doing business. These companies are characterized by:

- a high level of awareness of Internet technology and application;
- a high level of awareness of the potential of further intercompany collaboration.

These early innovators are already installing intranets and are keen to extend these to their business partners. Until now their old computer and communication systems and interconnection costs have prevented them from realizing this. With global Internet standards they now see the opportunity to overcome these obstacles.

Competitive Positioning

These early innovators know DT as a respected and capable supplier for all components of secure intranets and extranets. Moreover, DT can make available the high bandwidth that is necessary for GEN-like collaborative engineering applications.

DT/Globana would position itself as the only provider that has a solution that 'leaves the suppliers and the customers in control'. This is the idea of the distributed information store: each partner manages its own information, while ICS still makes all these distributed information stores uniformly accessible. This can be contrasted with the competitors' approach of having a central database of information, which is owned and managed by the provider.

Strategic Objectives

Deutsche Telekom's product-market strategy in the coming two to three years would be focused on building its name in Germany in this type of business. At the same time, DT wants to assess the commercial viability of being a telecommunications host and service provider of industrial collaboration platforms like ICS.

As a company, Globana aims to establish a reputation as a high-quality, innovative firm in industrial information technology. Rather than aiming to become very large, its interest is in focusing and strengthening its niche orientation in innovation for kicking off new businesses rather than implementing and growing such businesses. In a few years' time Globana may decide to move into new areas.

Marketing Mix

Product/Service

The ICS product offering will be provided in bundles, with subscription levels relevant for M:N business solutions. In addition, individual customer wishes are supported through customization.

Product and service development is market driven: technology, competition and customers all play a role. Much guidance is obtained from pilot work. For example, a pilot was done in mechanical engineering, involving 50 SMEs. Although DT/Globana intended to extend ICS to support spare shop-floor capacity trading, it found out that this was highly sensitive, as it required SMEs to divulge their production levels. Guidance is also coming from continuous and intense market research and strategic planning performed by DT staff and many personal contacts, in particular those of Globana with prospective customers. Although there is not yet a competitive system which is functionally fully comparable to ICS, potential competition such as GE-TPN is monitored.

As far as technology is concerned, although there are some proprietary developments, important components are licensed from and jointly developed with others.

Distribution

Deutsche Telekom's sales channels should be used. These are built up as follows:

- the top 200 companies are to be served by a fully dedicated salesperson per customer;
- large accounts are to be served by one salesperson per 10 accounts;
- one salesperson per 100 accounts is to serve business accounts.

SMEs are in the 1 per 100 category and therefore receive rather limited attention. DT has recognized this and intends to set up a DT-partner scheme for its electronic commerce business services.

Promotion

Both product and firm branding is considered to be important. Primarily it would use the reputation of Deutsche Telekom. Product branding consists of the concept name Global Engineering Network (which as a brand is owned by the GLENnet association), and the specific brand name ICS.

Promotion is to be undertaken entirely by Deutsche Telekom, in view of the priority of building a name in this type of business. The most important way to deliver the message to the customer is via DT's direct salesforce. The engineering world closely associates the quality of the offering with such personal and long-term relationships. Usual means such as brochures and journals as well as major trade shows like CEBIT support this, as do contributions to events organized by industry associations and individual sales promotions to the management of such associations.

Although the prime target group of early innovators is technology aware, it is most important to talk their 'supply-chain-oriented language'. The key element of the message therefore is 'we help you to manage your supply chain'.

Pricing

Price is not considered to be a competitive factor. Even medium-sized companies are willing to invest DM1-2 million in changing to effective TCP/IP-based solutions. The software is priced comparable to the pricing of packages from SAP. In addition to that, there are service fees and transaction fees. Interestingly, customers prefer service pricing, for example for access to design expertise, on a subscription basis rather than pay-per-use. The reason is that time to market requires a guaranteed response at the moment that the demand is there (which is often a matter of urgency).

Process and people

Pilot experiments have shown that in the acceptance of the ICS system the 'people factor' is key. This holds for the salespeople as well as for the customers. Proposing a partnership with the customer is considered the best way to deal with this. Customers' demands and wishes are monitored on the basis of this partnership approach, feeding information back to DT to tune marketing. However, this means a culture change for DT, as telecommunications is something completely different to industrial engineering.

The power base at the customer determines which aspect of ICS is emphasized most. If this is at design and engineering, e.g. in automotive, the emphasis will be on collaborative design facilities. If it is with purchasing, the procurement side of ICS will be promoted. If it is with marketing and sales, it will be the supply-side support.

Summary—Marketing Model

The core of the GEN concept is a collaborative design and engineering platform. Globana/DT's ICS implementation of GEN encompasses even more, up to full supply-chain support. As such, it is of an infrastructural nature and likely to be most effective if it is used throughout an industrial sector. Customers will not be running their business on more than one infrastructure. Consequently, the marketing strategy is aimed at achieving dominance within a sector ('be number one or nothing'). As Globana is too small to achieve that on its own (and besides is more interested in a very focused, niche activity), it was necessary to find a credible large partner such as Deutsche Telekom. While with this partnership at first sight all the conditions are fulfilled to achieve market dominance, success is by no means guaranteed. The market is at an initial stage only. It is not evident *a priori* that DT/Globana has an unbeatable competitive advantage compared to strong global and national current and future competitors such as EDS, GEIS and Siemens.

INFOMAR: REORGANIZING AN AUCTION-BASED MARKET

Business—Customers—Competition

Business

Infomar is a real-time information and communication system in the fishing trade, linking fish buyers, sellers and fishing vessels, including an electronic auction system. Infomar originated from the ESPRIT pilot project of the same name,[75] in which Schelfhout Computer Systems (SCS) from Belgium is the auction-building partner. Infomar, as an advanced development, illustrates the changes in the business of electronic auctions. Information was obtained from interviewing Luc Schelfhout,[76] CEO and owner of SCS, from background information about Infomar,[77] and from other examples of Internet auctions.[78] A recent detailed analysis of electronic auctions can be found in the *International Journal of Electronic Markets*.[79] The current section describes Infomar, putting it in the context of the market of time-critical auction systems in general. Infomar is being marketed by SCS under the name Multi-Trade.

SCS business is electronic auction systems.[80] Created in 1983, the company currently serves 150 customers throughout Europe, Africa and Asia with auction systems of varying technical sophistication. Some are very simple, clock-based systems with a push button at a desk to stop the clock. Others provide mobility through a radiographic device with a push button. Yet other solutions offer remote participation in screen-based auctions via an ISDN network and PCs. SCS also provides integrated solutions for the whole bidding–contracting–administration–delivery–payment cycle, where necessary linking to existing administrative systems (e.g. SAP).

SCS has a turnover of BF150 million (about US$5 million) and 35 employees. SCS and NIAFF Smit from the Netherlands together dominate the market for electronic auction systems: amongst them they have about 90% of the market, of which SCS's share is about 60%.

Customers

The direct customers of auction systems are the auctions themselves. SCS's systems are primarily supplied to sell perishable products such as flowers, vegetables, fruits, fish and livestock on a spot market. The actors involved in auctions are the producers (farmers, fishermen), wholesalers, individual supermarkets and the market maker, that is, the auction itself. Auctions are often run by a cooperative, owned by the farmers or fishermen.

As auctions have sprung up around a locality such as a port or a city, there used to be many of them all across Europe. Gradually auctions have started to merge and collaborate, a trend that is most advanced in sectors such as flowers and in a country such as the Netherlands (where only a few flower auctions still exist). Fisheries is still very fragmented, with some 400 auctions in Europe alone, and auctions in southern Europe are still less inclined to collaboration then those in the north.

Mr Schelfhout observes that the process of concentration and consolidation is irreversible, in Europe at least. In that sense, his market is shrinking in terms of number of customers. However, geographic expansion still offers plenty of opportunity to automate existing auctions in Africa, India or Latin America, or to help set up new auctions, e.g. in India, with the development of local agriculture.

Fragmentation is also reflected in the thinking about electronic auction systems. Customers tend to believe that their needs are unique and are not very aware of the similarities that exist, even between auctions for completely different types of products. Therefore they sometimes require exclusivity from suppliers. Effectively, however, 90% of their requirements are identical and each auction system requires only 10% customization. SCS's advantage is in knowing all these markets and leveraging the similarities. Therefore it will not enter into exclusive agreements.

Farmers and especially fishermen are generally speaking rather conservative. Mr Schelfhout observes that they tend to have little interest in the marketing and sale of their produce. Farmers work hard during a whole season and then, when their products are harvested and brought to the auction halls, sit back and let the price 'verdict' happen to them. Fishermen still largely have a hunter mentality, taking the sales process for granted and expecting a good price for all the risks that they took while out at sea. Fisheries is the most conservative sector, being years behind the other sectors in terms of use of market automation.

However, ultimately those producers will have to think more about the trading aspects of their business and participate more actively in the negotiation phase. Competition among producers, enhanced by cheaper transport, is leading to lower prices to the extent that some even run into losses. In the farming sector, the response has been to form larger farms to achieve economies of scale and to increase production yield. However, there are limits to this. In addition, this has turned out to be a dangerous route as markets tend to be cyclical, leading to oversupply and in some cases fatal loss of income in bad years. Lack of involvement of the producers in the trade increased their exposure to risk. As an example, it has happened that farmers, lacking information about the likely price for their products, were not even aware that the cost of harvesting and delivering to the auction would be more than the price they would finally receive. They would have been better off leaving the produce unharvested! Thus the limits of spot auctions, in the farming business, have become increasingly clear over the past few years.

This trend has happened at the same time as the power of large buyers such as supermarket chains has increased. These large buyers are sometimes so strong that they can manipulate prices. In fact, they are not very interested in having to negotiate every day—they prefer to conclude long-term contracts.

Finally, another trend, at least in farming, is that production is becoming increasingly predictable with controlled quality through modern farming techniques. Agriculture is industrializing.

The farming sector illustrates the changes that these trends are bringing about for producers and buyers. In farming, for example, futures contracting has developed next to the spot market. Large buyers purchase in advance of production to get guaranteed supply at lower transaction cost, while the buyers get guaranteed prices and less exposure to risk. In Europe, initially producers did not want to sell directly to buyers, being afraid that the negotiating power of the cooperatives would be eroded. However, with the development of the internal market in Europe, large buyers have started to bypass them, dealing directly with producers in countries such as Spain. Ultimately, the cooperatives had to accept futures contracts. The spot market is still needed, however, to 'clean' the market, that is, to even out fluctuations and uncertainties in demand and supply, through price negotiation. In addition, the small producers do not yet take part in futures contracting. In fact, a new generation of farmers is coming up quickly who are taking an industrial approach to farming, in terms of production, delivery and trading, and who are actively performing risk management. While these new producers account for only about 10–20% of all farmers, they already make up 50–70% of production value.

The next step in the farming business is expected to be the rapid growth of the emerging futures market, to trade futures contracts just as happens for minerals or shipping capacity.

An advanced information system like Infomar intends to support in fisheries the same trading changes as have been occurring in farming: while still at sea the fishermen can sell part of the catch in advance of landing and unloading. The remainder is sold at the physical auction. In this way the information chain is increasingly being split from the physical chain. In addition, the fragmentation of auctions within an increasingly open market is being addressed, by interconnecting auctions in the Infomar network and allowing buyers to deal at any market.

This has profound implications, not only for the auctions, but also for the role of the other actors and for the supporting systems. For example, trading without seeing the goods requires quality control and standardization of quality measurements. Judging the quality at sea would require new qualifications for fishermen. Trading the catch from a vessel would require a fisherman to be able to negotiate and select a bid. These changes together are too much of a change, however. There is still a need for a vessel's selling agent on shore to look at catch reports, put the supply offer into the information system, and negotiate on behalf of the fishermen. Currently futures contracting in fish is still rather small (about 10%) but it is growing rapidly.

However, new systems like Infomar are likely to cut out those middlemen who do not create added value and who take advantage of the fact that the market has not been sufficiently transparent and organized. Clearly, these middlemen, who might influence customers, are not in favour of the introduction of systems like Infomar. Figure 4.12 describes the relationship between the actors in fish auctions and the role of the Infomar trading system. It shows its two components, namely spot market support for short-term transactions and options market support (futures) for long-term transactions.

Competition

Competition is very limited; as has been said, there is really only one competitor, NIAFF Smit. An auction may exceptionally decide to liaise with a technology developer to obtain its own electronic system, based on the desire to have full control. In some markets, e.g. France, near saturation of market share has been achieved, which leads to some erosion of the customer base from time to time. In addition, this is a gradually shrinking market because of mergers of auctions.

The rise of the Internet has led to a plethora of online auctions. Turban[81] counted about 100 companies currently doing auctions on the Internet. Their business model is to sell trading information and to charge for transactions, rather than to support full trading with deep business

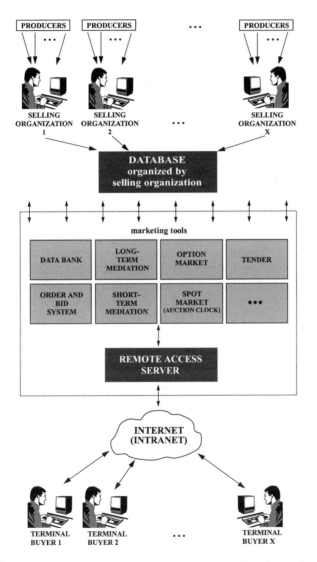

Figure 4.12 *Actors and their relationships in Infomar trading. (Reproduced by permission of Luc Schelfhout)*

knowledge as does SCS. However, Internet auction technology providers might well become a competition alternative to SCS's technology, as much of this technology is of a generic nature. In the future, auctions might be tempted to use such technology, supplying the business expertise themselves.

SCS, having monitored this development over the past few years without getting actively involved, has now concluded that the Internet is indeed going to be the key technology platform on which to compete and has consequently decided to concentrate its development resources on the Internet. It expects that its primary market will continue to be perishable product auctions, although it does not exclude moving into other types of auctions, e.g. for second-hand cars.

Competitive Advantages

SCS believes that its competitive advantage lies in understanding the role of the actors, the market mechanisms and the business processes in the rather conservative market of perishable goods auctions. This holds not only for the bidding part of auctions but for the trading cycle as a whole, including logistics and administration. While SCS is not a technology leader, it is nevertheless strong in applying advanced technology (e.g. Internet, radio, broadband networks). It considers that its technology strength is especially in dealing with time-critical processes. With respect to the application of new technology for electronic auctions, it believes that it is 'better to be a strong follower than take the first user risk'.

Structure of the Electronic Auctions Market for Perishable Goods

The main barrier to entry to this market is knowledge of the business. SCS has built this up over many years, having grown with the development of thinking in the perishable goods world itself.

SCS intends to maintain its market leadership, but does not want to grow much larger than it is today. Competition in the industry exists but, rather than fighting itself for the existing market, SCS seeks to sell into new markets, which are either in other countries or for auctioning of other time-critical products. Markets are becoming saturated (replacement sales are only small) and, because of the ongoing consolidation among auctions throughout Europe, the market is already shrinking in a number of European countries. SCS still sees plenty of opportunity, nevertheless, in Eastern Europe, Asia and Africa and to some extent in Latin America. In terms of auctioning time-critical products, fish auctions continue to represent an opportunity (of the 400 fisheries auctions in Europe, only

40 have until now been provided with automated systems from SCS, which is leading in this market).

In the past, large IT solutions providers have tried to enter the market. Although they could build a one-off system, they did not manage to achieve economies of scale fast enough, lacking intimate knowledge of the true nature of differences between auctions. In addition, the electronic auctions market was too small for them compared to other business opportunities. For suppliers of the underlying technology (PCs, networking etc.) this market is too small. Some small new technology developers are entering this market through a liaison with individual auctions.

However, SCS believes that as long as it does not itself become competition for the auctions, these entrants will generally not be tempted to develop an auction system themselves. Therefore, SCS is very careful not to eliminate any market actors, and in particular not to threaten its own customer base by moving into services that are supplied by the auctions, even though it might be able to deliver such services better and cheaper.

Altogether it looks as if SCS is in a very well-defended and defendable position in a niche market (although with limited growth opportunities). The only real threat is expected to emerge from Internet auction providers. For SCS it is clear that it will defend its niche at that side through innovation by means of Internet technology. Infomar is a critical development in this respect.

In summary:

SCS's product-market strategy is to stay market leader through:

1. continuous innovation by means of new technology with a view to adding value and achieving differentiation;
2. continuously moving into new markets as existing markets become saturated or even shrink. New markets are in other countries, or in the auctioning of other time-critical products.

Marketing Strategy

Internet Opportunity, Segmentation and Targeting

The Internet, although it is a near real-time system that is adequate to provide product information, cannot deliver the millisecond response times that are needed for real-time bidding. Therefore it is currently used to implement the market mechanism of futures bidding that is evolving next to the spot market, in order to do the following:

1. provide produce information to the selling agent (however, fish catch details such as day of catch, species, quantity etc. are not yet sent via the Internet but through the vessel–land radio network);
2. submit the supply offer to the auction, including demand price per lot—this is done by the selling agent;
3. collect buyers' bids and provide bid information for counter offers—this is the role of the auction;
4. accept an offer (by the selling agent);
5. register the deal and transmit information to sellers and buyers as well as into the logistics and administration system (the auction's task).

The main opportunities of the Internet for SCS are thus:

- standard, near real-time means of providing information and communication, implementing the separation between physical and information flows;
- international worldwide system, available at any PC with standard software at lower cost than previous dedicated solutions, broadening the number of parties that can participate in the bidding and reducing transaction costs;
- much easier and wider availability of information, which makes the market more transparent and reduces the opportunity for middlemen to make money at the expense of sellers or buyers;
- multimedia presentation of product information through standard browser technology, overcoming the lack of physical presence;
- lowering of customer-support costs for SCS itself.

The electronic spot market can also be dealt with when in the future the Internet provides guaranteed response times and time registration. One-to-one marketing based on the Internet is considered an option for the future.

SCS could also have chosen to develop an advanced system such as Infomar for other types of auctions, e.g. flowers or fruit. However, it targets the fish trade as this is considered the most difficult: a system that is capable of serving that market is expected to be suitable for other markets too.

The initial customers for the Infomar system are expected to be in the UK, France and the Netherlands. Other interested auctions will be in Germany, Belgium, Denmark, Norway, Ireland and Iceland (pilot customers include IJmuiden in the Netherlands and Oostende in Belgium, of which the latter decided at the end of 1998 to purchase the commercial version of the system). In total these comprise about 100 potential customers. Later markets in Spain, Portugal, Italy (in total about 100

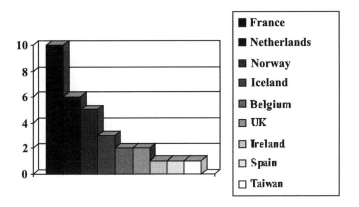

Figure 4.13 *Number of fish auctions with SCS systems*

potential customers) and Eastern Europe (Baltic, Russia, Poland, market size not yet assessed) are also to be covered. This geographic segmentation of the market is the result of considering factors like state of technology take-up at the potential customers, the potential size of the market and the current market presence of SCS in fish auctions (see Figure 4.13).

Positioning

This is very much a 'word-of-mouth' market, where reputation counts. Potential customers need to gain confidence that SCS can do the job and base themselves on references to existing customers. SCS positions itself as the market leader, highly respected because of its quality and innovation. It does not aim to be the lowest-cost provider.

Market Strategy—Summary

SCS considers that the new product, Infomar, is well adapted to the market and has a high growth potential. With Infomar and its existing product lines, it pursues the dual strategy outlined above.

Marketing Mix

Product/Service

The products are always customized. This is one of the added-value opportunities that SCS has built up over the years from its experience with the fishing industry. Customers expect a unique product/service, which goes far beyond the technical product only. In fact, each sale is a project. A high level of customer support is expected after the project has been delivered. SCS specializes in time-critical systems as needed for perishable products. Therefore support is aimed at minimizing loss of time and the time that an auction is out of operation. To this end, SCS maintains a full replacement capability for any auction component as well as private air transport to provide rapid service within 500 km. At a greater distance regional service centres take over that role.

Infomar is currently in a pilot stage. Advances in Internet technology imply periodic revisions to use new browser features. For the vessel application the same is true, for upgrading to newer communications technology. Additional links will be made between applications, so that the whole trading process may be automated.

Distribution and Sales

Typically a potential customer would visit an already automated auction, e.g. in Europe, to learn about the possibilities of improving the market operation for perishable products in its home location or country. SCS hears about this and contacts the prospect directly. Usually the potential customer has only a fuzzy idea of what he/she needs. SCS then offers to make an assessment at the customer's location of the opportunities for an electronic auction and may give a demonstration. The customer is asked to pay travel expenses for that first visit, which limits the sales effort to the more serious prospects.

Following this visit, SCS might suggest a technical-economic feasibility study. It would perform the study as coordinator of a consortium of experts called the European Auction Builders. EAB groups together expertise in electronic auction technology and operations, architecture, marketing, logistics and project management. Alternatively, the potential customer may have issued a tender to which EAB responds. Such a study can be quite profound, for example when a new auction is being set up, addressing industry analysis, market-structure analysis and proposal, market-concept development, technical implementation and business plan. Following the study, the customer can decide to award an implementation contract to SCS or to someone else.

SCS works with agents in various countries who establish the first contact. The subsequent assessment and study are usually performed by SCS Belgium. Direct sales on a project basis are the only way to sell in this business, with its high degree of customer-specific requirements.

Promotion

SCS uses newspaper articles, brochures, demonstration and word of mouth as promotional means. It considers all these means as secondary to the direct contacts and spends little effort on them. The Internet is hardly used for promotion, except to get international exposure for Infomar as an advanced pilot in the sector.

Price

A system like Infomar is either sold or offered for rent. Roughly half the customers are expected to buy the system. Prices for a single Infomar node are estimated to be about €100 000. However, there may be an initial phase during which the system is offered at a lower price in order to gain a large market share quickly. It is expected that service will be for free for a certain time after the pilot project.

Process and People

Infomar could potentially weaken the power of existing auctions and the middlemen, as it allows for direct buyer–seller negotiation. However, in the fishing industry the markets play a vital role to ensure the smooth functioning of the trade. They are in the first instance service providers, as collection centres and providers of the infrastructure for landing, grading, weighing, cool storage etc. They also take care of administration and payments and sometimes help the vessels to organize maintenance, delivery of fuel etc. Finally, they also play an important role in dispatching the sold fish to buyers.

Therefore, SCS states that any scheme that is introduced without the involvement and support of the markets will not succeed. However, it does expect that the role of traditional auctions will change over a period of years.

Physical Evidence

Separating physical and information flows, enabled by electronic auction systems (and more generally by Internet trading environments), introduces the need to provide physical evidence in another way. Quality standards are one way to achieve this. In the flower trade these are well established and harmonized. In the case of fish this is only at its very beginnings, and likely to be based on auction-dependent standards at first (e.g. 'Silver Sealed' at the fish auction at IJmuiden in the Netherlands). Some of the current quality assessment (organoleptic) is hard to perform at a distance. This is a barrier to the further development of international electronic trade in the fishing industry.

Summary—Marketing Model

SCS and Infomar provide an innovative electronic auction system for the fish trade, which creates a new market mechanism for trading in advance of landing at a port and in between auctions. This new market is to exist next to the traditional clock auction. This is expected to significantly reduce trading costs, which will lead to better prices for both suppliers and buyers. It also enables a much better match between demand and supply, leading to higher quality for consumers and less loss of catch. SCS generates income from the electronic auction software and hardware and from support. Its marketing strategy is based on using Infomar to gain market leadership in new product and geographic markets, while maximally exploiting its existing market leadership in established markets, and complementing its development of other geographic markets with existing auction systems.

SUMMARY

This chapter has presented a description of eight cases, which provide a variety of business models (some cases consist of several business models), as summarized in Figure 4.14.

The following two chapters provide a comparative analysis of these cases, with a view to understanding the market structure (in the sense of industry organization, competition, transaction costs) and their marketing strategies and programmes.

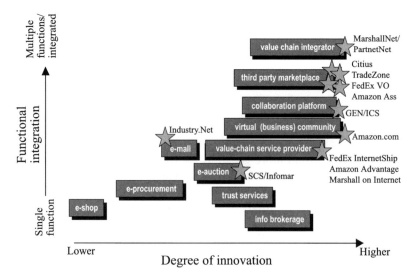

Figure 4.14 *Overview of business models in the case studies*

5
Markets and Competition

This chapter is the first part of the case-study analysis. It addresses the macro level, that is, the structure of industry and markets including competition among the market players, and focuses on the new features that emerge when doing business electronically. The next chapter will focus on the company level, the approach of companies to segmentation and targeting and marketing programmes for business-to-business electronic commerce in the Internet environment.

The analysis addresses industrial competitiveness, using Porter's competitive forces model (Porter, 1980). A generic analysis of the impact of electronic commerce on competitive advantages can also be found in Bloch, Pigneur and Segev (1996). Here in particular, the competitive structure of the industry of third-party marketplace providers is analysed in more detail. Several of the cases studied are pursuing this business model and their comparison leads to a number of conclusions, on the one hand about the extent to which the Internet reduces transaction costs and therefore brings 'perfect competition' closer and, on the other hand, about the challenges to intermediaries.

These two topics are then pursued further in the last two sections of the chapter. The first topic, transaction cost theory, is applied to the four cases for which more information could be obtained about strategic future orientations. This application of transaction cost theory leads to interesting insights into the functionality that will be needed either now or in the future for these providers to realize their strategies.

The second topic, the role of intermediaries, is analysed within the more general context of internal and external business organization. Within this context fit 'hot' topics such as disintermediation and reintermediation, as well as other business organization concepts of the late 1980s and early 1990s that gain a new meaning through the Internet, such as value networks or network organizations.

INDUSTRY STRUCTURE

A number of the cases considered are about generic catalogue handling (third party marketplace providers, electronic industry malls, value-chain service providers that extend into catalogue handling). This section analyses industry competition among these providers, applying Porter's competitive forces model for internal competition, suppliers' power, customers' power, threat of new entrants, and threat of substitutes (Figure 5.1).

Industry Competition

Electronic catalogue-based trading such as Tradezone, CitiusNet and even FedEx (VirtualOrder) seem to move towards a set of trading services that are strongly integrated and of a generic nature, that is, not specific to the industry sector. They start to implement a third-party marketplace provision model, and may become value-chain integrators in the future. Basic services offered by the third-party marketplace providers include:

- Web presence of the product offer;
- Web marketing;
- catalogue integration into the Web.

In addition they may offer:

- a multiple-catalogue marketplace (Tradezone, CitiusNet);
- order registration and order handling, either passing this on to the

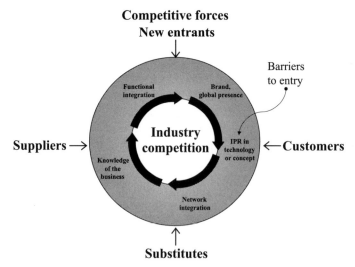

Figure 5.1   *Competitive forces and barriers to entry (Porter)*

suppliers, or handling the order automatically when there is integration with the supplier back-end system;

- financial transaction handling (Tradezone, CitiusNet);
- logistics handling (FedEx).

At one time Industry.Net was also starting to expand its information services with transaction handling, but this has now been reversed with a new owner.

Internal competition—that is, among third-party marketplace providers—and their positioning are along the following lines:

1. level of functional integration, providing convenience, cost reduction and new opportunities to the customers;
2. network integration, that is, how far parties are connected together through a single system that acts as an sector-wide infrastructure for trading; and related to this the extent of access to information, providing convenience and cost reduction;
3. brand;
4. global presence;
5. technology ownership/intellectual property;
6. business knowledge.

The first two of these, integration of functionality and partners leading to convenience and access to information, are important for purchasers of goods and for suppliers of goods who trade via a third-party marketplace provider. CitiusNet is offering additional integration, with adapted software, installation support and training at the purchaser site, as illustrated by the Texas Instruments example. The third, brand, might address the purchaser (e.g. the FedEx name can be used by the VirtualOrder merchant towards the purchasers), but is more likely to play a role for the merchant only. The fourth, global presence, is relevant for both the supplier or merchant and for the purchaser (e.g. international shipping or funds transfer, or access to a worldwide range of catalogues). These factors on which companies compete are at the same time the barriers to entry (Figure 5.1). An additional barrier to entry can be ownership of technology or concept. The cases show that this holds for Citius, Tradezone and DT/Globana with ICS, although all emphasize that this is not a very strong barrier. Finally, a further barrier to entry is business knowledge. Knowledge of the purchasing process is strongly emphasized by Citius and Tradezone, while FedEx clearly positions itself around its logistics strength. Technology ownership, business knowledge, global distribution or partnerships are key assets for realizing a system with global presence or a high level of integration or trust.

Internal competition can be expected to grow, as service providers are increasingly starting to implement the same integrated generic concept. There will also be more new entrants, since the investment to become a third-party marketplace operator will go down as technology becomes more readily available.

Specific characteristics of the Internet in relation to internal competition are as follows:

- Branding is key on the Internet. FedEx is leveraging its global brand in the Internet environment. Globana, CitiusNet and Tradezone are seeking financially strong international marketing partners and European or worldwide recognition.
- Internet presence is still growing fast and the market is far from saturated. Therefore competition is rather limited. At this stage all providers benefit from competition as it creates awareness and acceptance of the general concept.
- There is still ample scope to improve the quality of the basic offering, for example through enhanced Internet security, search facilities and negotiation assistance. For example Onyx, the parent company of Tradezone, is involved in the CASBA project, which seeks to extend systems like Tradezone with intelligent agent-based product search and price negotiation.
- Many providers are seeking to add value through Internet-enabled integration of information and functionality. This is facilitated most if the provider is capable to combine the Internet with back-end processing, i.e. legacy systems, EDI, financial transaction software, as well as network presence. This requires a profound knowledge of technology and business processes and practices. Some providers are engaging in 'strategic' partnerships, e.g. Onyx/Tradezone with Hewlett-Packard, CitiusNet with telecom operators like France Telecom, Bell Canada or Belgacom, for platform technology and network presence.
- Extending the offer with new Internet-based services also provides added value. Marshall has moved into customer training and design assistance.
- As there is still ample scope to grow in the market, price competition is not yet an issue (but is expected to become so in a few years' time—by then the scope to add value by extending integration or by offering new services will have to be exploited).
- One-to-one marketing is enabled by Internet technology. However, as of today this is not used much in the cases investigated. Nevertheless, this could become an important competitive tool.

Companies that are competing in this market have their origins in:

- single service provision (in logistics, Fedex; in catalogues, CitiusNet);
- industry marketplace (Industry.Net);
- technology provision (e.g. secure Internet technology in the case of Tradezone);
- sector-specific marketplace providers (for example, Tradezone now integrates computer products catalogues; there are several specialized computer products marketplaces);
- single-company 'marketplaces', that is, e-shops (e.g. CitiusNet integrates office furniture catalogues. Specialized office furniture companies also offer such products where they have a strong Web presence, e.g. Steelcase Inc., http://www.steelcase.com).

In the business models analysis in Chapter 3, the sources of new competition can readily be mapped. For third-party marketplace providers, Figure 5.2 gives the general trend and indicates three concrete possibilities for competition:

1. A vertical market catalogue operator extending its service with transaction handling for routine purchases, for a range of vertical markets (e.g. Vertical.Net with its set of vertical market industrial e-malls); or generic MRO catalogue operators, likewise extending with transaction handling (such as Industry.Net)—this is a likely development. An ISP or Web designer could likewise move up the curve, by first adding catalogues and subsequently adding support for ordering and payments, i.e. transaction support.

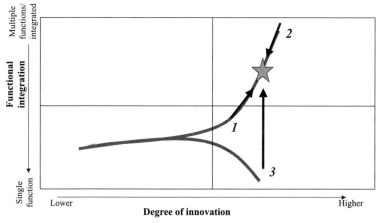

Figure 5.2 *Sources of competition for third-party marketplace providers*

2. An industry-specific value-chain integrator like Marshall, intending to create more turnover on the basis of its technical expertise by spinning off its information services department as a separate transaction-handling service for a wide range of industry sectors. Another example is a PC distributor such as Ingram that is hosting transaction-management functions for its resellers, leaving to them the branding and marketing.[82]

3. An information broker or portal like Yahoo extending its service with transaction handling, possibly first on the basis of B-to-C transactions or with products such as PCs or travel tickets that can be sold to both consumers and businesses.

Suppliers' Power

Suppliers in the cases investigated are technology and platform providers (e.g. Microsoft, Netscape, Oracle, Sun to Tradezone, CitiusNet, GEN).

Technology providers are not at all in favour of exclusive deals. Instead, technology is broadly licensed and often based on open interfaces. The intention is to encourage as many software developers as possible to write to these interfaces (even though the platform providers retain control of some strategic pieces of software). The objective of platform providers is to establish and control the dominant standard. This strategy is based, for example, on the success of Microsoft MS-DOS as the *de facto* standard operating system of the 1980s and Windows for the 1990s, control of which has given Microsoft enormous leverage in application software. Another example of such successful market dominance by being master of the standard is in mobile communications with GSM and European companies like Nokia and Ericsson.

The market-dominance strategy of the technology providers such as Microsoft and HP means that technology users (like several of the companies in the case studies) can obtain major parts of the basic technology rather inexpensively. On the other hand, those technology users cannot derive strategic advantages from the basic technology, as it is generally available. They may be in a strong position to negotiate especially advantageous price deals, as the technology providers are strongly interested in enhancing market share. In the future the situation might change, if relatively small companies with particular circumstances supply critical technology for highly specialized advanced services, for example technology for intelligent service assistance or one-to-one marketing. The users of that technology—that is, the marketplace providers or virtual community operators—might be building competitive strength on exclusive access to certain technologies.

Customers' Power

The cases show that the power of large purchasers (as customers of the trading systems) is highly respected. Mrs Rijsbergen of Citius expects that they will determine which provider will win in trading systems. Tradezone foresees that some of these large purchasers may become themselves operators of trading systems. DT/Globana has indicated that it is well aware of the power of the automotive sector and the impact that a choice of a specific system will have on *de facto* standards.

Backward integration of large purchasers, in the sense that they run their own purchasing system, is not unthinkable. In fact, this has already happened with GEIS/TPN, whose main customer is the parent company GE itself.

An additional reason for large purchasers to consider such a move could be that electronic trading systems capture a large amount of information that a large purchaser may wish to keep for itself in order to gain competitiveness through better tuning of its purchasing.

A consequence of large purchaser-operated electronic trading systems is that MRO suppliers also have to adopt the same system in order to keep the large purchaser as their customer. The recent past of EDI-based procurement systems has shown that the risk for suppliers was that they got locked into a specific purchaser, or that they had to accept participation in several incompatible trading systems. It is exactly these risks that open, interoperable third-party marketplace systems promise to avoid.

Citius Belgium and Tradezone franchisees, as well as Industry.Net, also have suppliers with catalogues as their customers. They seem to be considered as much less of a threat, as Michael Jeffries of Tradezone comments, because their system is primarily purchaser oriented. One reason is probably that (local) suppliers are much smaller than the large purchasers and there are many of them competing to deal with those large buyers.

Small purchasers are not considered to have much power, except when they are organized through industry-sector organizations (a target group for Citius, Tradezone as well as DT/Globana).

New Entrants

The threat of new entrants is coming in particular from the supply side. Already some of the suppliers are becoming Internet B-to-B operators themselves. Industry.Net has been acquired by the catalogue provider IHS (see Chapter 4). HP is contributing to the platform for Tradezone, but at the same time is also involved in a business-to-consumer electronic trading platform (e-Christmas) that could well extend into Tradezone's business. Value-added network service providers like GEIS or EDS have moved into Internet business, including trading services. These two, for example, are partners in the ANX automotive network, which could compete with a GEN-like offer. At the same time, some of their VAN services could be part of the offering of GEN or CitiusNet or Tradezone, in particular where the Internet is perceived as lacking security. In 1995 GEIS formed a joint venture with Netscape, ACTRA, to integrate the Web and EDI. Such technology is in competition with the underlying technology of third-party marketplace providers. In the meantime GEIS has sold its share in ACTRA to Netscape.

Netscape and Microsoft dominate the browser market and Web browsers are intrinsic to any of the B-to-B operators studied here. New competition can be expected from this corner too. Following its acquisition by AOL and its partnership with Sun, Netscape is repositioning itself as an Internet business transactions technology and services company. This brings it into competition with several of the providers studies here.

In many cases the basic platform is Windows from Microsoft. This company itself is now extending its product offering into electronic marketplaces with many individual pieces of related technology such as store-front builders, security and electronic payments (Merchant Server), as well as into value-chain integration (Value Chain Initiative). Indeed, for many companies the marketing clout and platform dominance of Microsoft pose the main threat to their business. Part of the motivation to grow so quickly is to be faster than Microsoft, in case this market leader decides to move into their specific area of business.

The incumbents have created certain barriers to entry. Technology companies like Microsoft and Netscape are likely to be most threatening to the generic trading service providers (such as Tradezone and CitiusNet), whose assets are based more on the technology than on specific business knowledge and therefore have relatively low barriers to entry. Others who are sector oriented, such as Marshall, or who specialize in specific business processes (such as the ultimate concept of GEN as being about collaborative design and engineering), have assets that can be better defended.

New entrants may also be deterred by their own legacy and at times a 'not-invented-here' syndrome that reduces their flexibility and agility to operate effectively in fast-moving markets. They may also be hindered by lack of strategic vision and direction.

Substitutes

With such new trading systems, especially for routine products, it seems odd to start considering substitute solutions already. However, perhaps

Marshall provides some indication of how the issue of substitutes has to be considered. While the competition is fierce in the trading of electronic components and the margins are relatively thin, Marshall is developing new businesses, namely design assistance and online training, that one day may be much more interesting than the 'core' business of distribution of electronic components. If that is true, Marshall might afford to run the distribution business at very low margins, in order to attract customers for its much more profitable services. The acquisition of components then becomes a 'non-issue' and customer focus shifts to knowledge acquisition. A substitution process would be happening, exerting a tremendous competitive force on the industry incumbents.

For the trading of goods that can become intangibles, substitution scenarios are actively being developed, notably for business-to-consumer trading.[83] Books can also be delivered in electronic form, likewise music or software. Those that build their strength in electronic commerce today exclusively on skills like electronic warehouse management and logistics may become threatened later by purely digital delivery mechanisms.

Generic Competitive Strategies

According to Porter, there are three generic competitive strategies that can be followed by firms to achieve commercial success:

1. *Cost leadership*: pursuing a position of being the lowest-cost producer through economies of scale and benefiting from experience curve effects in order to build and increase market share.
2. *Differentiation*: providing a product or service with a unique characteristic, which allows the company to charge a relatively higher price and thus generate better margins.
3. *Focus or niche*: concentrating on a specific market segment.

In order to pursue any of these strategies successfully and possess sustainable competitive advantage, companies need to build and exploit key assets. A number have been analysed in Chapter 2 in the context of the opportunities of the Internet. It is often considered that the niche/focus strategy is particularly vulnerable, as a company in such a niche may have difficulty in defending itself against a frontal attack from a better-resourced competitor. Porter also argues that companies have to watch out not to become 'stuck in the middle' between the three generic strategies. However, strategy development in the fast-moving and often turbulent electronic commerce world is particularly difficult, as will be further analysed in Chapter 7. Many companies will not be able to do better than 'muddle through' or stay as flexible as possible in order to adapt their strategy opportunistically to the rapid changes around them.

It is interesting to try to assess whether and where the companies in the case studies fit in the generic competitive strategy classification. The following is suggested from the analysis:

- Marshall, as an electronics components distributor, is following a differentiation strategy, positioning itself as the leader in bringing a rich set of electronic commerce-based benefits to its customers, both the manufacturers and the component buyers. Marshall follows a fairly clearly formulated strategy that is however, flexibly adapted to the opportunities arising from the new technologies and allows for learning from experiments and mistakes.

- Industry.Net set out initially to exploit its first-comer advantage and become the largest industry mall. It was not clear, however, what its business model would be, and therefore its generic strategy. Was it a differentiation strategy, being the portal for access to industry catalogues and later on for MRO purchases? Or was to a cost-leadership strategy, maximizing catalogue exposure in any form, Internet and non-Internet? Industry.Net, as is understandable for a pioneer, got into a mode of 'muddling through' strategy development.

- FedEx does not necessarily seek to be the cheapest package-delivery service, but rather emphasizes delivery time, global coverage, and ease of access and service availability. It is a differentiation strategy, supported by strong brand building. With its ventures into catalogue support it shows strategic experimentation, although it hints at uncertainty about the correctness of this choice. This experimentation is still fairly limited, however. Direct competitors such as UPS are likewise venturing into new areas, for example trust services and certified digital deliveries, possibly with the advantage of the follower in terms of reduced uncertainty about strategic choice.

- Amazon's business services (Advantage and Associate programmes) mostly seem to emphasize low cost and easy financial benefits because of likely high traffic for its business customers (publishers and online booksellers). Amazon's strongest asset certainly is its brand name, which supports the build-up of high traffic. Towards the business partners, this looks like a cost-leadership strategy. As will be argued elsewhere, Amazon for now forgoes differentiation opportunities with respect to its business customers. Its strategy towards book buyers, the consumers, is better characterized as differentiation: book buyers obtain a range of benefits, including lower prices, much wider choice, convenient ordering and delivery, and much appreciated supplementary information from the book readers' community. Even if a potential book buyer could get a lower price by comparing with tools like Acses, it is quite likely that Amazon will be chosen because of its reputation.

- Citius is potentially in a network integrator position as a critical market intermediary for hub–spoke purchasing configurations and could therefore consider pursuing a differentiation strategy. However, as the market evolves quickly while the roll-out of the system takes time, and with ownership changes, it is not clear that this can be pursued, or that instead a niche strategy would be better suited. The latter may also fit better with the concept of supporting specific trading communities of many smaller companies, within selected market sectors such as medical goods. The risk of changing strategy is to become 'stuck in the middle'.
- Tradezone likewise has to work on building a critical mass, where its franchising concept and catalogue interconnection technology may help in achieving this. Its strategy then can be characterized as differentiation, offering global coverage and an extensive and evolving set of catalogues. This concept is still pursued, not rigidly but instead with an adaptive approach to strategy development.
- GEN as a concept is potentially of wide applicability. Its collaboration dimension and engineering orientation make it different from catalogue industry malls or third-party marketplaces for engineering parts. This makes it very suitable for a differentiation strategy, even if specializations emerge for specific engineering disciplines (mechanical, electrical, construction). Implementations that emphasize the basic trading facilities of an open marketplace for standard engineering parts may be tempted to follow a niche approach. This would make them vulnerable to invasion by larger generic marketplace providers.
- SCS as an electronic auction provider with Infomar is following a niche strategy if compared to the approach of many of the Internet auctions. It is a planned strategy approach based on following rather than leading the technology. As discussed in the case study, there are several reasons that this is a well-defended niche.

Industry Structure—Summary

It has been argued (Wyckoff, 1997; Varian, 1997, Hagel and Armstrong, 1997) that Internet electronic commerce brings the ideal of perfect competition (Lipsey *et al.*, 1990) closer, in the sense that:

- barriers to entry are lowered;
- transaction costs are reduced;
- customers have improved access to information;

- marginal or customer-oriented pricing becomes possible;
- minimal legislation and regulation and other forms of intervention by public authorities exist.[84]

However, we also observe that new barriers to entry can be created, as is demonstrated in the case studies presented here. Such barriers can be based on the capability to manage complex business relationships, as in the interworking of many parties in the automotive sector (supported by concepts like ANX or GEN), or in the multitude of procurement relationships that exist around large firms (as illustrated by EDS/Citius). They can also, and at the same time, be based on building intimate relationships with the customer, as is central to one-to-one marketing. And there are plenty of opportunities for new 'middlemen', as illustrated by Marshall, who can wield considerable power, add value for both customers and suppliers and shift the focus away from pure price competition. Finally the cases confirm the importance that is attached by the providers to global branding.

TRANSACTION COSTS

Introduction

Transaction cost theory states that firms make rather than buy goods and services because they expect that the cost of internally coordinating production will be smaller than the costs of coordinating with their suppliers. Coase (1937) argued that the cost of obtaining price information, which is one of those coordination costs, is one of the reasons for the firm's existence (Coase, 1937). Transaction cost theory therefore makes the distinction between the hierarchical integration of economic activities within the firm's management structure and a market relationship with external firms. The 'governance structure' is this institutional arrangement within which transactions are negotiated and executed.

Williamson (1985, 1986) developed and structured transaction cost theory. He provided a mapping of governance structures taking into account three dimensions, namely:

- frequency of transactions, ranging from recurrent to occasional buying;
- specificity of the supplier's investment, ranging from non-specific to idiosyncratic;
- uncertainty of the transactions.

Considering first frequency and investment specificity, the reasoning is as follows. At one extreme, for non-specific investments such as purchases of standard items like office supplies or office equipment, the market mechanism is optimal, with classical contract law being applicable[85]. At the other extreme, for idiosyncratic recurrent transactions, e.g. transfer of intermediate products from one production phase to the next, it is more advantageous to internalize the transaction or in other words, to rely on unified governance. In between we find two more forms. First, there is idiosyncratic or mixed investment (that is, those where investment is partially specific to the buyer) for occasional transactions, which can be governed by a trilateral neoclassical contracting, i.e. involving a third party to arbitrate in addition to classical contracting. An example is a large construction project. Secondly, it is also possible to engage in bilateral governance with relational contracting, for mixed investment forms and recurrent transactions. This means that a bilateral relationship is created with contractual obligations and follow-on agreements.

Uncertainty (e.g. about who will be the specific buyer) does not influence the transactions of items with a non-specific investment, as via the market other buyers will be found in any case. However, if there are more specific investments it becomes more important to deal with uncertainty. After all, neither the buyer nor the supplier would wish to risk wasting their investment. Standardization on a limited set of product options is one way out. More elaborate negotiation and arbitration form another option.

In the following analysis the uncertainty dimension is kept fixed. What is being considered in more detail is the frequency of purchasing and the investment specificity. In Chapter 7, uncertainty will be reconsidered when addressing collaboration between companies under various governance approaches (more specifically, value networks and dynamic markets).

This mapping of governance structures as defined by Williamson on the dimensions of frequency and investment specificity will be applied in the following sections to four of the cases described above. Also included is their expected evolution. This is a useful procedure, as it provides a better understanding of the contracting support that needs to be provided, in order to match the governance structure.

Citius

Citius supports recurrent purchases of non-specific, 'routine' items. Multiple suppliers can trade with multiple purchasers, where the rules of the game are determined by an EDI contract that suppliers and purchasers sign up to. This is a classical contract situation. Citius is now starting to offer *ad hoc* purchases for non-registered users (extending in

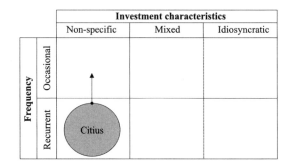

Figure 5.3   *Current and future (arrow) governance structures for Citius*

the direction of the arrow in Figure 5.3). However, classical contracting for occasional purchases, in an open environment like the Internet with anonymous parties, is of a different nature than the traditional closed environment EDI-based purchasing in which Citius has its roots. Principles for the necessary adaptation of trade procedures for this kind of open electronic commerce have been developed in a dissertation by Bons (1997).

Tradezone

Tradezone already covers both recurrent and occasional transactions. The latter happens when anonymous purchasers on the Internet use the system. Anonymous suppliers are not supported, however. The classical contract for the occasional case is virtually non-existent in Tradezone: purchasers have to rely on the supplier to deliver according to what they believe to have ordered. This approach is very similar to today's practice in business-to-consumer electronic commerce: given the absence of a contract and the incompleteness or incompatibility of the global legal framework for electronic commerce, aspects such recourse and customer (consumer) protection are not always well defined.[86] The risk for Tradezone is that this may introduce an element of uncertainty and lack of confidence in what is otherwise presented as a system that offers a very high level of trust and confidence.

Tradezone is considering extending in the future to support mixed type transactions (in the direction of the arrow in Figure 5.4), that is, purchases of critical items, the governance model of neoclassical contracting indicates that at least two types of support need to be added:

- negotiation and case-by-case contracting support[87];
- third-party arbitration in case of dispute.

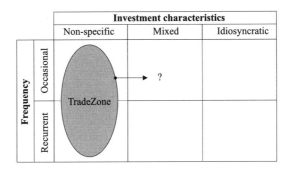

Figure 5.4 *Current and future (arrow) governance structures for Tradezone*

GEN

The Global Engineering Network concept is centred around online collaborative design and engineering. Suppliers, while starting with a catalogue of standard products, e.g. subassemblies, add to this basis customer-specific information. This is an example of recurrent transactions with a certain amount of customer-specific investment from the supplier side, the mixed category mentioned before. Deutsche Telekom/ Globana's implementation of the concept, ICS, also covers recurrent transactions of routine items. However, it is not clear that ICS fully covers bilateral negotiation and contracting, including the protection of intellectual property rights (indicated by * in Figure 5.5). Such contracting might have to be established outside the system, in other words offline.

The GEN concept also includes support for *ad hoc*, occasional transactions in design and engineering. As well as IPR protection, and as for Tradezone, negotiation support and third-party arbitration will have to be added in a future implementation of this aspect of the concept (** in

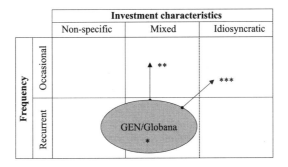

Figure 5.5 *Current and future (arrows) governance structures for GEN*

Figure 5.5). In addition, implementations are only feasible when the transaction cost associated with common use of design and engineering tools by both supplier and purchaser tooling is sufficiently low. This might be achieved through standardization or interoperability or low-cost, 'easy to use' design and engineering tools.

Finally, GEN implementations might in the future also support large construction and engineering projects (*** in Figure 5.5). Similar considerations hold. It is not unthinkable in such a case that the GEN implementation becomes internalized. For example, a high level of specific training might be needed for collaborative use of design and engineering tooling, that is, the cost of compatibility (which is a transaction cost) can become too high. In that case, vertical integration happens again and the specific GEN implementation would be operated as an intranet solution within the firm.

Infomar

Infomar has its origins in the automation of traditional clock-based fish auctions (spot market, indicated by the circle in Figure 5.6). The Infomar system effectively splits trading into two markets. Part of the catch is sold by means of bidding while the vessel is still at sea. This created a futures market. The remainder of the catch is sold on the spot market. In the first case, as Infomar provides low-cost worldwide Web access to transaction information (price, type of fish, quality etc.) occasional buyers can also participate in bidding. In the second case, as Infomar provides information from all auction nodes of the networked Infomar system, likewise occasional buyers from another auction in the Infomar network can participate.

Fisheries have not yet evolved as much as agriculture towards controllable industrial production. A system similar to Infomar, but for flowers

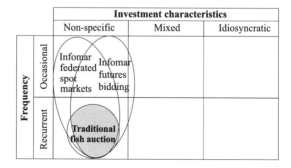

Figure 5.6 *Current governance structures for Infomar*

or vegetables or fruits, can be imagined as supporting mixed types of transactions (both recurrent and occasional). Especially for the occasional mixed case, it might be interesting to consider electronic support. An example would be online negotiation and contracting between a large supermarket in Sweden and a fruit farm in Spain to deliver during a specific season a certain quantity of oranges at a certain quality. Not only would third-party arbitration be beneficial to provide confidence in dispute resolution, there is also a need for a common quality system. Again, a third-party needs to be introduced, acting as certification agent for quality measurement procedures. In agriculture such quality systems exist, as opposed to fisheries.

Frequency Revisited

In traditional transaction cost theory, the frequency dimension is split between recurrent versus occasional. However, as has been pointed out[88], there are more patterns of relationships. For example, purchasing toner for an office printer is a recurrent but irregular activity (unless buffers are built into the system, which will lead to additional transaction costs). This is a routine catalogue product and no negotiation will be performed. However, this recurrent pattern may be interrupted from time to time when suppliers themselves change the toner offer. They may have a cheaper, lower-quality option, or may want to offer the purchaser a take-back service for used toner. Such recurrent transactions with interrupts will require a transaction approach that can deal with both routine purchasing and negotiation. Where suppliers are dealing with many purchasers they may want to automate both—current electronic commerce systems are not yet able to deal with this.

Yet another pattern is periodic but infrequent (sparse) purchasing. An example is companies giving their staff a Christmas present, as happens in some countries. It is highly predictable when this will happen, even though it is infrequent, and each year new offers will be made. In addition, the situation of the purchaser may have changed, with a different company policy. Suppliers are likely to have non-specific investments such as catalogue tools and Web sites, as well as additional personnel that are contracted around Christmas time. However, they may wish to offer negotiation on a case-by-case basis on the actual presents for that year.

Considering a diversity of patterns in time of purchasing or other business relationships leads to two related questions:

1. What are the economics of those patterns, taking into account that there could be varying mixes between online and offline support for transactions?

2.   What are the technical and marketing requirements for electronic and non-electronic commerce to support these patterns optimally?

Businesses that in the future wish to support *ad hoc*, variable as well as routine purchasing patterns will need answers to these questions, which until now have been little researched.

INTERNAL AND EXTERNAL BUSINESS ORGANIZATION

As the Marshall case shows, there is an internal and an external dimension to the business organization for Internet commerce. Internal aspects relate to the reengineering of business processes. External aspects address on the one hand networking with business partners and on the other hand the reallocation of activities in the value chain and redefinition of the roles of business partners, including the disappearance of intermediaries and the creation of new intermediaries.

Internal Business Organization

The effective introduction of electronic commerce for external relation-ships such as purchasing or interaction with customers is likely to have profound implications for the internal business organization. This is in line with the stream of thinking that IT is only one factor in enabling competitiveness. To get the maximum result out of the introduction of IT, other factors also need to be aligned, namely business process organization and human resource management (skills, responsibilities, roles etc.), as for example discussed by Brynjolfsson, Renshaw and Von Alstyne (1997).

The Citius and Marshall case studies provide some evidence of these kind of changes: Texas Instruments as a user of Citius significantly reduced its purchasing department, gave it a more strategic role, and delegated purchasing responsibility to a much lower level throughout the organization. With the introduction of Internet commerce Marshall has created an extremely flat organization, without an organization chart, with collaborative team effort in sales (where previously there was strong internal competition), and decision-making power vested in the person who is closest to the decision.

Venkatraman (1994) argues that ultimately the extent of change may not be limited to business process reengineering (BPR) but can even go as far as business scope redefinition. Again, Marshall seems to provide indications that the introduction of the Internet indeed enabled this distribution company to move towards a new business scope with its online design and training services.

A specific case as regards the internal business organization for electronic commerce is to use the Internet as an electronic marketing channel. Gartner[89] recommends for the internal organization that:

- an *electronic marketing management team* is formed, of marketing, sales, distribution and accounting;
- a *electronic market channel manager* is established to select the best offerings, develop pricing strategies, manage cross-channel conflicts and overseeing online market tests;
- *business plans and profitability metrics* are developed for electronic market channels;
- the channel manager together with business unit managers *reevaluate the product and service offering* and pricing to maintain a competitive offer, specifically where online price comparison will drive prices down and value-added services become more important.

Of the cases studied only Marshall showed evidence of following such a comprehensive approach. In fact, dissatisfaction with the sales approach in the direct channel was the starting point of Marshall's involvement in the Internet. However, Marshall's CEO Rod Rodin does not consider it important to develop separate metrics for its use of the Internet ('we don't see the Internet as a profit and loss centre') (Shaw, 1997).

External Organization—Disintermediation

In this section the topic of external business organization—cooperation with suppliers, channel partners and customers—will be briefly introduced. In Chapter 7, much more will be said about two evolving forms of external business organization, namely value networks (Porter, 1985) and dynamic markets.

Information and communications technology can lead to radical changes in business organization, not only within the firm, but also between companies and with customers. In particular, the question that has been much debated is what impact the Internet will have on intermediaries. It has been observed that certain intermediaries add significant costs to the value chain, while they could potentially be bypassed when manufacturers deal directly with customers. This is the 'threatened intermediaries' hypothesis (Wigand & Benjamin, 1995 and Benjamin & Wigand, 1995).

At the same time, Sarkar, Butler and Steinfield (1995) argue that one might just as well reason as follows. As coordination costs can be reduced with the help of information and communications technology, firms will externalize, that is, make use of other forms of organizing for the transaction than vertical integration. Therefore firms will seek to outsource certain functions (e.g. design, procurement, marketing, distribution, after-sales support), which will result in greater reliance on markets and intermediaries.

Clearly one way to reconcile these two views is to note that not all firms and industry structures are the same—it depends. Currently both phenomena can be observed on the Internet. Existing intermediaries are being bypassed in sectors such as travel and book retail. At the same time, new intermediaries are being created, for instance to mediate business purchasing.

The question of reinforcing or bypassing intermediaries is not only a matter of transaction costs but is also closely linked to competitive strategy. Reinforcing existing intermediaries, such as in a manufacturer–distributors chain, can be used to enhance loyalty and keep competitors out. However, when a manufacturer bypasses its distributors, it puts the burden on the manufacturer to put the marketing mix in order such that a strong competitive position can be maintained, which is usually not a trivial task. A cost advantage in the short term may then turn out to become a long-term strategic disadvantage.[90]

The case studies illustrate disintermediation (e.g. Infomar) as well as the creation of new intermediaries (e.g. Tradezone) in business-to-business electronic commerce. In addition, they illustrate that existing intermediaries can add value to their business by means of the Internet (Marshall). Furthermore, business can significantly reduce the cost of its internal operations, including the customer interface, by means of electronic commerce, as has been illustrated by several examples in Chapter 2. This is then an exhaustive list of possibilities of what can happen to transaction costs before and after introducing the Internet. Thus, the case studies concur with the analysis of Sarkar, Butler and Steinfield (1995) that any of the four scenarios for the impact of the Internet on relative transaction costs are plausible. In Table 5.1 an assessment of the impact on intermediation of the cases studied in this book is provided.

Whether disintermediation or (re)intermediation occurs, one would expect the Internet to lower transaction costs. Using the Internet for coordination with suppliers and customers instead of or as well as interpersonal relationships is expected to lead to a lowering of transaction costs and better-quality transactions. Surprisingly, Kraut and Steinfeld (1997) found empirical evidence to contradict this general assumption. In fact, they detected a weak negative relationship between the use of electronic networks with suppliers and the relative efficiency of transactions (that is orders arrived on time, without errors or meeting quality standards).

Table 5.1 *Impact on intermediation*

Case	Impact on intermediation
Marshall	The Internet enabled Marshall to change and strengthen its role as a distributor/intermediary, even leading to business transformation and redefinition
Fedex VirtualOrder	As a well-established intermediary for logistics, Fedex offers with VirtualOrder an option for companies to externalize certain sales and marketing functions, enhancing the intermediary role
Industry.Net	A new intermediary, which still has to prove that it lowers transaction cost in a profitable way for all parties (suppliers, purchasers and Industry.Net itself)
Citius, Tradezone, GEN (ICS)	New intermediaries themselves, with evidence of reduction of total transaction cost; at the same time they may well replace or absorb other intermediaries, such as traditional catalogue providers
Infomar	Introduces transparency (lower cost of access to information) and is thus likely to reduce the power of some traditional market makers/intermediaries
Amazon Associates	Amazon itself lowers transaction costs as it bypasses the traditional bookshops. At the same time, Amazon Associates creates and supports new intermediaries, namely the associates who provide the need for Amazon to externalize part of its marketing.

How to reconcile their statistical findings with the cases presented here and elsewhere is an open question.

External Organization—Value Networks and Dynamic Markets

Schwartz (1997) argues that the new opportunities are in first 'deconstructing' the value chain in order to subsequently reassemble it again with new roles and new business actors who use electronic commerce. Such deconstruction and reassembly are also the basis for the classification of business models presented in Chapter 3.

There, however, it is argued that classical value-chain analysis such as in Porter (1985) is not always fine-grained enough to understand all of the new ways of organizing business that are being enabled through electronic commerce.

It is also argued that commercial success is not self-evident for the conceivable business models (of which there can be an enormous number when considering value-chain integration, that is, using technology to combine information flows from various parts of the value chain). A marketing strategy for the business model is needed, which has been called a 'marketing model' in Chapter 3.

The business models form part of the complete organization of the business network, consisting of relationships between suppliers, customers and business intermediaries. This can take the form of a value network[91] or a dynamic market configuration (see Chapter 7). Rayport and Sviolka (1995) argue that increasingly businesses will organize themselves in a value constellation (Norman and Ramirez, 1993), virtual organization (Mowshowitz, 1997) or virtual value chain (Rayport and Sviolka, 1995), which are relationship patterns in a network of partners to create value.

Many companies need a wide range of skills, while they are also inclined to concentrate on their core competence under the pressure to cut costs. They need to compete globally, yet meet increasing customer-specific demands for customization and timely delivery. Information and communications technology reduces the transaction costs of obtaining skills externally, while improving core competencies internally. It also enables global sourcing and delivery, with reduced lead times. Information and communications technology is the key enabler of the trend towards such value constellations. Value creation is critically dependent on the collaboration in the whole network of companies and their customers. The dynamic market dimension of these networks is being continually reconfigured to find new ways of value creation, under the pressure of changing customer requirements and competitive forces.

Effective operation in a value constellation has to be accompanied by internal company adaptation. For example, as markets become more important internal hierarchies are broken down. The previous section provided an example of this (although cause and effect cannot be simply separated).

Van Alstyne (1997) argues that value constellations are critically dependent on affiliation, loyalty and trust. Interestingly, to build these there should be shared values and social norms of loyalty and/or frequent trading or collaboration with the possibility of review and arbitration, which is paradoxical in view of the dynamic nature of relationships that is also often seen as an intrinsic feature of value constellations. One way to resolve the paradox is by considering that such dynamic networks are usually organized around a lead or brokering firm. This is typically a pattern that is also sought by the third-party marketplace providers such as Citius or Tradezone, who consider themselves the hub in a wheel, with as spokes the customers as well as additional service providers (e.g. Web site designers).

The cases provide evidence of the emergence of dynamic value constellations involving the companies in the cases. Young *et al.* (1996) perceive Marshall as such a value constellation with its junction box role being subject to a progressive evolution of value creation. It considers not only suppliers and purchasers as its partners in the network but also systems integrators and technology providers. Partners in these latter two categories may well change as technology changes—Marshall is ready to sacrifice technology solutions as business needs change.

GEN/ICS, with its emphasis on collaboration (in design and engineering), may have the potential to catalyse value network building, but this still needs to prove itself. Certainly in the original concept, Rethfeld (1994) emphasized 'networked cooperation' and 'a working culture of large-scale collaborative engineering capable for fast change', enabling organizations to become 'agile'.

Amazon, at the centre of a network of Associates (online bookshops) and Advantage clients (publishers), is an example of a value constellation, the dynamic nature of which will be investigated in Chapter 7. However, there is little evidence that Amazon is actually building loyalty and trust. Its Associates, a large number, are anonymous and do not share clearly formulated values, even though they share the brand. For example, they do not get customer data around which common norms for customer service and quality, and thereby loyalty, could be built (see also Chapter 6). The same holds for publishers, potentially a huge number too, for whom Amazon is just another opportunity, with very low switching costs and even less sharing of identity or ownership than for Associates. This has to be contrasted with the much more intimate relationships that Marshall provides to the component manufacturers and privileged component buyers.

Citius and Tradezone are both engaged in a pattern of relationships with partners and are considering extending these with a view to enhancing customer value, for example by providing additional financial or marketing services. Both Citius and Tradezone are keenly aware of the potential for new forms of value creation that their position in the network brings. Citius mentioned the potential for improving financial flows. Tradezone believes that the further extension of shared catalogue definitions is key in building loyalty in the network of franchisees. However, their current relationships are mainly of a long-term strategic and static nature and do not involve the final customers (suppliers and purchasers) in value creation. It remains to be seen if these will develop or extend with new partners into more dynamic value network configurations.

SUMMARY

This chapter, the first part of the comparative case analysis, has investigated the competitive structure of industry, the impact of reduction of transaction costs and the changes in internal and external business organization that electronic commerce brings.

Some tentative conclusions from the analysis of the cases and electronic commerce literature are the following. First, companies seek to build competitive strength and barriers to entry on either a global brand and/ or a web of intimate customer relationships with profound knowledge of the specific industry in which they operate. Secondly, technology is not a strong factor in building a sustainable competitive advantage. Most technology is widely available, and technology providers are seeking a global market, preventing exclusivity. Thirdly, in most of the cases studied, it is felt that building global presence and market share are critical for success. Competition is already fierce or expected to increase considerably in just a few years' time, so the window of opportunity is relatively short. Partnerships with strong players are seen as essential for the upcoming players such as Citius, Tradezone and GEN/ICS to be able to achieve a strong market position in a short timespan.

Fourthly, transaction cost theory leads to interesting insights into the new aspects of electronic commerce that will arise when companies want to realize their strategies to move into more flexible and *ad hoc* business relationships with suppliers and buyers. Notably, support for negotiation and third-party arbitration will be needed. Fifthly, business-to-business Internet commerce can strongly affect internal and external business organization. Internal changes have been demonstrated for a purchaser using a third-party marketplace system. Third-party marketplace providers argue that internal reorganization of purchasers has important potential for deriving full benefits from such systems. External changes are often phrased in terms of value network terminology (reconfiguring the value chain, building value constellations, dynamic market relationships). Some examples are provided by the cases studies that suggest that the companies are becoming part of a value constellation.

6
Marketing Strategies and Programmes

This chapter completes the case analysis in the previous chapter, in the sense that it focuses on the company rather than industry level. It addresses approaches to marketing strategy and marketing implementation, including segmentation and targeting, marketing communications and new ways to interact with customers such as one-to-one marketing. The chapter investigates how companies deal with these key dimensions of marketing in Internet business-to-business electronic commerce, assuming that the usual marketing concepts can still be applied.

TRADITIONAL B-TO-B MARKETING

B-to-B, industrial or organizational markets are defined as 'individuals or groups that purchase a specific type of product [or service or information] for resale, for use in making other products, or for use in daily operations' (Dibb *et al.*, 1991).

Characteristics of B-to-B or industrial markets are listed in Table 6.1 (see e.g. Kotler, 1991).

The table shows that often in industrial selling a high degree of customization is required. This in its turn necessitates close and often person-to-person collaboration with the customer and support of a knowledgeable sales staff. It is not uncommon that the industrial sales process is a team effort, involving several persons from the buyer and seller organization, as well as possible intermediaries such as banks. Marketing communications emphasise product performance and business benefits rather than emotional appeal. In many cases, prices are negotiable and form only one of the factors to be considered as well as product specifications, delivery conditions, financing conditions etc. In addition to direct sales, distribution channels with various degrees of value added are also well known in B-to-B markets. Finally, industrial markets are often

Table 6.1   *Characteristics of business-to-business markets*

Characteristic	Explanation
Customization	Product and service customization; cooperative product specification and development with customers
Knowledge	Knowledge-based interaction, often requiring highly skilled sales staff to deal with professional customers
Personal	Person-based sales; often a direct channel from producer to buyer, next to distributors and resellers; interactivity (that is, communication is bidirectional).
Professional	Professional promotion through information-dense brochures, datasheets, videos, tradeshows etc.
Negotiation	Negotiation on price, product specifications, delivery time etc. (which might be fixed in a contract)
Multiparty	Possibly several persons or organizations involved in the buying process that can be complex, involving extensive purchasing procedures
Multichannel	Manufacturers may have several channels to reach different industrial customers (direct sales, distributors, VARs, retailers); with potential for channel conflict or channel synergies
International	In many industry sectors the market is international. Industrial marketing has to deal with differences in language, culture, business rules etc.

international, as a significant part of sales may be cross-border. For instance, in Europe total trade (imports and exports) was no less than 45% of total GDP in 1994, of which 63% is with other countries of the European Union.[92]

The analysis in the previous chapters has shown that electronic markets reinforce a number of these characteristics, such as increased globalization

Table 6.2   *Reinforced and new characteristics of electronic industrial markets*

Characteristic	Explanation
Globalization	The Internet increases global sourcing/buying and global selling/supply; considerations about location become secondary
Customization	Customization increases because Internet technologies facilitate specification, design, and pricing online
Networked	Value constellations, in which the linear model from producer to customer no longer holds, but value is instead delivered through a network of partners; see the argument developed in Chapter 5
Flexible/*ad hoc*	Business relationships are becoming more flexible, *ad hoc* and transient, and customers come and go
Branding	Brands become more important as a source of value where organizations have squeezed costs and reduced transaction costs, with greater choice for customers, and with remote seller–buyer relationships

and increased customization (the latter argument was developed in Chapter 5 in relation to transaction costs). Moreover, electronic commerce as a facilitator for B-to-B markets also appears to lead to other characteristics beyond these traditional ones, such as a higher degree of networked business relationships and increased dynamics in such relationships. These reinforced and new characteristics of electronic B-to-B markets are summarized in Table 6.2.

Chapter 7 will present several scenarios for the future of B-to-B electronic commerce. There it will be argued that for certain products, markets and business processes, new opportunities can arise from electronic commerce-enabled convergence between B-to-B and B-to-C.

SEGMENTATION AND TARGETING

Keeping in mind the broad and to some extent changing characteristics of industrial markets, the next step is to develop an understanding of customer base segmentation in B-to-B electronic commerce. To this end, it is useful to consider the case examples in electronic purchasing that are not sector specific (Citius, Tradezone, Industry.Net and their competitors like GEIS TPN). Typically, these use in the explanation of their product offer words like 'routine purchasing' and 'hub and spoke' or 'open marketplaces'. From this it can be inferred that they apply a product-market segmentation on the basis of the critical importance/ value of a good to the actual production at the purchaser and degree of structuring in the market in terms of organization around large purchasers (Figure 6.1).

This model became most explicit in the analysis of Citius. Customers in product-market A are typically in concentrated businesses such as chemicals or consumer electronics, as well as in monopolistic or oligopolistic public services such as the post or police, or they can be governments and public administrations. Customers in product-market B are sector organizations in highly fragmented, relatively unstructured sectors of industry, such as construction, publishing or agriculture. Product-market C consists of critical production goods (e.g. machinery) in fragmented/unorganized sectors. An example might be tractors for farmers, or trucks for the transport sector. Trading systems for these heavily rely on extensive and detailed but to a large extent standardized and reusable product information, complemented by personal advice and service. They are likely to be strongly industry sector oriented. Product-market D consists of large companies and high-value, one-off purchases, possibly with multiple suppliers. An example is the contracting of a complex project. The 'trading system' in that case is likely to consist of a

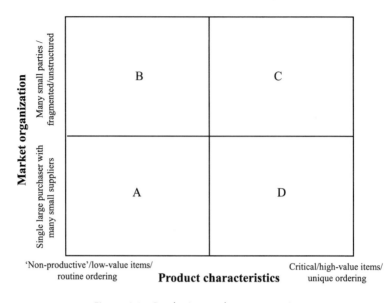

Figure 6.1 *Purchasing market segmentation*

multidisciplinary team doing person-to-person negotiation and following a case-by-case approach.

Having put this product-market segmentation in place, we can also see that it is too crude to capture all B-to-B trading systems. For example, between routine purchases of low-value items to one-off negotiation of very high-value items is trading in medium-value items. Currently, trading systems are not equipped to negotiate on such items (e.g. buying 10 personal computers for a 100-person company). This holds notably if such goods have to be delivered from another country. However, some recent developments started to address this area too, in auction systems and electronic trading systems with negotiation assistance.[93]

The product-market matrix may also limit the strategic view too much, by addressing solutions, namely the actual product, rather than problems/opportunities: it may fail to make explicit customer needs and benefits. With at least two kinds of customers in any of the B-to-B electronic trading systems considered here, i.e. suppliers and purchasers, these needs may be different, yet have to be met at the same time. Those needs are clear for the corporate purchaser (cost reduction in purchasing being the primary driver). The large purchasers pull along suppliers who do not want to lose market share. Those needs are less clear in the case of trading systems for sector organizations. They could include ease of access leading to more visibility and therefore extension of the market, as well as cost reduction for supply by the smaller players who need to reinforce their position *vis-à-vis* larger competitors in the sector. Cost reduction should correspond to a need on the purchasing side for a cheaper offer. New markets should correspond to interest by potential purchasers in new products. In the latter case there is a more profound need for information to be met (more than price information).

Again, it is the desire to control the cost of purchasing that is the driver from the customer side to differentiate between 'non-productive' or routine goods and 'productive' or critical goods.

Thus we can conclude that, within the context of the trading systems considered in the cases, there are three primary needs of potential *suppliers* for an electronic *trading* system: *reducing the cost of supply, maintaining market share* and *extending market share*. We also conclude that there are two primary needs of potential *purchasers* for an electronic trading system: *reducing the cost of purchasing* and *innovation* through information about new products. This leads to a different segmentation matrix, in Figure 6.2.

We can now take this customer benefit-oriented reasoning to its final stage by also considering other potentially relevant customer benefits along the lines developed in Chapter 2. There we considered a whole range of benefits: cost and capital reduction, time to market, brand reinforcement, market share defence or extension, quality improvement,

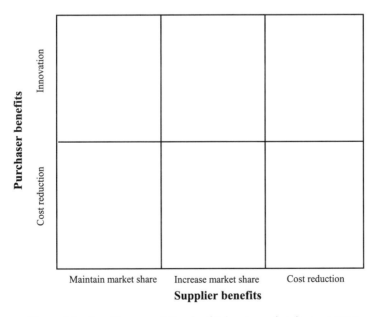

Figure 6.2 *Benefits segmentation for third-party marketplace provision*

convenience, availability, choice, customer loyalty and innovation. We need to consider which are the key benefits that can be provided to the customers of B-to-B electronic commerce systems, and on that basis reconsider customer base segmentation and—consequently—consider how companies can position themselves and build competitive advantages. Any of the electronic commerce systems in this study has at least two kinds of *business* customers: sellers and buyers (see Table 6.3). In all cases considered in this study, the B-to-B electronic commerce system acts *at least* as a 'switchbox with memory'. It connects sellers to buyers and at the same time stores information about products, sellers and buyers. In addition to business customers there may be consumers as customers, as in the case of Amazon.com. The 'memory' aspect is one resource to add value to the 'switching' function. As we have seen, in most cases there are many more ways to add value as the 'switching' is integrated with several other business functions, e.g. payment, logistics etc.

From the Marshall case study, as well as from the experience of Citius' customers, it appears that time to market—that is, reduction of lead times—is in that case a key benefit sought by purchasing customers. Reduction of lead time is also a benefit delivered by MRO trading systems like Citius or Tradezone, as demonstrated by the data from Citius' customer Texas Instruments. However, the extent of this benefit is likely to be more or less the same for each of these systems, as it amounts to reducing delays by electronic means throughout a fairly standard set of purchasing/supply steps. It is interesting to note that there is more opportunity in non-routine products like custom electronic designs to use reduction in time to market as a key element in competitive positioning. Marshall, by developing design support services for its

Table 6.3 *Customers (sellers and buyers) of electronic commerce systems*

Example sellers	Electronic commerce system 'switchbox'	Example buyers
Small book publishers	Amazon Advantage + Associates	Specialized online bookstores
Office supplies producers	Citius/Tradezone/ Industry.Net/GEIS TPN	Large purchasers
Mechanical designers	GEN/ICS	Automotive component manufacturers
Integrated circuit manufacturers	Marshall	Electronic equipment manufacturers
Fisherman	Infomar	Large supermarket chains

customers, has chosen to go that route. The same holds for GEN/ICS, where likewise reduced time to market is described as a primary benefit.

In the case of Amazon.com, benefits for customers include cost reduction, defending market share and access to new markets. In addition, we observe that opportunity for innovation is a key benefit for its business buyers, that is, the Associates (e.g. to enrich a virtual community or create a specialized online bookstore). We have also seen that opportunity for innovation might be a benefit for the purchasers that are customers of Citius or Tradezone. Marshall and GEN/ICS likewise clearly demonstrate the opportunity for innovation by their purchasing customers.

It is striking, however, that there seems to be far less emphasis on providing opportunities for innovation to suppliers in any of the systems. This holds for the MRO suppliers in the third-party marketplace systems, or in industry malls like Industry.Net. It also holds for the publishers that are customers of Amazon's Advantage programme. In GEN/ICS there is no mention of supplier innovation. Such a concept is also not being considered in the electronic auction Infomar. Only Marshall is an exception, as it sells purchasing customer profiles to electronics components manufacturers and also offers design-related feedback from purchasing customers to components suppliers.

Marshall points to two generic ways to provide opportunities for innovation to supplier customers:

1. providing customer profiling for one-to-one marketing;
2. providing product-related customer feedback.

MRO third-party marketplace providers could likewise consider building a new competitive advantage, namely to provide opportunity for innovation to the suppliers of the MRO products. First, they already collect transaction data and could easily construct purchaser profiles. Such data could then be provided to the MRO suppliers, which could then build much closer relationships with purchasers by providing them with specific discounts or bundling (one-to-one marketing). However, from the interviews and literature study there was little evidence that third-party marketplace providers were starting to exploit this.[94] Tradezone indicated some initial ideas about such a possibility, limiting it, however, to statistical and anonymous data.

Secondly, third-party marketplace providers could collect customer feedback about products, even in the case of routine purchases. As they control the user interface to the purchaser, it is possible to collect satisfaction ratings, perhaps triggered by detection of a change in purchasing behaviour or solicited by offering the purchaser an incentive. Such information can then be sold to the MRO supplier concerned.

SCS as an electronic auction provider does not mention anything about innovation opportunities for the sellers (that is, the fishermen). This is perhaps understandable from a historical and cultural point of view. When we look at the electronic auction literature there are, however, examples where seller innovation is enabled. AUCNET, a Japanese used-car electronic auction system, provides the sellers—the used-car dealers—with post-trading information (quality characteristics, prices paid by buyers of the most recent five transactions of the same car model). In this way the dealers are kept well informed on market behaviour regarding specific cars, enabling them to consider special deals, promotion etc. (Lee, 1997).

As demonstrated in the SCS case study as well as in the studies of flower auctions and used-car trading, a quality system is a key element in remote trading of perishable goods (which includes cars!). Such a quality system, provided that it is integrated with the electronic auction, is a potential source of innovation opportunities for suppliers.

Figures 6.3 and 6.4 capture the discussion above. They indicate, *qualitatively,* whether the capability to deliver a certain benefit is more or less a competitive advantage, as derived from the cases in this book.

Recapitulating what is expressed in these diagrams:

1. The provider of an electronic commerce trading system for *routine products* can increase its competitive position by delivering more benefits to its customers in terms of either:
    *   enabling the suppliers and purchasers of the products that are traded through the system to reduce their trading costs; or
    *   showing to suppliers that the trading system increases the supplier's market share.

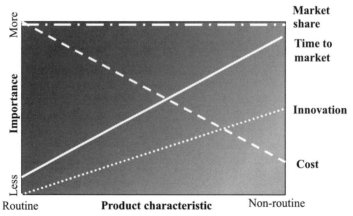

Figure 6.3   *Competitive advantage from delivering benefits to sellers*

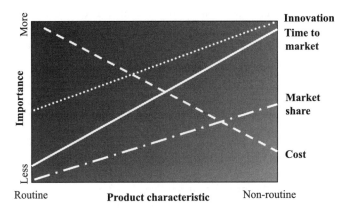

Figure 6.4   *Competitive advantage from delivering benefits to buyers*

2. The provider of an electronic commerce trading system for *non-routine products* can increase its competitive position by delivering benefits that its customers will appreciate, especially by:
    *   enabling the suppliers and purchasers of such products or services to reduce their time to market; and/or
    *   enabling particularly the buyers but also the suppliers to increase their capability to innovate; and/or
    *   show especially to suppliers but also to buyers that they can increase market share through the system.

PRODUCTS AND SERVICES

The cases studied have in common that they are all relatively innovative in terms of product and service development. It is striking, however, that none of them appears to emphasize a large proprietary advantage in technology. Mastery of the technology is critical, nevertheless. For example, in the case of Marshall this was considered essential, according to company accounts, to stay in the lead. In the case of GEN/ICS and Tradezone, distributed Internet technology was essential to realize key features of the system (in the first case to ensure access to data that is distributed across the network; in the second case to create a global set of catalogues). Although patents protect some of the technology,[95] the more important assets generally appear to be understanding of the processes and intimate knowledge of the business.

All the systems considered here seem to have matured sufficiently that product and service development is driven by market pull rather than technology push. This is even more evident for the technology user companies (such as Marshall, Amazon, FedEx, Citius) than for the technology provider companies (such as Tradezone or Globana).

DISTRIBUTION

The Internet and the Web can be used to contact potential customers and inform them about the product and service offer. In that sense it is a *medium* on which a message can be delivered. It is also a *distribution* channel to deliver the product or service. Furthermore, it provides the secure *communication and interconnection* infrastructure of the parties involved in transactions or remote collaboration. In the latter sense, the Internet is critical for all the cases studied here. Internet as a medium is dealt with in the next section.

A distribution or marketing channel is defined as a group of individuals or organizations that direct the flow of products from producers to customers (see Dibb *et al.* 1991). In this definition, direct producer–customer contact is also considered a channel, sometimes called the zero-level channel.

The combination of a telecommunications connection with customers and interactive software, as in the case of the Internet, performs in many respects the same function as a physical distribution channel. However, it is not quite the same as the zero-level channel of direct contact between producer and buyer. That is, the Internet is more than just a medium used in direct producer–buyer contact. The reason is, of course, that the buyer can perform many more functions than only information gathering, especially interactive functions such as software-assisted purchasing and support. An important aspect in this is to transfer more of the distribution, sales and support activity to the customer (see Hoffman, Novak and Chatterjee, 1995, and Michalski, 1995). The Internet is often considered to be an additional channel to direct product delivery or delivery through agents and distributors.

Kotler (1991) defines eight functions of a marketing channel. Most of these are also present in the Internet when viewed as a marketing channel. In addition, new channel functions are emerging. Kotler's functions are:

- *Information*: collecting and disseminating market research information. An example is the collection of transaction data to build customer profiles, as actively used by Marshall and Amazon.com.
- *Promotion*: to attract new or existing customers to products and services. Clearly, this is seen by most as the most obvious function

of the WWW and offered by all, although not always very strongly (see the next section).

- *Negotiation*: in the case studies only Infomar currently offers this possibility. As analysed in the previous chapter, it can be imagined that negotiation will also become part of next-generation collaboration platforms and third-party marketplaces.
- *Ordering*: except for Industry.Net, this is possible to perform via the Internet in all cases.
- *Delivery*:[96] in business-to-business electronic commerce this is one of the core functions. First it is information delivery to the customer, which can be fairly basic information (e.g. from catalogues as for Industry.Net) or much more extensive (e.g. designs, as for Marshall and GEN/ICS). Secondly, it is the set-up and delivery of a service such as training (Marshall), online collaborative design (GEN/ICS), catalogue updating (e.g. Tradezone) or online bookstore creation and operation (Amazon Associates).
- *Payment*: a typical example is the possibility of paying by credit or purchase card via the Web browser (e.g. Tradezone). Both online and offline payment are usually supported in the cases studied here.
- *Risk taking*: as an Internet channel function this means online trust services. For example, certification of parties involved in a transaction can be delivered in a fully integrated way at the customer user interface, cf. Tradezone. Possibly the service provider may have contracted such a trust service from a TTP (trusted third party).
- *Financing* is not really provided online. Tradezone offers this implicitly, as the franchisees that support purchase cards have to financially buffer transactions (which can be undone within a certain period of time).

In addition, the Internet as a distribution channel can bring new functionality to customers. Examples are:

- *Information brokerage*. This can take the form of software-assisted search for alternative product offerings, price comparisons, assessment reports, advice on usage etc. Several of the cases studied here offer such information search functionality within their own information domain (clearly not outside their domain).
- *Virtual community participation*. Notably the possibility of exchanging information with peer customers. When analysing the business customers involved in the cases studied here, we see that none of them offers such functionality (Amazon has virtual communities for consumer customers only). This is remarkable, especially as virtual community building has been one of the most highly praised opportunities of the Internet (e.g. Hagel and Armstrong, 1997).

Table 6.4   *Using the Internet as a distribution channel for products and services*

Company	Sellers	Buyers
Marshall	Online access to several services, such as customer profiles, sales data, catalogue updating	Online catalogue access, purchasing, training, design information, customer support
FedEx VirtualOrder	–	Online catalogue access, purchasing, tracking
Industry.Net	–	Online catalogue access
Amazon.com	Online sales and inventory monitoring	Online set-up of bookstore; sales monitoring
Citius	Offline computer-assisted catalogue integration (Altius)	Online purchasing; payment
Tradezone	Offline computer-assisted catalogue integration (bureau service)	Online purchasing; payment
GEN/ICS	Online catalogue and design integration; customer information capture; collaborative design	Online catalogue and design access; collaborative design; purchasing
Infomar	Online specification of offer and online negotiation	Online catch information; submission of bid; negotiation; purchasing.

The last two channel functions have been derived from the classification of Internet business models developed in Chapter 3. The single-function business models mentioned in that classification particularly lend themselves to being integrated into the channel and thereby to becoming a channel function rather than a self-standing service. Along this line of reasoning other examples can be readily identified, e.g. tracking of deliveries or certification of business actors.

Table 6.4 summarizes the main elements of the use of the Internet as a distribution channel for the cases studied in this book.

MARKETING COMMUNICATIONS

Marketing communication consists of advertising, sales promotion, public relations and personal selling (Kotler, 1991). The communications mix depends on communications objectives, target audience, nature of the message, available communication channels and communications budget. How the different nature of the Internet (as summarized in Chapter 2) is changing marketing communications is probably the most popular subject of electronic commerce books (see Hoffman and Novak (1995) for a discussion, as well as Kalakota and Winston (1996) and Vassos (1996)). Hoffman and Novak (1995), for example, state that the Internet enables marketing communications to become more interactive, available on demand, targeted (micro-marketing), or even individualized (one-to-one), and enabling differentiation that would help to reduce price competition.

However, in most studies business-to-consumer interaction has been addressed, rather than business-to-business. A model for business-to-business electronic commerce marketing communications does not yet seem to exist.

In developing such a model we have to take into account on the one hand the specific characteristics of industrial markets (as known from 'traditional' marketing theory and as listed in Table 6.1) and their relevance for marketing communications. On the other hand, we have to consider the specific characteristics of traditional marketing communications channels and of the Internet as a tool for marketing communications. The subset of characteristics of the Internet from Chapter 2 that could play a role in marketing communications are given in Table 6.5.

Such a model would also have to address 'channel coherence'. Business consultants make a plea for an integrated approach to channel management. Gartner points to the need for an electronic commerce channel manager (Kopriwa, 1997). George Colony, CEO of Forrester, advocates a coherent approach between channels, with each reinforcing the others.[97]

While this book will not attempt to develop such an integrated model for marketing communications in B-to-B electronic commerce, a number of observations are provided from the case studies on the use of the Internet as a channel for marketing communications, next to 'traditional' communication channels.

First, however, marketing communications objectives will be addressed, as this largely conditions the approach to marketing communications of the companies in the case studies.

Table 6.5 *Important Internet characteristics for marketing communications*

• 24 hours online	• Interactive
• Multimedia	• One-to-one and/or micro-marketing
• Ubiquity	• Integration
• Global availability	

Communication Objectives

In most cases studied here, the primary marketing communications objective is closely related to global branding. Marshall seeks to emphasize its capability to supply electronic components globally. It works with a European partner, SEI, to market the same service as it offers in the USA. Brand building is focused at this global sourcing capability: it is product/service focused. FedEx already has a strong global brand and is now seeking to leverage this in the global marketplace. It applies brand exploitation for its new electronic commerce trading service, VirtualOrder. Industry.Net, Citius and Tradezone are each setting up a new kind of business from no previous base. They all seek to build a global brand as *the* provider of electronic trading in the MRO market. The same holds for Amazon.com, in that case in online book distribution. SCS is operating in a global niche market, in which it is already well known. It now seeks to build a global brand name for Infomar, on the basis of its current reputation. GEN/ICS is to some extent the odd one out. Although the concept is clearly of a global nature, DT/Globana with ICS has for the time being a national focus. It is a question how long this can be sustained, as the main competition is global.

Target Audience and Take-up Process

The target market is a key factor in designing marketing communications. It determines the choice of means or channels (see next section), as well as the nature of the message and the promotion mix.

The products and services analysed in the case studies are of a wide variety and correspondingly they deal with a variety of target audiences and communication channels. For example, the Amazon.com Associates programme is targeting virtual communities that can be formed around any topic and is mainly using the Internet to contact them. Tradezone has a two-tier audience, namely in the first tier, for Tradezone International, potential franchisees such as large banks. These are mainly addressed by means of personal selling and PR. The second tier, the customers of the franchisees, consists of MRO purchasers and suppliers, which are approached through personal contacts and advertising. There seems to be little in common between the various audiences and communication approaches.

Therefore, as part of this comparative analysis, we focus on general characteristics of the target audience, such as their size, as estimated in Table 6.6.

While the following section analyses in more detail the use of communication channels, it is observed here from the case studies and

Table 6.6   *Target audience size estimates*

Case	Size of marketing communications target	Potential target audience
Marshall	100s	Electronic components manufacturers
	100 000s–1 000 000s	Professional buyers of such components
Fedex VirtualOrder	100 000s	Any company (in the USA) with a catalogue of standard products
Industry.Net	100 000s	Any company with a catalogue of MRO products
	1 000 000s	Purchasers of MRO products
Amazon bookshop	1 000 000s–100 000 000s	Book buyers
Amazon Advantage	10 000s	Publishers
Amazon Associates	100 000s	Virtual communities/online bookshops
Citius	100s (initially)	Large purchasers
	100 000s	Suppliers of MRO products
Tradezone International	10s	Franchisees
Tradezone franchisee	100s (initially)	Purchasers
	100 000s	Suppliers of MRO products
DT/Globana—ICS	10 000s	Manufacturing, engineering, construction
SCS/Infomar	100s	Fish auctions

Table 6.6 that the size of the target market is a key determinant in the choice between mass communications means (journals, newspapers, the Internet) and personal communications. A large target audience (10 000s–1 000 000s) will be addressed through PR and Web or newspaper/trade magazine advertising. The small audiences are dealt with on a personal basis. The one 'in-between' case, DT/Globana with ICS, is only capable of dealing with 10 000 customers on a personal basis by making use of the extensive salesforce network of Deutsche Telekom in Germany.

Another key factor in designing market communications is the product/service adoption process. For example, Dibb *et al.* (1991) argue that customers go through a sequence of steps: awareness—interest—evaluation—trial—adoption.[98] For each step the marketing communications approach might be different. For example, mass communication media, including the Internet, are better suited for the early stages, to create

Table 6.7 *Product/service adoption stages for Amazon Associates and SCS/Infomar (after Dibb et al., 1991)*

	Amazon Associates	*SCS/Infomar*
Awareness	Web banner ads; newspaper ads/articles; other Associates; direct/mail from Amazon; word of mouth	Visit to another auction; contact with sales rep; brochures; Website; Infomar at conferences.
Interest	Information at Web site: benefits, FAQ	Site visit by SCS (often by CEO himself)
Evaluation	Reference sites	Detailed analysis by experts and concept proposal, made by European Auction Builders, with SCS
Trial	Online set-up of links to Amazon.com after screening by Amazon	Onsite demo
Adoption	Same as trial phase; quarterly automated transfer of revenues	Actual installation, training
Loyalty	Weekly feedback on sales, but not on customers	After-sales support; company news

awareness and interest. At the later stages personal contact may be more appropriate. Table 6.7 illustrates the adoption process and communication means used for two of the cases.

In the adoption process the *loyalty* or *retention* phase has been added. There are two reasons to consider this step explicitly for Internet electronic commerce, namely where the Internet is a threat to customer loyalty and where the Internet is an opportunity to enhance loyalty.

1. As a *threat*: the investment to adopt a product/service can be rather low, as in the case of becoming an Amazon.com Associate or when ordering products online from a distributor like Marshall. In those cases all the customer invests is his/her time. Therefore switching costs are low and customer loyalty or retention becomes an issue (as argued in Chapter 2). This holds less for systems like Infomar or Citius that require substantial upfront investment by both purchasers and suppliers.

2. As an *opportunity*: the Internet provides means to automatically capture information about customers, which can be used to create incentives for customers to come back.

The cases demonstrate a number of ways of using the Internet for customer retention:

- online product news, implemented or foreseen in all cases;
- virtual community elements such as discussion lists offered by Industry.Net to its members;
- access to sales data. Of all those studied, Marshall applies this most actively. It offers the component suppliers extranet access to buyers' data. Component buyers are offered purchase history through PartnerNet. Amazon.com also provides sales data, but not up to the level of the individual book buyer.
- customized product offer. Marshall has customized Web pages for its buyers;
- additional services. FedEx VirtualOrder provides a Marketing Alliance Program to assist its customers in their marketing on the Web.

Although we classified the Internet earlier as a mass communication medium, it also exhibits some characteristics of a personal communication channel, such as interactivity and one-to-one relationships, as argued in Chapter 2. These may be particularly useful for the later stages of the product adoption process, as argued by Dibb *et al.* (1991). In practice, the cases show that the more personalized communications capability of the Internet is only used—if at all—for the retention stage.

Where the Internet is used for communication in the cases studied here, this is mostly, as expected, as a one-way impersonal mass communications means for the early stages of product adoption, to generate awareness and interest.

Communication Channels and Promotion Mix

Kotler (1991) distinguishes between personal and impersonal communication channels. As in traditional business-to-business marketing, personal contact is quite important in most of the cases studied here too. Citius and Tradezone depend heavily on personal marketing. In their market-dominance strategy it is key to sign up large purchasers. Tradezone's franchising marketing programme is clearly directed towards large potential franchisees, with a strong emphasis on the professional approach through its marketing partnership with Arthur Andersen. DT/Globana's marketing of ICS is centred on the direct salesforce of Deutsche Telekom, and in the first phase of roll-out is directed at the larger customers (at least medium-sized). Likewise, in SCS's approach with Infomar there is no doubt about the central role of direct person-to-person contact with the customer. Marshall employs about a quarter of its total staff in field sales illustrating the importance of personal contact for its business. The extent of direct sales is less clear for Industry.Net, FedEx VirtualOrder and the Amazon.com Associates and Advantage programmes.

Direct sales is supported by traditional marketing communication means such as brochures, videos, journals, as well as in a number of cases by exhibitions and trade shows (Citius, Tradezone, DT/Globana).

Public relations are actively pursued by some of the companies. Industry.Net (until recently), Marshall and to some extent Amazon.com and FedEx are the most outspoken examples, their CEOs featuring in business journals and appearing at prominent conferences. GEN and Citius have sought international PR via the G7 label and presence at a number of conferences, but this has had fairly limited impact. Possibly the difference in approach reflects differences in business culture between the USA and Europe, from which GEN, Citius, Tradezone and Infomar originate.[99]

The use of the Internet as a communications channel shows some interesting variations in approach. Citius, Tradezone and SCS/Infomar, although having an Internet presence, are all fairly low-key in their use of the Internet for promotional purposes. Even though Tradezone has foreseen a sizeable promotional budget, it is understood not to be used for Internet advertising.

The GEN concept is promoted more strongly via the Internet, among others by means of an interactive demo of collaborative design. However, DT/Globana has not (yet) provided its own specific version of this demo. FedEx does not heavily advertise VirtualOrder via the Internet, although it does actively promote the FedEx brand in general. It channels traffic to its site by means of banners (see Box 6.1). Once at the Web site, extensive information is available about VirtualOrder. However, the VirtualOrder service itself does not feature prominently on the FedEx site. Marshall has an active approach to the design of its Web site for customer retention. Its Web site has received several awards. Marshall has an explicit channel-integration approach, not only for its communications but also for its services. For example, its Web support is complemented by personal phone support, both available on a 24-hour basis.

Finally, Amazon.com is one of the largest advertisers on the Web. Its advertising is exclusively directed to consumers and highly focused on brand building. This is understandable in view of Amazon's objective to build global market share. However, it has to be taken into account that Amazon basically sells a commodity—books—with little opportunity for differentiation. Amazon's Associates and

Advantage programmes are well explained on its Web site. However, they do not feature prominently, nor is any specific online advertising being done for them.

Box 6.1   Banners

Banners are areas of screen space with a message on which the user can click. Banners are used for advertisements, aiming to direct customers towards the vendor's site. They are also used for sales promotions, special offers etc. From the click stream sophisticated direct-response measurement and analysis can be done. Banners are therefore useful to incite direct response. They also serve the purpose of building the brand when they are shown to the potential customer. They always lead to an 'impression'—that is, that the customer has been confronted with them as soon as the Web page is accessed—and therefore are sold on the basis of CPM—cost per thousand impressions. As an impression does not say much about the actual customer interest, the trend has become to pay for click-throughs only, that is, to pay only if the customer clicks on the banner. However, the effectiveness of online ads and banners has been decreasing markedly, with click-throughs dropping from 1.4% in May 1998 to 0.5% by the end of 1998, according to NetRatings, Inc. (Everett-Thorp, 1997). Moreover, it is claimed that 80% of all Web ad space goes away unsold and that CPM rates are likely to drop from a level of $25–35 to $8–10 (Kroll, Pitta and Lyons, 1998).

Neither Citius, Tradezone nor DT/Globana has offline advertising in order to attract potential supplier customers (who could provide the catalogues of products and services). It might be that FedEx contracts offline advertising directed at suppliers with product catalogues, or similarly Amazon.com to bring publishers into its Advantage programme. However, this study did not find evidence to that extent.

This leads to the following observations:

- only marginal use of the Web for targeted promotion towards supplier customers (i.e. MRO producers for the third-party marketplaces or industry malls and publishers for Amazon's Advantage program);
- somewhat more but still very limited use of the Web for targeted promotion towards business buyers (i.e. purchasers for the third-party marketplace systems, or online bookstores and focused communities of interest for Amazon's Associates programme), with the exception of Marshall and Industry.Net.

This is partially understandable as a strategic marketing communications choice. Although all of the third-party marketplaces need large catalogues to implement their global dominance strategy, they tend to build those in the first stage through a few large customers. Citius reasons that large purchasers will bring their supplier network into the system. The same probably holds for DT/Globana. Tradezone expects that large franchisees will be able to bring many suppliers in through their business contacts (e.g. being a bank or trade association). Amazon.com was launched with a huge catalogue from a large distributor. However, there are potentially many more MRO suppliers that could become customers of these systems, as this is a highly diverse and fragmented industry. The same holds for publishers (10 000–50 000 in the USA alone). Not addressing these, mostly small, business customers leaves these systems exposed to competition. It seems reasonable, however, that in an early phase the focus is on the larger customers.

As for the buyer customer side, these are treated a little better through the Web sites of the electronic trading systems. However, small, *ad hoc* purchasers are not served very well nor explicitly attracted by means of targeted promotion. As for the supplier customers, this leaves a potential market underaddressed. Again, this may be a matter of strategic choice (e.g. DT/Globana expresses this explicitly). In the case of Amazon.com it is somewhat surprising, as for book publishing a global presence strategy seems to depend critically on working with many focused niche outlets (focused in a geographic or community sense).

There may be yet another explanation of the observations made above, namely that Internet-based promotion is not well understood for business-to-business marketing. This fits with the other observation made before, that there are no marketing communications models available for business-to-business electronic commerce. It also fits with the observation in Chapter 5 that most of the current systems that support full transactions do not seem to have been designed to address *ad hoc* small suppliers and possibly anonymous purchasers. Either their technical or their commercial concept is not fully suited. This does not contradict the fact that an industry mall like Industry.Net has thousands of suppliers and 'buyers' as Industry.Net supports only the first step, access to product information, of a business transaction.

ONE-TO-ONE MARKETING

Introduction

A key marketing concept that is often discussed in the context of Internet commerce is one-to-one marketing. In this section an assessment is made of the applicability and actual application of this concept for the case studies.

The one-to-one marketing idea has recently attracted a great deal of attention, notably through the work of Peppers and Rogers. They define one-to-one marketing as 'using customer databases and interactive communications to sell to one customer at a time as many products and services as possible over the entire lifetime of that customer's patronage [instead of selling one product at a time to as many customers as possible in a particular sales period]' (Peppers and Rogers, 1997a).

One-to-one marketing is based on knowledge of the customer and company flexibility to deliver customized products and services:

- knowledge of the individual customer, assessment of the lifetime value (LTV) of a customer, rather than their one-off value, increasing the level of interactive communications with the customer, keeping customer records, development of the customer needs; and
- development of the internal flexibility to respond to a potentially wide variety of customer needs, by customized development, production and delivery of products and services.

How this could work is illustrated in Figure 6.5, applying Peppers and Rogers (1997a) to the case of a third-party marketplace of office furniture. In such a marketplace customers can buy standard products from office furniture suppliers (position ①). When the third-party marketplace operator is capable of bundling information from several catalogues,

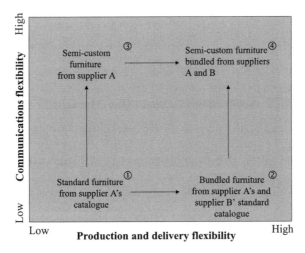

Figure 6.5 *Increasing customer value by increasing company capabilities. (Applying Peppers and Rogers 1997a; reproduced by permission of Don Peppers)*

and thus increases its delivery capability, it can offer bundled office furniture (position ②). The third-party marketplace operator can also decide to communicate with the customer about specific requirements and to negotiate with the supplier on behalf of the customer for support for customization. The latter may be possible because the third-party marketplace operator achieves economies of scale when aggregating the requirements of many buyers. It then gains an increased level of communication flexibility with both buyer and supplier and thus moves to position ③ in the diagram. Finally, when the third-party marketplace provider can deliver both bundling services and customization services, it reaches position ④.

Peppers and Rogers argue that it is possible in many cases to move customers from a situation of a single or a few uniform needs to a wide variety of individual needs. They also argue that analysing your customer base will lead to a differentiation of customers on LTV, from high LTV to low. Comparing customers' LTV with their actual value to the company leads to a variation of strategies. Customers who already realize their LTV and are the most valued customers are to be retained. Customers who have significant potential should be grown (in terms of their needs and actual sales to them). Customers with an LTV lower than their actual cost should be shed. By improving the company's flexibility, it is supposedly possible to move at least part of the customer base from uniform customer valuation (a single one-fits-all product) to high customer valuation.

Clearly, Peppers and Rogers' recommendation is to implement one-to-one marketing, even if this requires substantial business reorganization in customer communications and in production. First, this is a compelling approach to improve the company performance. Secondly, this is a strategy that the competition is in any case likely to adopt. Finally, Internet technologies are particularly suited to implement one-to-one marketing, as explained in Chapter 2.

Application of One-to-One Marketing

In certain areas of B-to-B one-to-one marketing is well known, notably where there is a limited number of individual customers, tight supplier–buyer collaboration (for example project-based business) and a strong customer-oriented attitude at the supplier's side, which may be due to fierce competition. Some of the cases studied here exhibit such characteristics, namely the third-party marketplace providers Tradezone and CitiusNet, in their sales to large purchasers. However, these providers also have an additional customer base of much smaller customers, suppliers and purchasers. One-to-one marketing techniques can be readily imagined for those smaller customers too. However, Tradezone does not consider it to be in its interests to exploit such knowledge of the customers. Citius is only starting to consider this option. It is claimed that FedEx implements one-to-one marketing through its VirtualOrder system. However, the case presented is not very convincing, as VirtualOrder provides only limited support for capturing information about buyers and leaves the handling of that information to the supplier itself.

Amazon.com has a profound implementation of one-to-one marketing for its book buyers (the consumers). It also has certain one-to-one features for the publishers that subscribe to the Advantage program, signalling low-inventory status to them and helping them to reorder automatically if wanted. As for online bookstores and others that subscribe to the Associates programme, Amazon does not provide them with one-to-one support, and is even rather explicit about not providing additional information related to the selection of books sold by the particular online bookstore. This is understandable, as Amazon needs to protect itself against its own associates which it does by not giving away one of its key competitive advantages, namely customer (reader) specific information.

Beyond exploiting customer information and building delivery flexibility, a third-party marketplace provider could also consider providing suppliers with one-to-one marketing tools, helping them to improve their marketing. This would require that the supplier's customer-oriented sales proposition be transmitted all through the third-party marketplace system to the purchaser. As of today, none of the electronic commerce systems studied here provides such a service to its suppliers.

To implement one-to-one marketing (even for 'named accounts') requires additional technology support in an electronic business environment. Interactive and multimedia technology is needed to overcome lack of direct person-to-person contact.[100] Recording, security and data-mining technology is needed to deal with anonymous and *ad hoc* service usage, or to deal with large numbers of customers.

Pricing and One-to-One Marketing

Varian (1997) argues that in industries with increasing returns to scale, large fixed costs or economies of scope, the appropriate guiding principle for pricing is to equate marginal willingness to pay to marginal cost. *In extremis*, if marginal cost to supply is zero, the price would be set at what the buyer is willing to pay. However, in practice, this would be likely to have adverse effects on the willingness to pay of other customers. Therefore, driven by profit seeking, firms would be expected to introduce differential pricing (price brackets or categories). The Internet is a significant enabler for operating certain business-to-business services with increasing returns to scale. This would hold for services and information that can be delivered to large markets, e.g. globally, and whose delivery or reproduction can be automated (B-to-B services such as Amazon Associates or Marshall's NetSeminars, or digital information such as digital designs in ICS).

The one-to-one marketing philosophy, especially when combined with emergent online negotiation technologies, fits closely with the use of differential pricing. Determining the customer's willingness to pay, on the basis of historical knowledge of the individual customer, an assessment of actual customer needs from an interactive dialogue (e.g. negotiation) and service or information delivery flexibility, allows pricing to be much closer to the willingness to pay rather than applying flat-rate pricing.

However, use of one-to-one marketing to exploit the differential pricing opportunity for the delivery of services and information via the Internet still seems underdeveloped. The case studies did not provide evidence of experimentation along these lines of thinking.

Assessment of One-to-One Marketing

A conclusion from the current research is that, despite the huge publicity given to one-to-one marketing, these ideas do not seem to have really caught on for most of the cases studied here. One reason might be that it is still early days for some of these systems to go beyond their basic functionality. The reasons mentioned by Peppers and Rogers possibly do not yet apply: company performances are not yet perceived to be under pressure, and competitive pressures are not yet strong. However, if the predictions are correct about the speed of market development, we should expect one-to-one marketing soon to become a hot topic for industry malls, third-party marketplaces and collaborative platforms.

SUMMARY

This chapter dealt with the second part of the comparative case analysis, addressing marketing strategy, segmentation and targeting, marketing communications and one-to-one marketing.

First, a number of general observations were made about industrial markets, namely that characteristics such as globalization and customization are reinforced through the Internet, while new characteristics also emerge, such as networking with business partners in flexible constellations, and an increased role for branding.

With this understanding of industrial markets, the next step was to investigate how companies segment the customer base, select target markets and build competitive advantages for their competitive positioning. The most complex in this respect are generic trading systems, as these have two types of customers (suppliers and purchasers) in a wide range of industry sectors. On the basis of the case studies and the Internet benefits analysis in Chapter 2, it was possible to define a benefits segmentation scheme. This was done first for the third-party marketplace providers, and then generalized for providers of trading systems for routine and non-routine products or services.

Products and services, distribution and marketing communications have been analysed as key elements of the marketing mix. While generally products and services in the case studies are advanced and strongly dependent on Internet technology, they use little proprietary technology. The Internet as a distribution channel (for services and digital products) supports most of the functions of traditional distribution channels, although in a modified form. In addition, it provides new functions such as automated information brokerage and virtual community participation.

Marketing communications, although much discussed for business-to-consumer electronic commerce, is not yet well described for business-to-business. In particular, there seems to be no business-to-business marketing communications model that provides an integrated approach to deal with several possible marketing communications channels, including the Internet (channel coherence), and also takes into account the characteristics of Internet-enabled industrial markets. However, for the cases studied, marketing communications objectives such as global brand building and the corresponding approach to creating customer awareness can be understood with standard marketing communications theory. It seems useful—and the case studies demonstrate this—explicitly to address marketing communications for customer retention as a stage in the product-adoption process. The reasons are that retention can be both threatened and reinforced through the Internet. Marketing communications seems to be mostly addressed to buyers rather than suppliers in case of the trading systems, and the Internet is used only to a limited extent.

Finally, this chapter addressed one-to-one marketing, as this is often seen as an important new trend in marketing that is enabled by the Internet and technologies like databases, customer profiling and data mining. The assessment is that despite the huge publicity given to this concept, it has not yet really become part of the approach of most of the cases studied.

7
Roadmap for Business-to-Business Electronic Commerce

There is no lack of predictions of a bright future for electronic commerce. Speculation is rife that a 'new economy' is being created, governed by 'new rules' (Kelly, 1998). It is argued that the exciting new possibilities will especially benefit fast-moving small companies that are not held back by a legacy and history, the 'gazelles that are willing to take the plunge' (Uyttendaele 1998). Others, however, are emphasizing that companies should not, above all, forget about basic and well-established business principles (Shapiro and Varian, 1998).

Predicting the future is always a risky undertaking, and this is especially the case in the Internet world. Uncertainties are plenty in this fast-changing environment. Many assumptions have already proved wrong due to lack of market research, the unpredictability of technology development, or incomplete understanding of market and other social mechanisms. This chapter first analyses such critical assumptions in strategic Internet business planning. Secondly, and with due reservations given the high level of uncertainty, a perspective is given of the future of B-to-B electronic commerce. Finally, the chapter provides the overall conclusions to this book.

CRITICAL ASSUMPTIONS AND STRATEGY DEVELOPMENT

There are some qualifications to statements about the Internet. In many cases the underlying assumptions have not (yet) been thoroughly verified. For example, wrong but hidden assumptions in the marketing models may show up only after a while.[101] In addition, there are still problems in agreeing on definitions and a common language for electronic commerce. The following sections address some of the critical assumptions for business strategy development in electronic commerce. In essence, it is argued that while electronic commerce is developing very fast, this goes along with a high degree of uncertainty. As a result, business strategy development is truly a challenge!

The next section argues that care has to be taken with the interpretation of market research in electronic commerce. The definition that is used as the basis for measurement of the electronic commerce market is often not clear and usually definitions are not comparable. There are also some more fundamental problems with traditional market research in fast-moving markets that are discussed in subsequent sections. The degree of uncertainty about electronic commerce is increased particularly because of the high degree of dynamics in technology development. Yet another uncertainty is introduced by the confrontation between electronic commerce over the Internet as an intrinsically global phenomenon and the lack of a global legal framework for electronic commerce. Despite all these uncertainties, there is some hope. Strategic management thinkers have analysed various approaches to business strategy development and provided some guidance on how to achieve the 'strategic fit' between the turbulent and fast-moving environment, the organisation and its legacy, and the business strategy.

Quality of Market Research

One problem with the statistics on the electronic commerce market is that there is no single accepted way of defining or measuring electronic commerce. The OECD (1997) has published a report, '*Measuring Electronic Commerce*' which makes a systematic inventory of the different reports about market size and growth of electronic commerce. It finds that predictions are wildly different (e.g. predictions for the total value of electronic commerce in the year 2000 ranging from $580 million to $775 billion).[102] The statistics do not usually include all of the transactions that are enabled by information and communications technology (and in fact cannot do without it). For example, the huge daily financial flows would fit into most definitions of electronic commerce but are not factored in. For some market researchers (e.g. Killen Associates) electronic commerce also includes interactive TV, infomercials etc. The wide definition used by the European Commission in the European Initiative in Electronic Commerce[103] includes many forms of electronic business and work. It also comprises business collaboration, for example collaborative design and engineering. Economic statistics have also not been designed to measure what Goldfinger (1997) calls 'the intangible economy'. Finally, the statistics are likely to be based on an extrapolation of the past and the present, rather than on visionary insight such as Negroponte's, who predicted that electronic commerce would be in the order of one trillion dollars by the year 2000.[104]

The same comments about inconsistencies in statistics of market size can be made about data on user acceptance. Many reports state that security is the key barrier to the take-up of Internet commerce. Others state exactly the opposite, and instead see lack of evidence that electronic commerce has business relevance as the prime reason that companies are holding back from the Web (European Commission, 1997c). Other reports find a mix of reasons, none dominating. In addition, the perception of barriers to electronic commerce seems to be quite different between the USA and non-US parts of the world.[105]

At the firm level, the cases in this book provide striking illustrations of the difficulties of market research in an emerging market. The various third-party marketplace providers that have been analysed have an incomplete picture of their competitors. For example, both Tradezone and Citius, although offering very similar systems and having a similar strategic objective, namely rapidly to build global market share in the online MRO market, did not know the details of each other's offering. Similarly, industry analysts mentioned different systems than were being considered by these third-party marketplace providers as their potential competitors. This is an understandable phenomenon in emerging markets.

However, at the same time the providers are convinced that the window of opportunity is only relatively short. The combination of the lack of complete market research and shorter timescales may introduce higher risks than in traditional business. There is less time to learn and to correct a possibly wrong strategy. How to adapt market research methods to deal with the dynamics of Internet commerce is a key question for the Internet world! Where it is being said that Internet time goes a factor of three times faster than normal time, market research that does not adapt itself will face an increase (by the square root of that factor) of the error in its predictions. However, the solution is not simply to reduce the timescales for market research correspondingly. There are inherent limits to lead-time reduction in certain tools for market research, e.g. in response times to questionnaires, or the cost may be prohibitive, as these, in the worst case, increase by the same factor. In addition, the impression is that changes in the Internet world are more outspoken. If indeed fluctuations are wilder (which may be the case, witness the stock markets!), conventional market research will also be faced with more uncertain predictions.

An indication for one possible way forward comes from following the online discussion lists about Internet marketing. These can bring together the experiences of many people, leading to a consolidated opinion about market trends or about the effectiveness of new marketing approaches in a fairly short timespan. In other words, perhaps the Internet and electronic commerce can themselves provide the tools for effective market research. Further research is needed into these and other forms of what I would call 'networked market research'.

Dynamics of Technology and Growth of Electronic Commerce

The take-up of the Internet was accelerated tremendously by the invention of the World Wide Web in 1991 at CERN by Tim Berners-Lee and Robert Caillau, and the subsequent development of browsers like Mosaic, Netscape and Explorer. This 'killer' technology combined the worldwide accepted computer-to-computer communication protocol TCP/IP, which gives access in a uniform and simple way to the Internet as a 'network of networks', with a straightforward visual way to access information from any of these sources.

Electronic commerce is now developing rapidly on the basis of the Internet and the WWW. However, much more is needed than access to information to make electronic commerce work. Essential functionality first of all includes reliable and high-capacity communications infrastructure. The Internet is still too congested, making users reluctant to commit to electronic commerce or even leading to them turn away. It also includes electronic payment in all its modalities, from electronic cheques to digital money for micro-payments, security for privacy protection and the protection of copyrights on digital content, application-to-application communication, search and navigation to deal with large amounts of information, and user interface design.

The take-up of electronic commerce is also still considered to be hampered by difficulties in easily deploying the available, let alone emerging, technology (see e.g. the e-Christmas report, mentioned before, or the Marshall case study). When the technologies become easier to use and more powerful, they will become mainstream tools to implement competitive marketing strategies.

Furthermore, many new technologies are being developed, for example to provide 3D animation and video over the Internet, information broadcasting based on push technologies, online negotiation, customer profiling, and automated user assistance with the help of 'intelligent agents'. Their rapid development creates new opportunities for early adopters as well as new uncertainties. The majority of companies are likely to adopt a 'wait and see' attitude because of uncertainty about which technology will be the winner in the marketplace and the immaturity of some technologies. The challenge is in choosing the moment to start using new technology. Many consultants—understandably—argue that early experimentation is critical in order not to be left behind.

Companies may temporarily have a competitive advantage in proprietary new technology. However, the general pattern in the Internet environment, confirmed by the case studies, is to make technology widely available and leverage on mass-market deployment and other key strengths (such as knowledge of complex systems integration or business practice knowledge). An ultimate example of this is that Netscape announced in February 1998 to make the program code of its browser publicly available, whereas this technology was its core asset only a few years ago, at the founding of the company. Netscape's strength now is its access to a huge customer base (it still has a large share in the browser market) and its strength in electronic commerce server software, which is the back-end to the front-end browser.

The name of the game is to set a *de facto* standard through rapid and large-scale roll-out of new technology. Being either the owner of the standard or in the lead of standards development is perceived to bring large benefits to technology suppliers. Standards wars in Internet technology are numerous and lead to confusion among technology users. Examples are the Netscape versus Microsoft browser war, Sun and others with Java versus Microsoft with Active-X for the programming of interactive Web elements, and (in the recent past) the fight between the ANSI X.12 and UN/EDIFACT electronic data interchange standards.

Figure 7.1 illustrates the Tower of Babel in electronic commerce land with many different approaches to standardization or interoperability. One of the difficulties is to find a common terminology and common

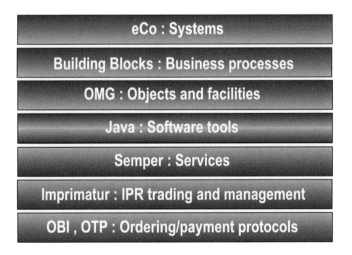

Figure 7.1 *Different approaches to interoperability in electronic commerce (reproduced by permission of Man-Sze Li, IC Focus Ltd)*

view of an electronic commerce architecture, in order to be able to assess exactly which part of electronic commerce is being addressed by each of these initiatives. In the diagram, eCo is a framework developed by CommerceNet and applied in, for example, the RosettaNet PC supply-chain experiment. 'Building Blocks' refers to a study performed by EBES, which addressed the business processes as building blocks for electronic commerce (and subsequently breaks this down into technical building blocks). OMG, the Object Management Group, has a working group for electronic commerce, focusing on business objects and their exchange via CORBA object request and brokerage facilities. The Java approach is driven by Sun's Java Electronic Commerce Framework and addresses Java-based tools and the programming environment for electronic commerce (as well as specific facilities such as wallets and payments). Semper was an ACTS project that designed a secure set of services, with a strong focus on financial services support. Imprimatur was an ESPRIT consensus-building project on intellectual property management of digital content. Finally, OBI and OTP are ordering and payment protocols for B-to-B and B-to-C electronic commerce. Many more standards-oriented activities could be mentioned here, addressing specific services, e.g. SET for secure credit-card payments. The Open Information Interchange Guide to Electronic Commerce provides a more extensive description of the various standards (http://www2.echo.lu/oii/en/commerce.html).

The rapid and often unpredictable technology developments, the confusion caused by standards wars, and the hard-to-foresee influence of technology limitations all risk invalidating our assumptions about the development of Internet business. Market researchers, of course, only take continuous changes into account in their extrapolations. The impact of *discontinuous* technological change, on the other hand, remains pure crystal ball gazing. An example of this is push technology, which only came into the picture in 1996 and has greatly changed the way of thinking about marketing on the Web. An example of technology limitations is in network capacity. The rising popularity of the Internet, and especially heavy multimedia use, might be self-defeating, as network capacity might not be able to keep up, causing congestion or even breakdown, which would severely damage business confidence in the Internet. Such a case occurred during the Asian stock crisis (end October 1997). At that time stock-trading Web sites were not able to deal with the flood of access attempts. Exactly at the moment that rapid information provision was critical, these sites were letting their customers down. It was reported that as a consequence many customers lost their confidence in this form of online stock trading.

For electronic commerce to continue to grow rapidly and to become pervasive, considerable improvements will be needed in its usability.

Particularly the general consumer and many small companies require more intuitive and direct access. This may include new devices offering TV-based and mobile access, as well as voice support, and ideally intention-driven interaction rather than today's syntax-driven approach, which at times makes the user into a grammarian. But even those with high keyboard and mouse skills increasingly find the Web less usable. Today's relatively unstructured and non-intuitive access, even with the help of search engines, is inadequate to cope with the ever-growing and already enormous amount of Web pages. Finding the right information item becomes searching for the proverbial needle in the haystack.

Another condition for achieving widespread take-up is cheaper access. In Europe, for example, as well as in a number of Asian and Latin American countries, telecommunication tariffs are still rather high, although they have been coming down in recent years. New uses of the Web require increasingly more bandwidth, but it may be hard to see for the individual consumer, and even for small businesses, that high-speed access like ISDN pays off. The Forrester research quoted before identified telecommunications liberalization issues as the main impediment to Internet growth. It foresees penetration for the total consumer population to be limited to 13% by 2001 in Europe, versus 34% in the USA.

Continuous technological improvements in computing and communications power, together with increased competition among providers, will bring prices of equipment and communication down. With improvements in usability these are a range of smaller, quantitative steps rather than a quantum leap towards pervasive presence and use of electronic commerce. This may well be enough to grow electronic commerce such that critical mass in take-up and actual daily use is achieved.

Towards a Global Legal Framework for the Digital Economy?

The legal conditions for electronic commerce are still not fully clear. This creates uncertainty and may cause hesitation among businesses in adopting electronic commerce. For example, as mentioned before, during 1998 Andersen Consulting polled some 350 European and 30 US companies for their views on electronic commerce in Europe. The researchers stated that this showed that a major barrier to electronic commerce was the risk-avoiding and hesitating attitude of European companies. A significant part of business in Europe seemed to be waiting for clear legislation before moving into electronic commerce. Lack of certainty about international mutual recognition of secure electronic commerce services (such as certification and digital signatures) is holding back international Internet commerce. Large companies can overcome this by installing their own secure infrastructure.[106] Smaller companies may be inclined to wait for the global secure framework to be in place. However, it is not inconceivable that international electronic commerce suddenly takes off once a critical mass of mutually recognizing, trusted parties are in place. The question is when this will be, and whether a business should wait for this to happen or contribute itself to building trust and confidence by taking the risk and setting an example. Forrester believes that countries—that is, the public and private sector jointly—will have a short window of opportunity of some 18 months to two years to take away barriers and to catalyse the development of electronic commerce. They need to use this time in order to provide maximum impetus to the prolonged phase of hypergrowth that may follow. For the USA the window was predicted to be around 1999. The main European countries are believed to be lagging behind the USA by one to three years (Forrester, 1998).

Table 7.1 provides an overview of the legal issues that were under consideration internationally at the end of 1998. It also provides a (much-simplified) status of developments in the EU and in the USA at that time.[107] Following a series of international governmental and industrial conferences, a broad consensus has emerged that these are the key issues to be tackled. It is also generally accepted that solutions in the first instance have to be found by the marketplace, taking the global and unique character of the Internet into account, and that there should only be a minimal number of laws that stimulate rather than suffocate electronic commerce. Nevertheless, these are principles only—the actual solutions in a number of cases still need to be agreed. While it looks as if much of the current business-related legislation and regulation remains as applicable to electronic commerce as it is for physical commerce, it is also clear that there are some areas where legislation needs to be revised, e.g. in the import/export rules for encryption products. In other areas the applicability of the existing regulatory framework needs to be ensured, e.g. the GATS rules in the case of electronic deliveries. In the domain of taxation, the generally agreed principle is that of tax neutrality (no discrimination between online and offline business). Whether new taxes will be introduced in electronic commerce is still an open question (in the USA a three-year moratorium has been adopted; the EU has declared itself to be against the introduction of a new tax, including the so-called 'bittax' on data communications. There are also areas in which new legislation seems to be unavoidable (despite the general agreement to keep legislation at a minimum), such as for the legal recognition of electronic signatures.

International electronic commerce policy making happens among a number of public- and private-sector organizations. This is a world of acronyms, such as WTO (World Trade Organization) for issues like

Table 7.1   *Overview of key legal/regulatory issues in the EU and the USA*

	EU	USA
Data protection/ privacy	EU Directive came into force in Oct 1998; discussion with the USA about guarantees	Call for self-regulation/codes of conduct, 'safe-harbor' approach
Taxation	VAT principles (neutrality, simplicity); based on country of consumption; no new taxes	Three-year moratorium for new taxes (Internet Tax Freedom Act)
Customs	Supporting WTO—'duty-free Internet'	Supporting WTO—'duty-free Internet'
Security (authentication/ electronic signatures)	Digital signature laws in Germany, Italy, UK (draft); EU Directive on Electronic Signatures	DS laws in many states, preparation in others
Intellectual property rights	WIPO ratification; Directive on Copyrights in the Information Society; Green Paper on counterfeiting and piracy	WIPO ratification (Digital Millennium Copyright Act)
Establishment, commercial communications, electronic contracts, liability, redress	Draft Directive on certain legal aspects of electronic commerce (internal market related) Nov 1998, based on 'country of origin' principle; also extends consumer protection	Some elements covered by UNCITRAL model law, proposed to become international convention (contracts, recognition of electronic signatures)
Harmful content	Self-regulation and EU action plan; supporting filtering and rating	Child Online Protection Action and self-regulation; supporting filtering and rating
Domain names	Support for private-sector organization (ICANN)	Support for private-sector organization (ICANN)
Electronic payments/digital cash	Update of recommendation about consumer information; draft Directive on issuance of electronic money; monitoring developments	Monitoring developments
Consumer protection	Resolution confirms building on and extending existing consumer protection	Part of new five-point action plan (Dec 1998)

customs, OECD (Organization for Economic Co-operation and Development) for issues such as consumer protection, WIPO (World Intellectual Property Organization) for IPR issues, and UNCITRAL (United Nations Commission on International Trade Law) for contract law. Private-sector organizations that are active in the policy debate include ICC (International Chambers of Commerce), GBDe (Global Business Dialogue), BIAC (Business and Industry Advisory Committee of the OECD), GIIC (Global Information Infrastructure Commission), and TABD (Trans-Atlantic Business Dialogue).

Many countries and regions have now started to develop their own electronic commerce policies and action plans.[108] An overview of national initiatives as at early 1999 has been conducted by the G8 Global Marketplace for SMEs Pilot.[109] Timmers (1997a, 1998c) provides an overview of electronic commerce policy related to the European Commission, addressing the period up to the end of 1997. Vittet-Philippe (1998) and Johnson (1997) compare policy approaches internationally in more detail.

Companies that are completely new to the legal issues in electronic commerce may benefit from familiarizing themselves with the general principles and developments at national and international level through their industry organizations or any of the organizations or references mentioned above. As a next step, they may wish to get advice about the specific legal issues that are most relevant for their business. For example, if internationally personal data are being collected, they may wish to study in more depth approaches to privacy protection and possibly to seek professional advice. An understanding of the relationships between electronic commerce technology/business and law (and self-regulation) is gradually being built up among business consultants and lawyers, with a new profession of 'techno-lawyers' emerging. The relationship between advanced technology developments and legislation is studied among others by the European E-CLIP project, in areas such as taxation, liability of intermediaries, copyright protection, applicable law, contract law etc.[110]

Strategy Development—Strategic Fit

The large degree of uncertainty about Internet electronic commerce is likely strongly to influence approaches to strategy development. Managers and strategic planners in business are confronted by this uncertainty. It is not uncommon to hear CEOs talking about survival-threatening changes in their industry. At the same time, they perceive that there is a very wide range of strategic options. Then they go on to admit to hardly having a clue which strategic choice is the best even though they are forced to make a choice anyway! But equally, this uncertainty affects policy makers in governments and industry associations. They struggle to understand the developments that are happening at breakneck speed. The hype that is surrounding electronic commerce isn't helpful either. Scores of pressure groups are now focusing on the Internet and trying to influence governments and parliaments. And, with more difficulty than in the past, governments and public administrations in particular are confronted with the fact that the Internet and electronic commerce do not fit neatly within any single established policy-making area like industrial policy or international trade relations. Instead, they are challenged to overhaul policy making, demolishing walls between departments and disciplines, leaving the lead increasingly to their constituency, business and consumers. Political decision making is hard when the world is changing so fast and in such a turbulent way. Politicians are reconsidering their role. Mr Bangemann, a former EU Commissioner, called for politicians to be careful about their role and to take into account that the development of a legal framework would always lag behind technological development.[111]

Some guidance for strategy development in this fast-moving environment can be obtained from management studies. In *What Is Strategy— and Does It Matter?*, Whittington (1993) presents four generic perspectives on strategy development:

1. *Classical*: planning and (technology) tools.
2. *Evolutionary*: emergence of different initiatives, selection by the market.
3. *Processual*: a political view on the process of strategy development.
4. *Systemic*: integration of factors including the historic context.

As Egan (1995) explains, the *classical* approach assumes that it is possible to define and plan for a single outcome and to arrange resources accordingly. The *evolutionary* approach is Darwinian in nature, assuming that the market ensures that the fittest of options will survive. In this philosophy, given the dynamism of the environment, *in extremis* deliberate strategy development is a delusion. The *processual* approach is behaviourally oriented, assuming that decision making is a matter of 'muddling through' or trial and error, that human understanding is basically limited, and that decisions are often a matter of political bargaining. This corresponds closely to the incremental strategy development observed by Quinn (1980). The *systemic* approach is sensitive to the interrelationship of factors. It is—similarly to the classical approach—assuming that planning is possible even in complex environments, but contrary to the classical approach it relates more to history and context. The four approaches can be mapped in two dimensions: processes, from deliberate or planned to emergent, and outcomes, from pluralistic to single best result (Figure 7.2).

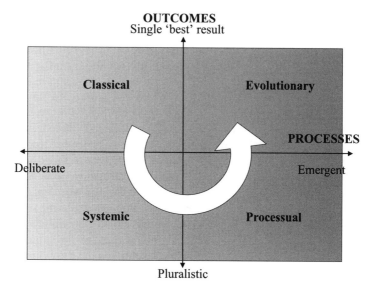

Figure 7.2   *Generic perspectives on strategy, after Whittington (1993); reproduced by permission of Taylor & Francis Ltd*

It seems unlikely that a planned approach to strategy can be successful in the current stage of the Internet. Instead experimentation is expected, fitting more closely to a processual or evolutionary approach. Nevertheless, in some of the cases studied here it seemed that strategy development approach was nearer to a planned approach, especially of the companies that were longer established in B-to-B electronic commerce or in 'classical' areas of information and communication technology, such as telecom operators (e.g. EDI/telecom-based Citius/Belgacom). If they can break out of the mould of classical strategy development, they may get into a systemic or processual approach, which may result in pursuing several objectives at the same time. For example, established companies will also have to take into account their legacy in terms of the organization as it is and in terms of existing business relationships and commitments towards customers and suppliers. In other words, they may need to follow a systemic approach. The risk is that by not focusing on a single clear target, performance will be insufficient towards *any* target. If such organizations become highly politicized, strategy development may move towards a processual approach, with less grip on both process and results.

Egan (1995) adds that a 'strategic fit' has to be obtained and maintained between environment–strategy–organization, in other words, adapting strategy and company organization to fit with the type of business environment. The Internet as a business environment is likely to be perceived by many as turbulent, uncertain, risk prone and complex. It is character-ized by rapid technology changes, hypergrowth of new competitors that are coming out of the blue, unknown response from customers and uncer-tainty regarding the legal frameworks. While there are many options for constructing a business model (See Chapter 3), there are still few 'best-practice' examples.

Exactly these factors have been identified by Ansoff (1987) in order to quantify the degree of turbulence in the business environment. Ansoff *et al.* (1993) have developed a framework for environmental analysis in which turbulence ranges on the scale repetitive–expanding–changing–discontinuous–surprising. Ansoff observes that discontinuous (or even surprising) change is a key characteristic of the modern business environ-ment rather than evolutionary change. Where the turbulence level is high and change is discontinuous, Ansoff *et al.* (1993) propose that the appropriate strategic approach is to be entrepreneurial and creative, rather than being based on precedents and experience. Again, this seems to be a characteristic of the current Internet commerce world. For example, Gebauer and Segev (1998) found from a survey of 79 companies involved in electronic procurement that over 50% of these companies perceived their business environment as very to extremely dynamic (and only 24% perceived it as very to somewhat stable). In the 'strategic fit' philosophy, the organization also needs to be adjusted to such an approach, being organic and flexible, allowing for fast tactical reaction to safeguard immediate survival and also allowing for organizational learning to capture benefits in the longer term. The dilemmas of (incumbent) telecom operators who intend to go into electronic commerce illustrate the difficulty of obtaining strategic fit (see Box 7.1).

Box 7.1   Strategic dilemmas for telecom operators

Becoming an ISP?
The evident route for telecom operators into Internet commerce is to become an Internet service provider and thereby exploit their asset of installed base of phone customers. The reasoning is that this will help to grow the core business of 'phone ticks'. Similarly, telecom operators are interested in bandwidth-demanding applications such as collaborative design and engineering. However, these require much more than just offering high bandwidth. For example, a professional salesforce is needed for application and business services. An established telecom operator will have to assess its organizational capability to deal with such new business.

More revenues from Web development or business information services?

As a next step, beyond basic Internet service provision, it is quite natural to extend into Web site development. However, the question is why a telecom operator would be better at such creative services than the many small and flexible Web designers? The telecom operator can also act as an electronic commerce information broker, exploiting its white and yellow pages. However, just bringing the phone book online does not help much in differentiation. Information brokers like Yahoo or AltaVista consider white and yellow pages as no more than just another add-on to their much richer set of information services. Moreover, there is usually little or no synergy between a telecom operator's ISP/Web design business and the information brokerage business. Therefore, whether a telecom operator becomes a Web house or whether it becomes an information broker it faces tough and flexible competition, while its added value is questionable. Which strategic direction should a telecom operator then take?

Providing essential value-chain services—trust?

To answer this question other assets of telecom operators can be considered. For example, a strong brand can be exploited by offering trust services. Some telecom operators are becoming a certification authority, offering digital signatures in particular for business-to-business electronic commerce[112]. The global telecom operators that are emerging through mergers and acquisitions can increase added value through cross-border trust services. Of course, here too they face stiff competition from banks, postal services and fast-moving Internet start-ups.

Payments?

Yet another asset of telecom operators is their knowledge of handling very large number of (small) payments. This takes a variety of forms, including a monthly (automatic) bank transfer or credit-card payment of the accumulated smaller charges of individual phone calls, or deducting charges from a stored value magnetic or smart card. The incumbent telecom operators particularly have the expertise and sophisticated and complex software systems to handle such payments for millions of customers.[113] Such systems are also suited to payment of small purchases on the Internet, that is, those typical business-to-consumer electronic commerce (e.g. Deutsche Telekom with T-Online). Telecom operators may be tempted to extend into other online financial services (becoming a value-chain service provider). Nevertheless, competition will also be fierce from banks, credit-card companies, and other financial service providers.

Fully supporting business transactions?
Finally, another potential synergy is where business collaboration and transaction handling also require high bandwidth and trust. If such a market exists, a telecom operator could extend its trust service with full transaction support (i.e. becoming a third-party marketplace provider) or collaboration support (collaboration platform provider). Additional added value can be created from the transaction or collaboration data that are flowing through the platform of the telecom operator. However, telecom operators have traditionally kept themselves rather distant from analysing the content that flows through their networks. This tradition may hamper them from developing added-value services as fast as newcomers would do.

Finding the strategic fit
In summary, telecom operators, and especially the 'old giants' that held a monopoly (in Europe in most countries until the beginning of 1998 for voice telephony), are particularly challenged by the turbulent environment. They have to cope with uncertainty about customer reactions, fierce and rapidly changing competition, a range of unproven business models, and a heavy legacy in terms of their own organization. At the same time, they cannot escape from strategic choices because of the relentless erosion of their market position by new entrants to their core telecom business.

SCENARIOS FOR THE FUTURE OF BUSINESS-TO-BUSINESS ELECTRONIC COMMERCE

The case studies and business models provided various pointers to the future of B-to-B electronic commerce. We have already seen how business relationships become more dynamic, how collaboration between companies is being enabled, and how value can be extracted from information that is flowing through the value chain. We can also catch a glimpse of the future from macro trends such as the advance of globalization, ever-increasing computing and communications performance, and the continued growth of networked connections between companies and between people. The future of electronic commerce will also be influenced by lifestyle and working-life trends, such as growing mobility in consumption, leisure and work, and the increase of portfolio working (Handy, 1994). Extrapolating all of these leads to a hypothetical future of any consumer, any worker and any company being connected to any other person or service, without barriers such as national or regional borders, in ever-changing configurations, with access to virtually unlimited bandwidth and computing power at virtually zero cost.

Taking into account the lessons learned from the cases, business models and trends, the sections that follow present a number of concrete scenarios for the future of B-to-B electronic commerce. While these do not go as far as the hypothetical future sketched above and while they are all substantiated by real-life experiments, it will be clear that they remain speculative. Taking them too literally can be dangerous for the health of your business!

The scenarios are summarized in Table 7.2. They are not mutually exclusive and some are in fact complementary. For example, those value networks in which companies are continually seeking new partnerships are likely to be accompanied by greater use of dynamic markets to find partners and to collaborate with them. Large amounts of information will be flowing around within such value networks and digital markets. Such trade information may be turned into valuable and tradable digital information products. The convergence and cross-fertilization between B-to-C and B-to-B can be identified in any of the other scenarios. New technologies will be necessary to realize dynamic value configurations, digital markets and digital information products, and will enable the cross-fertilization between B-to-B and B-to-C. Finally, beyond its enabling capability, technology may also dramatically change the rules of the game in any of these scenarios.

It is not the intention to present an exhaustive set of scenarios here. The future will surely have more in store than we can imagine today. For example, not addressed are possible futures in which the emphasis on teamwork increases. Already teamwork is being greatly enabled by the Internet and new workflow tools can be expected to emerge that easily span organizational boundaries—for example within a value network. The scenario would then be to bring competences together in the best configuration to fulfil a given task, and thus to see an organization rather as a support structure for human resources (providing a legal, financial and technological infrastructure). Yet another scenario is one in which the role of people greatly increases. This is in the sense that people provide the real competitive advantage, while electronic commerce serves only to deal with the routine functions, to communicate easily and to support people in delivering the added value. In such a scenario, companies differentiate themselves because they are able to deliver a better personal service, or better person-based expertise or better person-based relationships in business. This would be a world in which lots of niche players can find

Table 7.2 *B-to-B electronic commerce scenarios*

Scenario	Description
Competing and collaborating in value networks and dynamic markets	
Participating in value networks	Companies get engaged in multiple interenterprise relationships, driven by customer-specific demands. They seek to enhance customer value, reduce costs and time-to-market through a web of partners, focusing on the integration of information flows between them and exploitation of intra- and interenterprise knowledge.
Transacting in dynamic markets	Companies and markets increasingly become interwoven and interchangeable. Through markets companies seek increased dynamics in buying and selling and in contractual relationships, some of which are very short lived. New market mechanisms enable products and services to be traded that were previously locked inside companies.
Thriving on information	Existing and new businesses exploit the large amounts of information by pushing digitization even further and by bringing together information from many sources in a knowledgeable way. Their business models include direct and indirect revenue streams from digital information.
Converging B-to-B and B-to-C electronic commerce	Attractive B-to-C interactivity and personalization concepts overflow into B-to-B. Conversely, product and service lifecycle management and direct marketing concepts from B-to-B find their way into B-to-C.
New technologies, new business models, new policies: new rules?	Not so much a scenario but rather a helicopter view of the nature of the changes: companies use new devices, new interaction technologies and new information/ knowledge management technologies to explore new business models that create new trading channels, and to bypass incumbents by changing the rules of the business; favourable government policies may help to unlock the potential of such technologies and business models.

a place, as there are so many differences in interaction and personal preferences that can be dealt with on a person-to-person basis.[114] As before, this scenario can be 'stand alone', that is, it could be applicable to a number of individual companies only, for example those that address product/markets that are characterized by high complexity and customization. Equally, this scenario could be a way of working within any of the other scenarios mentioned before, for example within a value-network configuration.

The following sections analyse each of the selected scenarios (value network, dynamic market, digital information business and B-B/B-C convergence) in more detail and outline challenges for marketing strategy development.

Competing and Collaborating in Value Networks and Dynamic Markets

In the quest for efficiency and agility, companies continually need to reassess what is core to their activities, which relationships are strategic, and in which markets they need to be active. Companies need to consider rearranging their cost structure, trading off production that is organized in-house against sourcing from the market or partners. In other words, they can shift between activity costs (consisting of the cost for producing an item in-house plus the opportunity cost) and transaction costs (consisting of the infrastructure cost and coordination cost for procuring the same item from the outside). Beyond just the cost base other competitive factors need to be considered such as time-to-market, access to markets and market share, building of a strong brand and others, as discussed in Chapter 2.

The make-or-buy question has always existed for companies. Information and communication technologies have become part of answering that question as they have been helpful in reducing production costs and information-acquisition costs, even if not always in equal ratios. But the opportunities from recent new information and communication technologies and in particular from the Internet have put the make-or-buy decision very much into the spotlight again.

All these considerations lead to a rethink of how business processes should be organized, that is, both inside the company as well as in relationship to other companies and to the market. This goes beyond business process reengineering (which has an internal focus), and even beyond interenterprise process engineering to build extended or virtual enterprises. It also includes 'market process engineering', that is, analysing and defining market processes and their interface to the (extended) enterprise. In fact, all processes that add to value creation should be analysed to assess their intrinsic efficiency and the appropriate position inside the organization or external to it, whether in a value network or in a dynamic market configuration.

For the purpose of further analysis, the following definitions for 'value network' and 'dynamic market configuration' or, in short, 'dynamic market' are used:

A *value network* is a multienterprise network of relationships focused on integration of information flows to exploit information and knowledge in the network for strategic business objectives.

A *dynamic market* configuration is a market-mediated set of relationships focused on increasing flexibility and opportunity for strategic business objectives.

Value networks that were not based on information and communication technologies (ICTs) have existed for a long time. It is very common for companies to buy from and supply to each other. Here, however, we focus on value networks that are strongly facilitated by ICTs, sometimes also called virtual value networks or digital value networks, to contrast them with the existing 'real-world' networks between companies in supplier–buyer or co-maker relationships. The argument is that significant improvements can be achieved in electronic commerce-based value networks. While these improvements seem to be quantitative only at first sight, it will be shown that they add up in such a way that they lead to opening up truly new business opportunities, that is, they lead to qualitatively new ways of doing business.

For dynamic markets the same reasoning could be followed, namely that market-mediated ways of creating and delivering value have existed for a long time, but that completely and radically new opportunities arise because of market mediation through information and communications technology. Clearly, we are addressing these new forms of dynamic markets, which therefore could also be called dynamic digital markets, or dynamic virtual markets, again to distinguish them from the 'real-world' forms of markets. However, as will be shown, the dynamics of these digital markets are qualitatively different from the markets known until now, such that we can really speak of a scenario that is a revolution rather than an evolution.

A comparison of value network and dynamic market on some key characteristics is given in Table 7.3.

Value networks generally consist of relationships between a limited number of companies. The focus is on deepening these internal

Table 7.3   *Characteristics of value networks and dynamic markets*

	Focus	*Timescales*	*Mutual commitment*	*Investment per relation*	*Relations*
Value network	Increasing value through internal relations	Medium– long	High	High	Few
Dynamic market	Increasing value through external relations	Short– medium	Low	Low	Many

relationships, that is, between companies and inside each of the companies. The set of partners may change gradually over time as new, more competitive suppliers or buyers are added and others are dropped. The actual value chain at any given moment may involve a subset of partners from the value network, and this may also change over time.

Dynamic networks typically involve a larger or very large number of parties, with a focus on seeking to maximize value from those external relationships. In a dynamic network the approach is to maximize price or delivery opportunity, or flexibility or agility by selecting the most appropriate business partner (buyer, component supplier, service provider etc.) at any moment.

Figure 7.3 shows how value networks and digital markets relate to each other by reorganizing value-creation processes. It suggests that a company can evolve to become a member of a value network by setting up ICT-supported relationships with other companies that provide goods and

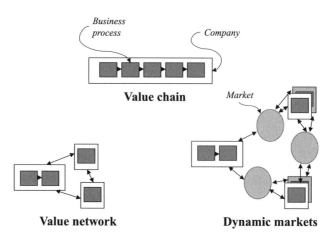

Figure 7.3   *From value chain to value network and dynamic markets*

services that are no longer produced in-house. It also suggests that these relationships can become more dynamic by being contracted from digital markets for goods and services. In other words, the value network can evolve into a dynamic market configuration. Certainly an evolution in this direction, from single company to value network to dynamic market configuration, is not the only path that a company can take. It may also make sense to strengthen the ties with some of the *ad hoc* partners in a dynamic market set-up and thus go in the direction of a value network. It may even be appropriate to merge with other companies in the value network and thus internalize the business relations (vertical or horizontal integration). Furthermore, new Internet businesses can start in any configuration. By the very nature of the Internet, many of them in fact will start with a dynamic partnership with market parties, rather than as a traditional, tightly integrated company.

The definitions show that there can be overlap between the two forms, namely where market-mediated relationships are combined with tight integration of information systems. Hybrid forms are also conceivable (and we will see several of them in the following sections), where a company is at the same time a partner in a value network for some of its business processes, as well as operating in a dynamic market setting for other processes. This can happen when collaboration with suppliers is tightly integrated and relatively static or of long duration, while collaboration with distributors is loosely integrated and more dynamic and of shorter duration. Another example is when critical components are sourced from a limited number of pre-selected suppliers, while the less critical parts are obtained from one out of many suppliers, dynamically selected on the basis of best price or fastest delivery.

Participating in Value Networks

The value-network scenario of future business-to-business electronic commerce is that companies will increasingly engage in a variety of relationships with partners—be it with suppliers, distributors, information brokers, trusted third parties or other intermediaries, as well as in partnerships with customers. The ultimate objective of each participant is to obtain better value for money, whether through cost savings or through increased innovation, or to realize other strategic business objectives. The approach that they seek is to get better access to information within and across business processes, and to optimize and rearrange business processes across the value network.

Much of the thinking about value-network configurations originates from virtual enterprise and business process (re)engineering work (Hammer and Champy, 1994; Hammer, 1996).[115] Value network configurations use shared information systems that support business processes *across* individual companies. Value networks do not take the business processes as a given, neither within companies (as is the premise of traditional business process reengineering) nor across companies. Value networks can only be realized if there is a commonly understood semantics of these processes in terms of their inputs, outputs and internal flow, and of the items that are the object of these business processes (business objects, including resources). Almost unavoidably value networks require a great deal of standardization, whether *de facto* or *de jure*. The vision of value-network configurations is that to a large extent the creation of such a network can happen online, enabled by common business semantics and syntax.

Online partnering is gradually becoming a reality and value networks will take a further step in this direction by attempting to increase exploitation of the knowledge that is underpinning the information flow inside and in between companies:

- The case of Marshall Industry's PartnerNet, discussed in Chapter 4, is a clear example of a value network. Selected customers and manufacturers of electronics components can, via Marshall's extranet, access product characteristics (like customer specific prices of the components) and sales data (like customer purchasing patterns, in order to improve supplier's production planning). Marshall is thus running shared applications with either its customers or its suppliers, tying them more tightly into Marshall's business, bringing Marshall the benefit of better stock management, as well as the benefits delivered to manufacturers and customers.

- The Aerotech case that was mentioned in Chapter 2 illustrates how Aerotech, as a new intermediary in the supply of aerospace components, has enabled Boeing (at the time McDonnell Douglas Aerospace) to build a 'virtual factory'. Exchange of largely standardized component information with hundreds of suppliers, selecting one of them through a bidding system, and tying production together with shared scheduling software enables dramatic cost and time reductions. As a next step it was foreseen that the set-up would become increasingly dynamic in the aircraft spare-part end of the business, by offering brokerage of technical information about such parts and Defense Logistics RFQs to large numbers of small suppliers.

- The ANX communication and security infrastructure in the US automotive industry, while set up for the original ANX partners only, has been opened up to any automotive component supplier. The common infrastructure enables component suppliers and subassembly or car manufacturers to engage in a variety of supply-chain configurations.

- The canned vegetable producer HAK in the Netherlands is setting up close electronic relationships in its supply chain (e.g. with vegetable farms and glass manufacturers) and in its retail chain. It sets out with this form of electronic commerce to achieve 'chain reversal': based on information flowing from customer to farmer, to go to customer-driven production and farming, instead of the other way around, supply-driven production. Its key motivations include safeguarding and reinforcing its quality brand in order to fend off 'white labels', and flexibly to address changing customer preferences and the influence of weather on production, both of which are rather unpredictable. It is implementing concepts such as supply-chain management and category management for the retailers (Electronic Customer Relationship management—ECR) (Leerink, 1998).

Other cases of 'greenfield' exploration, where collaboration in a value network did not exist before, include the following.

- The ESPRIT VIVE project (VIrtual Vertical Enterprise) introduced the concept of a business broker, who assembles a set of companies around a common business approach with the aid of a shared set of electronic commerce tools to integrate their operations. The concept was inspired by a case of severe competitive pressure experienced by a group of small companies in Emilia Romagna, Italy, in the field of oleodynamic and mechanic components. They lost their business from one day to the other to a Japanese competitor who developed an integrated subsystem for earth-moving machines, replacing components supplied separately by the Italian small companies who left assembly to the final client. Subsequently, the small companies developed a coordinated process for supplying the same subsystem as the Japanese competitor.
- Commercialization of concepts such as the Global Engineering Network allows companies to access, share and collaborate on the basis of a common information base for more complex forms of information sharing such as collaborative engineering. The ESPRIT AGENTISME project, which sets out to create awareness about the GEN concept, illustrates the relevance of this concept for Klotz, a German manufacturer of special machinery for the automotive, household and nuclear industry. Klotz needs increasingly to meet customer-specific requirements for these production machines. For example, at the moment of ordering an assembly or testing machine, the design specification may not yet be complete and collaboration with the

customer is needed to get to the final specification. Machines also need to be frequently adapted following changes in the customer's product for which concurrent access (with the customer) to the customer's product specifications is needed. Customers also ask for reduced time to installation and Klotz needs to be able to install and service globally. In order to meet these needs and access the global market without having engineers all over the globe for prolonged periods, tighter integration of the information systems of Klotz and its customers, suppliers and technology partners is required. This is realized through a shared engineering environment as envisaged by the Global Engineering Network concept.[116]

- RosettaNet[117] has been conducting a value-network experiment in the PC supply chain (between PC manufacturers and distributors and resellers). It has been leading to common definitions for PC and accessories features, captured in a Common Business Library. CBL is a shared resource for the industry sector, and potentially across industry sectors, enabling reconfiguration of the value network at lower integration cost. As RosettaNet states, it is the intention that this sharing will help to improve manufacturers' production planning, reduce the complexity and cost for distributors to bundle product information for their resellers, simplify return handling at resellers, and increase procurement efficiency for corporate purchasers of PCs.

Characteristics of Value Networks

A number of observations can be made about value-network configurations:

- Not all value-network configurations are equally complex, formalized, and 'intimate' in terms of level of interenterprise integration and collaboration. Ontology.org[118] distinguishes between extended trading networks, which are more formalized, EDI and process-automation-oriented versus virtual collaborative organizations, which have a higher degree of coordination and communication. Ontology's third configuration, a governed marketplace, is closer to the digital market concept of the next section. Snow, Miles and Coleman (1992) distinguish between three configurations, namely stable networks, where long-term relationships exists (cf. the value-network concept presented here), internal networks, which are a loose association of business units each subject to market forces, and dynamic networks (cf. dynamic markets presented below).
- Value networks provide opportunities for both SMEs and large enterprises. Large companies can use value networks for outsourcing.

Small companies can look bigger as virtually they command more resources.

- Standardization on a common set of tools is needed, e.g. common online project management, EDI—Electronic Data Interchange, PDM—Product Data Modelling, STEP—Standard for the Exchange of Product Data etc.
- Information will be built up in shared online databases such as project-management data, customer characteristics, engineering data etc. Ownership and intellectual property rights become issues to be dealt with. This is further discussed in the digital information business scenario.
- Where in the past companies tried to enhance value and control through vertical or horizontal integration, the name of the game becomes 'network integration' or 'from ownership to relationship'. Rather than pursuing a path of ownership of related companies, the participants in dynamic value configurations seek to add value and exercise control (on key competitive factors like time-to-market, quality and market access) through relationships based on the interconnection and integration of information flows.
- Linear relations (supply chain, value chain) are likely to be the dominant arrangement for a value network. This also includes 1:N configurations (like those of a manufacturer with its distributors, i.e. a distribution network), or N:1 configuration (supply chain). N:M configurations may have interesting added-value opportunities by introducing dynamic market elements (e.g. building virtual communities of distributors, or distributor auctions, or *ad hoc* supplier selection, see Figure 7.4). This illustrates, as stated before, that different levels of dynamics in the supply chain or distribution chain are quite possible, in other words that mixed forms of value networks and dynamic markets can also occur.

Transacting in Dynamic Markets

Many assumptions about the organization of production and distribution are being undermined as a consequence of increased globalization, flexibility and time-based competition. Existing value chains are thrown into disarray as parties seek to make optimal use of opportunities in the global marketplace. Relationships between economic actors become more varied, some being only very short lived, others being deepened in order to achieve a distinctive competitive advantage. Being able to operate in a multiparty, multicultural business environment, and being local and global at the same time are increasingly key competitive factors for success.

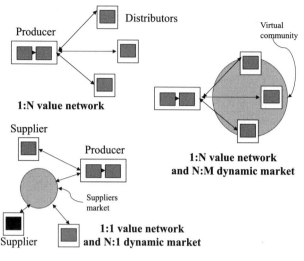

Figure 7.4 *Example network relations*

In a much more dynamic business world, the role of markets is increasing in importance. Electronic commerce will greatly facilitate market-based forms of value creation and value delivery—that is, dynamic digital markets—for businesses as well as consumers. Dynamic digital markets first of all provide a wide variety of mechanisms to match demand and supply quickly and efficiently. This holds not only for end-user business or consumer markets, but equally for business-to-business markets, that is, markets that facilitate cooperation within value chains or value networks, as well as for markets within companies. Secondly, dynamic markets go beyond simply matching homogeneous demand with equally homogeneous supply. They are also mediators to meet individual specific requirements through customization and by helping individual customers to find the supplier that can meet their specific needs, as well as helping suppliers to perform micro-segmentation and thereby locate the niche customers that are interested in their specific offer.[19] Thirdly, dynamic markets enable increasing added value, as market operators recognize unmet needs and supplement their basic matchmaking role with value-added services such as financing or logistics support, transaction bundling and virtual communities. Such services are not only attractive for the individual buyer but also bring along positive network externalities, as they usually become increasingly efficient and relevant as the number of parties grows.

Markets, by their very nature, are dynamic, in the sense that the ultimate transaction relationship between buyer and seller is not predefined. However, digital online markets enable exciting new possibilities to increase further the economic dynamics, such as the following:

- *Buyer or seller coalitions*: buyers or sellers with similar requirements are assisted in forming coalitions before or while engaging in the market negotiation in order to increase their purchasing or sales power.
- *Dynamic product/service bundling*: recognizing purchasing patterns allows buyers and sellers to be guided towards complementary products and services for which an additional marketplace is created as necessary.
- *Flexibility and learning while negotiating*: while establishing the match, buyers and sellers can change negotiation strategies depending on the product and service characteristics that they wish to include in the negotiation. Negotiation software can assist in suggesting a deal, learning from successes and failures in past negotiations.
- *Transient or ad hoc markets*: beyond markets with pre-defined product categories and a pre-defined market operator—but dynamic trading relationships—appropriate technology will enable transient markets that are themselves temporary. The market operator is either internalized, i.e. is with the trading partners themselves, or is owned by no one specifically. They will be based on distributed intelligence, such as intelligent agents that autonomously seek out counterparts to negotiate a deal. Such markets could be created only once there is a trading opportunity and disappear again after the deal has been made (i.e. the market is created by either the offering or the demanding party, without a third-party market operator).
- *Fuzzy markets*: in addition, dynamic markets will arise that are much more flexible in terms of products and services that can be traded. Such flexible or 'fuzzy' markets will support weakly defined product/service categories, namely where extensive interaction and negotiation are needed, for example in construction. Dynamic trading procedures will allow the involvement of additional market intermediaries, for example extending the negotiation procedure for a new construction site with an expert, who provides a third-party assessment on request.

The business models analysis in Chapter 3, among others, identified auctions, virtual communities, e-malls and third-party marketplaces, which are all specific forms of dynamic markets. Such dynamic markets are emerging rapidly on the Internet, with some of them reaching staggering stock market valuations, and several experimental dynamic markets are being proposed and piloted:

- Third-party marketplaces for routine purchases are rapidly growing in importance for business-to-business trading. Likewise, such market-places attract consumers, routinely shopping around for standard items to find the best buy, and increasingly assisted by shopping bots like Acses,[120] Jango[121] and others. In Chapter 5 it has been argued that MRO marketplaces may have a future growth path towards negotiated non-routine purchases trading.

- One of the most striking phenomena of B-to-B trading is the increase of auctions as a specific form of negotiation in online markets. Forrester foresees that auctions will grow in three categories: com-modity trading (such as bulk items like energy), private auctions (i.e. between a company and its partners, adding dynamics to value networks) and independent auctions (bargain auctions, liquidators etc).[122] Negotiated trading will also grow in importance in B-to-C markets. This will happen in the form of auctions of standard products (already happening for surplus items like PCs, white and brown goods, e.g. by Wehkamp[123] in the Netherlands), as well as by means of more sophisticated forms of interactivity and negotiation support.

- Dynamic markets between companies in a value network are already being created, with channel partners in the distribution chain and with suppliers in the supply chain. Ingram Micro, a $22 billion worldwide distributor of computers and computer-related products, has used auctions since 1998 within its network of over 115 000 resellers for new products that for some reason cannot be returned to the computer manufacturers. General Electric Information Services with TPN Post supports bidding and request for quote submission among pre-selected suppliers within a secure Internet environment.

- The Amazon Associates approach nicely illustrates how a critical business process, namely marketing, can be implemented through dynamic relationships. The approach also shows a high degree of built-in dynamics: at any moment an associate can terminate the relationship, and conversely it is only a matter of minutes for a new associate to become a partner in Amazon's value network. The hyper-growth of the number of Associates mentioned in Chapter 4 shows how dynamic such a configuration can be. Amazon has the leverage in its web of associate partners, as this is a 1:N network rather than a true web, with Amazon controlling the central hub, and as it is Amazon's brand that is being marketed rather than Amazon marketing any of the brands of its associates. However, there is no doubt that both sides in the partnership realize an increase in value.

- The SUPPLYPOINT pilot (Kerridge *et al.* 1998) builds virtual supply chains in public procurement for collaboration between contractors and subcontractors. This enables particularly the smaller companies to take better advantage of large procurement opportunities, by jointly undertaking such contracts. Interestingly, part of the concept is a partner brokerage service to identify contracts and possible virtual supply chains to fulfil the contract. This is typically a dynamic market approach.

The Internet is manifesting itself not only as the public network but also in the form of intranets and extranets. Likewise, market technologies (the set of technologies needed to establish and run markets and to participate in online markets) may also be applied in intranets and extranets, in other words for online markets *inside* companies as well as *between* companies in a value network. Inside companies markets can also be seen as a more efficient way of communicating: posting and settling requests through market mediation for company resources like human resources may just be more efficient and faster than having to reallocate staff through the personnel department (or leaving them idle).

Market technologies, in addition to the usual search and navigation facilities, also include support for brokerage and negotiation. A whole range of technology companies provide support for auctions, either of a generic nature such as Moai (http://www.moai.com) which is used for anything from Web advertising space to computer parts reselling (by Ingram Micro), or the Danish TAT-Systems (Trade and Auction Technology Systems International, http://www.colorweb.dk/tat) or those designed for specific markets such Schelfhout Computer Systems' Infomar system for fisheries described in Chapter 4. The European ESPRIT MEMO project provides negotiation support for open market-places, notably for small businesses, based on a formal language for business communication. The European ACTS COBRA project has defined a reference architecture within which the roles of actors and protocols for negotiation and brokerage are described.[124] Several groups around the world are investigating automated negotiation between software agents experimenting with various paradigms (e.g. based on market forces, game theory, auction models such as Dutch auction or English auction, behavioural or decision-making theory, and automated learning/ evolution theory[125]).

Characteristics of Dynamic Digital Markets

Figure 7.5 illustrates how dynamic digital markets might look like. This is a hypothetical scenario in office furniture purchasing. It works as follows.

A business intends to buy office furniture: tables, chairs, cupboards etc. The purchasing department goes on to the Web and browses through a variety of catalogues to form an idea of available furniture. Instead

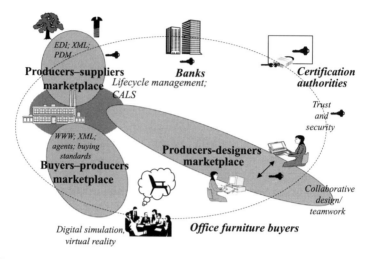

Figure 7.5   *Dynamic markets in the office furniture sector (after ECOM (1996) and European Commission (1997b))*[126]

of selecting a pre-defined model, however, a number of preferences are indicated, like colour, material and design requirements, perhaps including references to existing models that have desirable features. The potential buyer then posts this request profile on to an already existing or a dynamically created marketplace. Any furniture producer can now consider making an offer in this marketplace. Additional intermediaries in this market may help to aggregate offers. The negotiation between buyer and producer(s) may be supported by agent software and the buyer can ask several producers for an offer (RFQ).

Interested producers need to assess whether the furniture can be designed as desired, and at what cost it can be produced. To this end, a producer may want to post an enquiry on to a designers' marketplace for an indication of feasibility and cost. It is likely that more than one designer is going to be needed, for example one for the shape and construction and another for the artistic design. A tentative collaborative project can then be launched involving the potential producer and the designers.

At the same time the producer can inform its existing supply chain about material requirements, or alternatively post material requirements (or perhaps a request for an offer of production capacity) on to a suppliers' marketplace. It might also be that the producer postpones these requests, and will acquire the necessary materials and production capacity from an auction by the time that they are needed. In that case the producer may be able to react more quickly to the buyer of the office furniture with an offer (and thereby get the order). However, this will be at increased financial risk for the producer, as it might be that the producer is going to be forced to acquire materials or capacity from an auction at a disadvantageous price.

When finally the buyer has selected a specific producer, the production, design and delivery chains can be confirmed and set up. In order to realize this supporting technologies are required based on standards for ordering and delivery like XML and EDI, for production and computer-aided design such as STEP and PDM, as well as technologies implementing concepts for collaboration and lifecycle management like GEN and CALS. Further intermediaries may be needed to arrange payment guarantees, or to provide the logistics. The whole trading environment can only function if there is an appropriate level of trust. Secure technologies (indicated by the keys in the diagram) and trusted parties such as certification authorities can provide critical trust functions.

This example shows that doing business in dynamic markets also means making certain trade-offs:

- Dynamic markets are on the one hand about realizing current opportunities. At the same time, they are about relationships, which hold potential for future opportunities (and liabilities). To operate in dynamic markets may mean being able to trade off current against future opportunities.
- Customization may make just-in-time delivery and fast response times more difficult to realize.
- Exposure to financial risk can be reduced by internalizing operations, that is, through in-house production, or by organizing part of the operation as a fixed supply chain or in a tightly integrated value network. However, this may be at the expense of profits or flexibility for customization. Financial risk can also be reduced by means of contracts, guarantees, third-party underwriting and arbitration. All of these means will increase costs for either buyer or supplier however.
- Increased flexibility will lead to increased complexity. While flexible production and design in a dynamic market set-up may seem to fit neatly with the agility of small companies and self-employed professionals like designers, these smaller actors also risk being overwhelmed by such complexity.
- Customization requires increased and more time-consuming customer involvement. The customer needs to be convinced that it is worthwhile spending more time interacting with the marketplace. At the same time, such involvement provides much more information about the customer, which can be exploited as a commercial asset. Steelcase, mentioned before, sets out to engage in a profound dialogue with the business customer interested in buying office furniture by involving

them in a strongly visual virtual-reality environment. In the online consumer world, the example of garden planning Garden.com is well known as an attractive approach to customer-driven customization.

- Ownership of information, security, liability, global standards and multicultural support are among the issues that come to the fore in dynamic markets.
- The dynamic configuration that ultimately delivered the office furniture as desired will in principle be dissolved, and consequently cannot be called on any more. However, not all customers will be willing to forgo repairs or supplementary deliveries for increased customization. Lifecycle management, as a way to organize after-sales support and to safeguard repeat business, becomes critical, but has hardly been addressed until now in light manufacturing, services or information industries.[127]
- It is questionable whether such dynamic markets can exist of only small firms, as trust and confidence play an important role for many customers. For example, small buyers of customised furniture will demand strong quality guarantees, as their means of recourse in case something goes wrong is rather limited. This may favour the larger, branded producers. These will have more power if they work with smaller players in the supply network. Therefore such dynamic markets may become biased around large producers (or any large, branded intermediary who provides the main interface to the final customer, e.g. a global Web 'office furniture portal'). An alternative to provide trust is labelling or qualification of parties that engage in dynamic market trading. This could also be a role for industry associations. For a label or qualification to be credible, industry collaboration or recognition by a trusted third party will be needed, either of which carries a cost. Some of the industry associations are even inclined to set up their own industry-wide dynamic market system, with preferential treatment for their members. Such an approach is being considered in the print and publishing industries in the Netherlands.

Strategic Marketing and Value Networks versus Dynamic Markets

Companies will want to assess whether a value network configuration or a dynamic market approach, or a mix of these, is relevant for their business. 'Strategic fit' thinking tells us that this choice of organizational form should be made dependent on business strategy and business environment. Investment in the organizational form can be considerable: business processes have to be reengineered, employees have to be trained for new communication and coordination skills and complex information systems have to be put in place that may span company boundaries. The organizational form can also have profound implications for key assets such as market reach, brand image etc. Therefore this choice is not of a secondary nature, and not one of the last steps in a traditional strategic marketing-planning process. This does not mean that there will not be situations in which the choice is more opportunistic than strategic. For example, dynamic market configurations will also be used as an opportunistic add-on facility to optimize regular operations, for example auctions to sell off surplus stock from time to time or to maximize use of spare production capacity.

Textbook strategic marketing planning would take us through the exploration of the market and identifications of opportunities and threats, as well as analysis of strength and weaknesses, into portfolio analysis. This is then taken further into the definition of marketing objectives including segmentation, targeting and positioning, and the development of the marketing elements, such as 4Ps for products (product, price, place, promotion) or 7Ps for services (4Ps plus process, people, physical evidence). It is not the intention here to go through these steps in detail in order to determine the relationship between organizational form—value network or dynamic market—and business strategy (in other words, determining the marketing model in the sense of Chapter 3). This would only be possible by zooming in on specific businesses and markets. What will be addressed below are the generic aspects: what to consider in order to find the opportunities to create more value and thus grow revenues, how to reduce costs, and how to build assets for the future?

In an abstract sense, we can say that business is about creating and exchanging or trading value. The three key questions for marketing strategy development, in relation to the choice between value network and dynamic market configuration, are then about:

- increasing the current opportunity for value creation and value exchange;
- increasing benefits and reducing costs of value creation and value exchange;
- building key assets for future opportunities in value creation and value exchange.

Opportunities

Traditional market research into market opportunities should be extended in order to provide insight into those opportunities that are related to the choice between value network and dynamic market. Market research into opportunities for new markets or new products could include the following.

- What is the value that can be obtained from an existing set of relationships? Customer relationship management, for example, can be used to increase loyalty (countering the turbulence and dynamics of the digital economy mentioned before). The starting point for this is marketing communications, but as shown before when one-to-one marketing was addressed, this also needs to lead to adapting delivery and production processes and ensuring that the company has the required capabilities.
- Are there opportunities for externalizing business operations through procurement from online markets? This implies a profound and continuous reassessment of business organization to identify outsourcing opportunities. It also requires strategic considerations about what the core business is and knowledge of what is available from online markets. This is a kind of 'internal market' research with a view to finding externalization opportunities.
- Are there new places to create markets, such as in-company intranet-based markets or markets for selected customers on an extranet or with membership schemes, or markets in the distribution channels or in the procurement chain? For instance, Freemarkets Online (http://www.freemarkets.com) has managed to introduce a market-place in the procurement process of large purchasers. It performs the selection process for potentially hundreds of suppliers interested in large procurement, limiting them to a few highly qualified, that can then online and in real time participate in bidding against each other, resulting in large cost savings for procurers.
- Are new customer groups accessible by virtualizing distribution through dynamic market facilities? This could be, for example, new geographic markets or niche markets, for which otherwise the investment would be too high in a physical distribution network.
- Can optimization of current business operations be realized through market mechanisms such as auctions or event-related sales?
- Is there a possibility of participating in existing dynamic markets by offering value-added market services, for example by adding intelligent search facilities or risk coverage? FedEx online shipping service or Gigex (http://www.gigex.com) shipping service for digital packages are examples of facilities that are a value-added service to many dynamic markets for physical and digital goods.

Benefits and costs

According to economic rationality, a subsequent step would then be to calculate the investment required for each of the alternatives of a value network and a dynamic market-based approach, as well as to calculate marginal cost for each. Transaction cost theory provides a tool for such an assessment. Brynjolfsson *et al.* (1994) break down total cost into activity cost (which in itself is the sum of production and opportunity cost) and transaction cost. (See also Cordella and Simon, 1997.) Transaction costs find their origin in uncertainty (about alternatives, prices, quality etc.). It includes an external cost component as defined by Williamson (1986) to have a presence in the market and to establish contracts with external parties. The external cost thus consists of the cost of the infrastructure for external communication and coordination with market parties and the external coordination cost itself. The latter includes the costs of transaction services, such as trust services or insurance costs, or price mark-up of suppliers who wish to cater for increased risk. The transaction cost also has an internal component, namely the cost of the internal infrastructure needed for internal coordination, management and control, and the internal coordination cost itself, including maintaining procedures for transactions.

Figure 7.6 gives the total cost breakdown. Infrastructure costs tend to be in the first approximation fixed as a function of the number of transactions. Coordination costs may be proportional to the number of transactions, but they can also be related in a more complex form. An example of the external infrastructure and coordination costs is given by

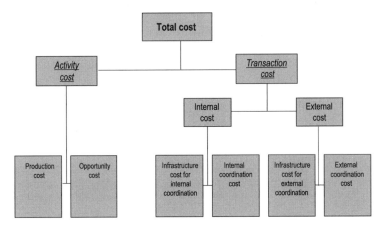

Figure 7.6 *Breakdown of activity and transaction costs*

Citius's pricing scheme in Table 4.2. The marginal cost contribution is the part of the price that depends on the number of transactions, that is, the transaction fee.

Clearly, introducing information and communications technology (ICT), and thereby reducing external costs to a larger extent than internal costs, should lead to smaller firms due to increased outsourcing—and therefore more opportunity for a dynamic market or value network configuration. Brynjolfsson *et al.* (1994) have studied the impact of these technologies on firm size and did indeed find that ICT leads to smaller firms (which, they state, is not due to increased productivity!).

Transaction cost analysis focuses on cost reduction as a competitive factor. However, while activity costs are usually well known and accounted for, it may well be that the reasoning of economists about transaction costs sounds abstract and difficult to apply in practice for most business managers. Moreover, findings have shown that many CEOs are not even aware of marginal cost concepts. In addition, even though Williamson's transaction cost theory assumes that managers display opportunistic behaviour and are limited in their cognitive capabilities (bounded rationality), it does not take account of 'non-traditional economic behaviour' that also influences managerial decisions, such as the pursuit of power instead of profits. The theory does take into account the history of transactions and thereby issues of trust and reputation, which, as we will show, strongly influence the choice of organizational form.

Pure cost reduction, with or without transaction cost analysis, ignore risks to investments in assets for the future of transactions, that is, assets to create revenues in the future. However, by investigating key business factors, it is possible to make decision making about the organizational form (value network, dynamic market or hybrid forms) more understandable and complete. In addition, it can usually at least qualitatively be identified to which cost elements in transaction cost theory these factors contribute. Key business benefits pursued by companies include trust, customer orientation and adding value through integration. Companies will also consider investing in business assets for future revenues like brand and market access. Assessing their importance provides guidance for the choice between value network and dynamic market configuration, as will be addressed now.

Trust

Initial information search costs are greatly reduced on the Internet. The cost to get at least one answer to the search for an information item is much lower than through traditional means. Nevertheless, uncertainty remains whether the right information item has been found. Usually many responses are returned and it is not known how one answer should be compared to another. The reliability of the information item that was found is usually not explicitly known. Spending more time in searching (increasing cost) or using search agents or 'shopping bots' can decrease the first type of uncertainty. Such agents also increase search costs as they require more time before the initial answer arrives, or you may be charged for their use, either directly or indirectly through advertising, as is not uncommon in information brokerage business models. However, their use should still cost less than a 'manual' search and comparison.

Uncertainty about the trustworthiness of a potential supplier can be decreased by authentication, credit worthiness verification and other trust services, or by establishing a contract or obtaining insurance (all of which increase external coordination costs). Likewise, individual information items can in principle be certified and verified with the help of IPR technology and digital certificates, which can guarantee the integrity of the information. In practice, however, this is still limited to fairly large ticket items, namely those that we call digital products, rather than being used for very small information items, like the price of an individual product (how do you know that the price quoted onscreen is the same that will appear in the invoice?).

Despite these uncertainties, many economic actors decide to participate in dynamic markets, accepting the potential risk that information is un-reliable or incomplete or that their business partner is unreliable in some sense. They compensate for the risk by focusing on lower-value items, or by increasing their price mark-up, as a kind of insurance. It is evident that better trust-enhancing technology, the availability of better trust services or a lower cost of trust services could lead to the following:

- *Attracting more actors to participate in dynamic markets.* In the business-to-consumer area this is the hoped-for effect of introducing increased security in credit-card processing, such as through the SET protocol; in the business-to-business area it is hoped that electronic certificates will have such an effect. Within sectors of industry specific trust services are envisaged. We saw an example in the fisheries sector, where electronic auctions as a dynamic market mechanism would benefit from a broadly accepted quality scheme that allows for reliable quality assessment of the catch at a distance.
- *Increasing the value of the product/services in those markets.* Even if Amazon wanted to it could not currently leave much of its valuable trading information with its Associates (which can be considered as a dynamic distributors' market for Amazon). The company has no efficient way to ensure the trustworthiness of those Associates.

However, it could start to segment its distributors' market, differentiating between them on some criterion that would fit with its strategy. It could then authenticate those and build closer relationships and increase loyalty, for example by providing them with more customer information. This could be considered in order to establish a reliable local presence all over the world much faster than having to create local Amazon.com subsidiaries.

- *Lowering the cost of tradeable items.* Obviously, reducing the need for a blanket insurance against risk by means of mark-up can reduce prices. However, it could also be the case that risk becomes better understood once dynamic markets develop, fine-tuning the risk-coverage instruments to the specific purpose. The development of negotiation tools, assistance to electronic contracting, online insurance and other financial services aims at better handling risks in dynamic and global markets (currently an area of intense research, see for example the earlier mentioned MEMO project in Europe, as well as a likely topic for future research identified in the EU and the USA[128]). However, in most cases where today recurrently high-value items are being traded electronically between businesses, this is still in a tight relationship between buyer and supplier, in other words in a value network configuration.

Increasing trust may indeed prove to be the onset of a virtuous cycle: as it pulls more buyers into dynamic markets, there will be more suppliers and more service providers or intermediaries, which will increase competition, leading to lower prices, which will make the dynamic market grow even further.

With increased trust and more sophisticated risk assessment, the borderline between dynamic markets and value networks can be expected to shift towards dynamic market configurations. In the cost base equation, this means shifting from production costs to transaction costs and within the latter from internal towards external coordination costs (while lowering total costs). It also means that fewer opportunities are forgone, as they can be realized in a dynamic market setting without a prohibitively high cost for trust assurance. In other words, an increase of overall economic activity should result.

Customer orientation

Purchasing standard items (e.g. MRO goods) will have lower transaction costs than acquiring non-standard items. Therefore trading in such products has been the first type that moved to dynamic markets, with the help of third-party marketplace platforms. The above analysis of such systems showed, however, that they have significantly different levels of support for the dynamics of such trading. Citius limits itself to pre-defined relationships between purchasers and suppliers, while Tradezone supports in addition *ad hoc* buyers, who pay by credit card. In both cases they do not (yet) support a dynamic approach towards suppliers: *ad hoc* suppliers are not possible in such systems, partly because of lack of open standards for catalogues. The fact that there are limited supplier dynamics shows up in the limitation of choice for buyers to pre-defined sets of products.

As a next step, as was analysed in Chapter 5, purchasing of non-routine items might move towards dynamic markets. Non-routine items generally require specific asset investments and therefore will have higher transaction costs for both suppliers and purchasers. Companies needing such non-routine items will be forced to produce them in-house, as there are no suppliers willing to make such an idiosyncratic investment *and* incur part of the coordination costs. Customization of a recurrent nature, rather than one-off (the mixed case in transaction cost theory, see Chapter 5), would be more suitable for specific investments, as in that case at least some fixed costs can be spread out. A supplier will seek guarantees for such recurrent customization to justify its investment. One way to obtain such guarantees is by binding customers into a long-term relationship, that is, making them participants in a value network, rather than by doing business in a dynamic network configuration. An example of such a value network relationship exists between sportswear producer Adidas and Pixelpark Germany (which calls itself 'Adidas's lead new media agency'). Pixelpark has created a shared information and workflow system primarily to support adidas in the quality control and cost reduction of the production of commercial information that has to be seasonally updated and delivered for a variety of media such as CD-ROM, Web and point-of-sale displays.[129] *In extremis*, such a relationship can lead to forward or backward (i.e. vertical) integration. Alternatively, to reduce customization cost, a supplier could also choose to rely on the aggregate demand of many purchasers, each with their specific customization requirements. With information technology to support modularization and standardization (see below), it is then possible for the supplier to organize the business in a dynamic market fashion, working with many customers in *ad hoc* relationships, and possibly also contracting sub-assembly suppliers in a similar dynamic way.

The above shows that two types of technology are needed for customization:

- *Coordination technology*, that is, information and communications technology for brokerage, negotiation, workflow and project management, complemented by electronic commerce technologies such as security, transaction handling etc. to reduce the coordination part of transaction costs. This will enable companies to engage more often in dynamic market business models.

- *Product-specific customization technology*, e.g. to support modularization and to make products customizable, through ICT as well as through other technologies.

The most interesting element of such emerging technologies is that they may enable customization to be offered as a complementary service for firms that could not previously offer this. They will reduce the critical threshold for customization, thereby opening up completely new business opportunities and making it possible to meet new needs. A particular business model for dynamic markets that is based on coordination technology is collaboration platform provision, as with the Global Engineering Network concept, which sets out to support collaborative modification of designs and specifications.

While generally coordination costs will be lowered through information technology, external coordination costs may not always be reduced as much as internal coordination costs. For example, coordinating internally on the basis of intranet and workflow technology may well be more efficient than external coordination with such technology.[130] Therefore, companies that already offer customized products or services may seek to improve internal efficiency further through new coordination and customization technology. Companies such as Andersen Consulting, which are by their very nature as consultants providing customized services, claim to have achieved such improvements on the basis of Lotus Notes workflow and document-management software.

Nevertheless, mass customization is still elusive in many industry and service sectors. The PC and network equipment industries are moving in that direction. Dell, Gateway, Compaq, Cisco, Sun and others offer online customization based on a high degree of standardization of components. A key and common element in their approach is also self-customization, that is, customers perform the customization themselves. While these companies maintain dynamic and loose relationships with their customers, their supply chain is often much more tightly integrated, implementing value network concepts like supply-chain management. Interesting examples are also emerging in online music publishing, where the dynamic market approach can be realized on the buy side as well as on the supply side (i.e. the artists). However, examples are still rare of companies that have already managed in business-to-business electronic commerce to combine a high degree of customization with a dynamic market approach, either in their supply or in their relationships with customers and distributors.

Adding value through integration—the need for interoperability/ standardization

In electronic commerce, great efforts are being undertaken to arrive at standards. One of the drivers is that increased added value can be based on integration of components or on combining information from the various production and delivery processes. In order to achieve such integration, interoperability of some sort has to be achieved. If there are no common standards, companies will be inclined to seek tighter integration, in a value chain or network, or even in-house production. Conversely, standards will lower integration (i.e. coordination) costs and thus enable dynamic markets. The rise of dynamic markets will go hand in hand with the emergence of broadly accepted electronic trading standards.

An example is in product definition and catalogue standards. With such standards, search and comparison functions—that is, information brokerage—would be greatly enabled. While this may on the one hand lead to increased price competition, it would also lead to increased sales, as a lower cost for customers to obtain good product information is an incentive to buy. Or consider a function such as lifecycle management, following a product during its whole lifetime with a view to providing improved maintenance, repairs and upgrading. This has great potential for complementary and lifetime sales to the customer and building customer loyalty. Lifecycle management, until now only known in large defence or construction projects—although experiments are ongoing in order to learn from this concept for other environments too—can only be realized if information flows throughout the value network are linked. Information has to be able to flow from the customer and product in use all the way back to the component suppliers as well as in the other direction. Information-management tools that span the whole value network would then be able to detect upgrading opportunities or automatically schedule maintenance. However, the difficulties in arriving at the required standards and the current confusion about interoperability and standards have already been discussed. This certainly forms an impediment to the full exploitation of the potential of electronic business.

Building key assets for future opportunities

The economic reasoning presented above takes current costs into account. Often in practice *expected* costs and benefits are also taken into account, in other words, investing today in assets that are expected to deliver benefits in the future and provide the basis for sustainable competitive advantage. Building a strong brand, building trust with partners, increasing market share etc. are all considerations that will enter the business manager's mind, and are probably often based on 'gut feeling', rather than on a strictly rational assessment and cost calculations. Such reasoning can strongly influence the choice between value network and dynamic market configuration. Amazon.com has to trade off investing in building strong loyalty among its Associates by making them more intimate partners in a value network configuration against rapid expansion of its presence in the Internet by offering a very low effort scheme to become an Associate. Obviously, it has chosen the latter strategy with a scheme that has a low barrier to participation, but consequently also a low barrier to exit. Associates may well start shopping around for a 'better Amazon'. The Associates scheme is not nearly as strongly integrated as is a traditional value chain of a central book warehouse with its distributors. It forms a dynamic market from the Associates' point of view. No one can tell (would any one ever have done a calculation?) whether this will pay off in the future for Amazon.com, although the stock market seems to believe that it will.

The question is whether a value network (or even internal integration) or a dynamic market set-up is better suited to building a specific key asset and sustaining a key competitive advantage. Table 7.4 summarizes an assessment for a number of key assets that correspond to most of the assets mentioned in Table 2.2.

Market access can obviously be enabled through a dynamic market configuration in which many distributors or other channel partners provide a conduit to customers. This is Amazon.com's Associates approach. It is unlikely that such an approach could be practised for complex products, which require intense interaction with customers and for which the salesforce needs substantial training. In other words, if the investment per distributor (i.e. the external infrastructure cost) is rather high, a value network with tight links is more suitable. Likewise, if there is by the nature of products or markets only a limited number of access points to the market, a value network will be the choice (or even horizontal integration). Currently, a dynamic market configuration is only suitable for simple, standardized or easily customizable products. However, information technology might change the balance. If it is possible by means of such technology to transfer complex customer information and customer interaction deeper into the value network, then the end points of the value network can still be based on a dynamic market configuration. The solution in such a case might be the integration of simple and complex services on the same distributor's site. The

Table 7.4   *Building assets and the choice of value network or dynamic market*

	Value network	*Dynamic market*
Access to markets	For complex products (and also when there are limited access points to the market, as in certain niche B-to-B markets)	For simple or mass-customization products
Brand	Image, e.g. high quality	Awareness: widely known
Cost leadership	If dependent on optimization of processes	If time available to get cheapest deal
Time to market	In the case of continuous production and continuous product improvement	For *ad hoc*, non-routine solutions
Customer service and convenience	For complex service or customers that need personalized interaction	For rapid, ubiquitous but fairly standard service; in case of simple products and self-reliant customers
Customer loyalty	If the customer interface is critical (especially where trust is an issue) and in case of complex customer information	If customer loyalty is based on simple measures, such as lowest price or fastest service
Network integration	Lock-in of customers and thereby locking out would-be competitors to create exclusivity in commercial relations	Ensuring that within the dynamic market the company continues to be the point of reference for commercial relations, like being in the central hub position while having dynamic relationships with the spokes

distributor handles the simple services and a professional service provider deals with the complex services in the value network.

Brand image can be built around many qualities, but the condition *sine qua non* is brand awareness. Clearly, a dynamic market approach towards the distribution channel is helpful in establishing brand awareness by making points of contact that mention the brand to the customers widely available. On the other hand, specific brand connotations, such as 'we are the quality brand', 'we know you' or 'safety first', require a thoughtful and controlled approach to the customer, which is more likely to be guaranteed through tighter relationships, i.e. a value network or even fully under the control of the company itself.

Cost leadership is better realized through a value network (or even vertical integration) if the largest efficiency gains are achieved through optimization of the production or distribution processes. However, where small-scale production is more efficient, and a market mechanism like bidding can ensure competitive pricing, a dynamic market approach may be chosen. The latter can be expected to be the case for services where economies of scale do not hold. These could be, for example, consultant services. The company Human Focus (http://www.humanfocus.com) provides such manufacturer-independent virtual consulting in usability issues (by its very definition no geographic location can be associated with such a company). In the construction industry, SUPPLYPOINT has set out to enable dynamic market collaboration between small companies in order to become a competitive bidder in large construction projects.

Time to market has traditionally implied increasingly tight integration between companies. Concepts like just-in-time and supplier-managed inventory adopt this approach. They favour a value network or even vertical integration approach. This is well suited to predictable production and planned product and production changes, e.g. in the automotive industry, and even in the microprocessor industry where product generations come out almost in a law-like fashion ('Moore's Law'). If a rapid response is needed for a non-standard, non-planned solution, such an approach breaks down.

Customer service's dependence on the information and knowledge content of the relationship with the client determines whether a value network or dynamic market approach is more suitable. Professional and complex service requires significant investment in the service provision. Organizing this either internally in the company, or in a close relationship with value network partners, is likely to be less costly than attempting to contract it from the market, or it may not be available at all. On the other hand, call centres are market-based solutions that are suitable for providing cost effectively a basic level of rapid and ubiquitous service. Virtual call centres and advances in call-centre technology are adding further dynamics to this market-based approach. Interest in call centres is steadily increasing, with over 16 000 predicted to be in operation in Europe in 2002, up from fewer than 10 000 in 1997, and with 15% of them expected to be Web enabled in 2002.[131] A similar reasoning to the type of products and customers holds for convenience. In order to excel in convenience and still work within a dynamic market approach, products should be relatively simple and/or customer self-reliant.

Customer loyalty is related to the previous point. Where trust is an issue and where the customer interaction is complex (including customer service), a value network approach is more suitable. However, if customers return because they expect always to find the lowest price, or where complexity can be reduced as customers themselves are sophisticated (and are less concerned about trust), a dynamic market approach combined with brand awareness may be a less costly solution. Surplus stock auctions may well develop into dynamic market platforms because of these reasons. They would have to ensure brand presence. On the basis of information about transaction patterns and by proactively notifying buyers as well as suppliers about opportunities, they can increase customer loyalty.

Network integration is about partner loyalty: it means creating value configurations around a company. In other words, the competitive advantage is built on attracting opportunities for dynamic value configurations, being the 'attractor' in the network, the spider in the centre of the value web, and thereby locking in customers and suppliers and locking out competitors. Cool (1997) argues that increasingly the competitiveness of firms will not depend on their resources and capabilities alone, but will be decided by their capability to mobilize their whole value constellation. This may be easier for a heavyweight like GE, Shell or Unilever, which are large procurers and which may even be able to enforce adoption of shared information systems, i.e. set up a value network with their suppliers. Generally, with a value network approach the key asset is in the investment in integration of information systems and business processes. A large company can also choose to maintain loose business relationships—that is, to operate in a dynamic market configuration—as its clout in the market will in any case make it the dominating central hub that can choose dynamically which of the smaller spokes it wants to do business with.

A dynamic market approach may seem less suited for small companies as a means to build up a key asset and sustainable competitive advantage in network integration. Nevertheless, even for a small company it is possible to become the centre or the hub, by starting with easy technical provisions for relationships to suppliers, customers, or added-value service providers. An example is Adobe, which by making its PDF reader freely available has become a central reference point for read-only document presentation; or Amazon with its low-barrier and immediate benefits service for potential Associates. Subsequently, proactive research into the value opportunity of that relationship can ensure that the company stays in the centre (going beyond what Amazon does in its Associates scheme). The free online service that subsequently leads to true value-enhancement opportunities is also pursued in the graphics industry, where some companies are making free online pre-press support available for preparing professional publications, combined with an optional—but likely to be chosen—electronic link into the subsequent printing processing.

Competing and Collaborating in Value Networks and Dynamic Markets—Conclusion

It would not be realistic to expect that the trade-off between in-house production–value chain–value network–dynamic market can be expressed in a few simple parameters. Nevertheless, it is striking that many of the factors influencing this trade-off seem to correlate with two main dimensions:

1. *Specificity of the investment required*: this correlates for example with trust, complexity, customer loyalty, value added through integration, building distinctive brand features.
2. *Flexibility/dynamic behaviour*: this correlates with customization, time to market for non-routine products, brand awareness/wide access to markets, service availability, capability for dealing with uncertainty.

Similar dimensions have been identified by Williamson (1986), with his dimensions of uncertainty and frequency of transactions relating to the dynamics dimension. Likewise, Ticoll, Lowy and Kalakota in Tapscott *et al.* (1998) arrive at similar dimensions, called 'value integration' and 'control'. Their analysis is based on a detailed study of about 30 'e-business communities'.

Figure 7.7 indicates the positioning of dynamic market configurations and value networks on these dimensions. It also suggests where some of the business models can be located. It depends on the realization of the business model to what extent dynamic behaviour is being supported. For example, an information broker could be a relatively static single-enterprise configuration, say when it is a credit-rating agency. However, it can also be much more dynamic, in the sense that the information base is dynamically enhanced and created by other market actors. This is the case for some of the search engines that invite submissions of information from the Web community at large.

The dimensions for the organization of value creation and value exchange are also not the same as those for the business models. Functional integration in the business models diagram in Chapter 3 correlates with investment specificity but is not identical to it. The level of innovation in the business models analysis is about comparing today's way of doing business with yesterday's: it is about the level of innovation relative to the 'traditional' way of doing business. The dynamics dimension, on the other hand, is about the scale of changes in the actual operation of the business model.

The above has been a qualitative and to some extent speculative assessment. The research challenge is to define the various factors that

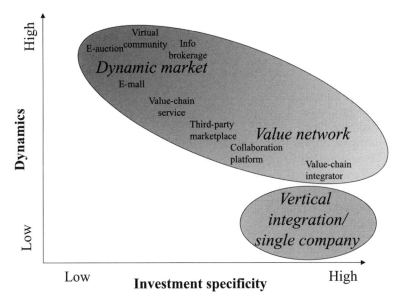

Figure 7.7 *Key dimensions for organizing value creation and exchange*

influence the strategic choice for the electronic commerce business organization in a much more precise way, to measure their influence and to determine how they are correlated and whether indeed they can be represented by a few key dimensions only.

Thriving on Information

This section addresses the digital information business. It will first define what doing business with digital information is all about. A number of examples illustrate the types of digital information business that are emerging. It then addresses characteristics of the digital information business, and the consequences for dealing with key issues such as management of copyrights, uncertainty and trust, and pricing. Next, opportunities are analysed for building and exploiting key business assets, in the context of strategy development for digital information business. Finally, an outlook on the future of the digital information business is provided.

Defining the Digital Information Business

There are high hopes for the growth of the digital information business. The stakes are high indeed. The digital content business in the USA and

Europe is predicted to grow to about $10 billion in 2001 out of total Internet revenues of some $270 billion (Forrester, 1998). This digital content consists of all products that can be digitized and are in digital form sold by online means. However, from those figures it looks as if the digital information markets are still going to be dwarfed by trading in physical goods. But equating the digital information business to the 'bit' business is underestimating the importance of the information-based economy. For example, even in MRO trading a large part of online purchasing will happen on the basis of digital information only. A new printer can be announced to potential purchasers in companies by means of a commercial delivered by means of push technology on an online channel. The purchaser may subscribe to an online report of a business magazine that has assessed the new printer. The purchaser may be a member of an online purchasers' club, a virtual community, and go there to collect experiences from peers—still receiving information by digital means only. When finally the new printer is being bought, e.g. through an online third-party marketplace provider, the purchaser accepts a completely digital trail of delivery as sufficient proof for payment. At the end, the purchaser (and perhaps even the supplier—that is, the distributor, who may schedule deliveries directly from the factory to the customer—have never physically seen the printer. This too is digital information business, and it requires many of the same technologies and many elements of the same legal framework that are needed for the 'true' digital content business. This whole chain of events has in fact been a chain of digital processes that deal with digital products. Another example of business that is enabled by digital information is provided by services based on embedded intelligence in products. Cars are equipped with a computer and memory to monitor and record the state of the engine, brakes etc. Several groups are now working on Internet-enabled vehicles. This will make it possible in the near future to provide an online 'car health-check' service.

Buying on the basis of non-physical information alone is in fact a continuation of a centuries-old commercial practice. People have always been buying 'in good faith' on the basis of a reference that they trusted. They have routinely been ordering from the milkman for this week the same amount of milk as they used last week. Likewise, in all the cases studied here, purchasing is to a large extent done on the basis of non-physical information. Books are bought from Amazon.com without the buyer touching the book and without ever turning over a single page, just because a large number of other readers have written an enthusiastic review according to Amazon's Web pages. Amazon Associates never need to see an Amazon.com representative eye to eye, nor touch the books that are sold through their referral, and still engage in a trading relationship, simply through embedding a Web link in their site. Printers, paper, chairs and other office equipment are bought in large quantity through Citius or Tradezone, just on the basis of a reference in an electronic catalogue. The difference to the past is that the information is now provided digitally and online. However, that difference may have tremendous consequences.

It is thus useful to make a distinction between 'doing business with digital information'—that is, selling digital content—and 'enabling business through digital information'. The first shows up in the statistics about the digital content market: it is doing business by charging for digital information. The second can range from Internet advertising, to transactions enabled by Internet auctions or third-party marketplaces, to customer co-design services enabled by value-chain integration. Its value is thus sometimes but not always directly measurable such that it shows up in straightforward economic statistics. Nevertheless, it is important to be aware that in electronic commerce every business is in the digital information business![132]

The case studies have pointed to opportunities to enable business with digital information and digital processes, or to charge for digital information. In some cases these opportunities were in the transposition of a physical business into an electronic version. In other cases these were new forms of purely digital information businesses. Most of them are not selling digital information but rather doing business enabled by digital information.

- Industry.Net and the many other industry malls, such as the set of malls created by VerticalNet, are in the information business, based on electronic versions of what previously were bulky physical product catalogues. They never need to touch a product physically, as they are only working with digitized representations of such products, bringing catalogues online in the industry e-mall. Their business model is not to charge for catalogue usage but rather for hosting of catalogues, which is close to the business model of a traditional catalogue business.
- Infomar/SCS has moved into providing a digital process, namely online auctions, as an evolution from physical (on-the-floor) electronic auction systems. Its trading system can report statistics for a variety of commercial and administrative purposes, including information needed for the enforcement of fishing quota. It charges for the system rather than for the digital information itself.
- Marshall Industries has been able to create an online professional training business. Its customers needed more than simple online delivery of technical information about electronic components such

as datasheets. Marshall responded to this need with an Internet-based training solution.

- FedEx and other shipping companies now allow for online calculation of shipping costs and for online package-delivery tracking. IShip, an Internet start-up, is building a new business on such information by allowing users to compare shipping costs and delivery times from UPS, FedEx and other delivery services.[133] In both cases the business model is not to charge for the logistical information itself. In the case of FedEx, the expected additional business is in attracting more shipments, on the basis of increased customer convenience and customer loyalty. In the case of IShip, the business model is that IShip charges 50¢ per shipping order to the participating courier companies. These are applications that have never existed before.

- Amazon has a physical book warehouse for the most frequently demanded items, where fast delivery is key. However, to a large extent it also works with third-party warehouses, in which case it only handles digital information about books and stocks. The Amazon Associates scheme is a purely digital marketing arrangement. As noted in the analysis in Chapter 4, Amazon does not (yet) exploit the large amount of information that comes via its associates. For example, it could create dedicated online bookstores on the basis of segmenting the customer base through its knowledge of the characteristics of the associate and data mining the related customer profiles.

- GEN/ICS is currently offering a digital process. The new digital information business is a perspective on the future. Not only digital information derived from usage patterns could be sold (as in the case of Citius and Tradezone), but digital professional services could also be provided (such as online training, as for Marshall).

- Citius and Tradezone are purely in the information business, providing a digital process. Their position as a new intermediary in the MRO market provides them with huge amounts of data about purchasing patterns. This potentially provides them with new information products, such as (statistical) purchaser profiles, which could be sold to suppliers, or purchase bundling, which could be sold as a service to the purchasers, and financial services for both.

In particular, the last two points above illustrate a digital information business that covers and integrates multiple business-to-business processes, as also indicated in the business models classification diagram, Figure 3.2. The other examples are addressing a single or just a few business-to-business processes.

Examples of companies that are doing B-to-B electronic commerce and charging for digital information include the following:

- Market research companies like IDC, Gartner, Forrester and business news companies like Reuters, Economist etc, who are all offering online subscription schemes. These grew as online information services out of a previous physically delivered information service.
- Lawyers that provide online advice, e.g. De Kreek, a lawyer in Amsterdam, offers 'do-it-yourself' legal packages, which can be downloaded for a charge to individuals and companies (http://www.advocaat.nl/). This is again a gradual transposition of a previously existing 'real-world' service.
- MusicTrial.com and Byline.com have been piloting electronic copyright-management systems (ECMS), in respectively digital music for value-added resellers and news syndication for journalists. The ECMS technology allows for identification, copyright protection and charging for such digital information. Both pilots based their business model on work done in the Imprimatur copyright-management project (http://www.imprimatur.alcs.co.uk/imprimatur).
- A precursor to the Imprimatur project was the TISSUS project.[134] This focused on the digitization of textile designs, storing them in an image bank and making them accessible via the Internet for commercial use under copyright protection, creating a marketplace for textile images and patterns. Another example is Museums Online (http://www.museums-online.com), selling digital copies of works of art. Both these and the previous two examples can be thought of as a transposition of existing physical businesses. However, moving into the digital world with potential online delivery requires such a significant step forward in terms of ECMS support and commercial relationships that one can speak of a newly emerging business model.

Characteristics of Digital Information Business

These examples illustrate a number of issues related to digital information business, as also identified by Choi, Stahl and Whinston (1997) and Shapiro and Varian (1998). The issues originate in the specific characteristics of the digital information itself (Choi, Stahl and Whinston, 1997):

1. *Indestructibility*: digital objects are intangible and their quality never deteriorates. This can be a disadvantage, to the extent that replacement sales of digital objects because of wear and tear or repairs are never needed. In B-to-B electronic commerce this will be of less concern if the digital information is highly time dependent, which is often the case for transaction data such as purchasing patterns. When information becomes quickly outdated there is a continuous need for replacement sales. However, indestructibility may be an issue if the

digital information is of a more static nature, such as catalogues or digital designs of products. Catalogue companies that go online find out that they only have to update parts of their catalogues instead of having to reprint the full catalogue regularly. Users will not be willing to pay a hefty fee for such minor updates. Therefore the companies have to adapt their pricing and packaging. One way is to use the digital catalogues as an enabler of other digital business, such as advertising (as in Industry.Net) or transaction handling (as in the third-party marketplaces).

2. *Transmutability*: digital objects can often be easily modified and customized, unless specific measures are taken to prevent this, by distributing only an encoded form. Technical means are available such as secure technologies like watermarking and hashing that can help to detect that a digital object has been modified. For B-to-B electronic commerce that charges for the information itself, transmutability is of concern as it creates additional cost for protection: normally businesses would like to be sure of the correctness of the information received. If, on the other hand, services are built on top of digital information, transmutability will be of less concern, as the data themselves are not directly exposed to the customer.

3. *Reproducibility*: digital objects can be copied without loss of quality and usually at very low cost. Where digital information is provided that can be reused in another business environment, this is potentially of concern. However, in particular in B-to-B electronic commerce there is great potential for customizing information, which will reduce the threat of reproduction. Moreover, where information can also be accompanied by a customized service, e.g. consultant advice that is specific to the business situation. Customization of this kind will also reduce the risk of copying. However, even if customized information and services cannot easily be reused in another business, since business situations will tend to be unique, they are nevertheless sensitive to industrial espionage and would therefore have to be protected. Non-customized digital information, such as product catalogues, is indeed at risk of being copied. Amazon.com restricts the copying that its Associates can do of its catalogue, by making the potential Associate accept an online contract that effectively limits such full copying by specific display requirements. However, both the validity of the contract (who signs?) and its enforcement (with hundreds of thousands of Associates) are questionable. It must be said that it is also technically difficult to download all of Amazon's catalogue. Catalogue-based marketplaces are, because of reproducibility, caught in a peculiar dilemma: on the one hand they would benefit from open and interoperable catalogues, as this will increase

their information offer for transactions. Tradezone, Citius and Globana all declared that they expect to be moving away from proprietary catalogue formats. On the other hand, freely accessible catalogues increase the risk of being bypassed by competitor transaction operators. Suppliers are likewise caught in a dilemma: freely accessible catalogues with an open interface mean that more third-party marketplace providers can market their products. However, at the same time this will make price comparison easier, which will lead to reduction of their margins.

These characteristics lead to a 'trust gap': for the information user, the fact that the information is provided in a transmutable form raises questions about its reliability. For information providers, the reproducibility and indestructibility raise questions about commercial viability—what is the appropriate marketing model? In addition, for both providers and users the fact that information is delivered at a distance in the online environment introduces further uncertainty as information gets decoupled from physical presence and evidence. Therefore, in order to 'thrive on digital information' the key issue to be addressed is *trust*. More specifically, the following questions have to be addressed:

Copyright management

Is this necessary and feasible? Technology to control copying and technology to manage the rights associated with content are gradually becoming available. However, there is not yet a global legal framework to give adequate legal protection for digital works. Also, online rights-management systems are not yet generally in place (they do exist for specific environments). These would have to register authors' rights and track usage and usage rights, such that payments can be channelled to authors and other rights owners accordingly. Certain, but not necessarily all, rights-management systems would have to be able to interoperate or develop into a single global rights-management system. Protection is currently feasible within closed environments that also subject themselves to specific contractual conditions (e.g. a closed user group as in the case of the trading of textile designs). However, copyright management in open environments like the Internet is expected to become available soon, partly as a result of the experiments mentioned before. As argued above, copyright protection is not always necessary. It may depend on the half-life of the information, its value, its exposure to the customer and its customer specificity. Copyright protection in specific product-markets may not even be desirable, given an appropriate marketing mix (see for instance the discussion below on pricing of digital information).

Moreover, in B-to-B the information is often sold into a market of mutual competitors, who have no incentive whatsoever to copy the information for which they paid dearly to their nearest competitor. B-to-B customized information and professional services based on digital information will therefore have less of a need to invoke copyright protection means. They may, however, have a need to track usage, for example, within a closed intranet to be able to charge for the number of users in the company.

Ownership and liability

While copyright protection can help to safeguard ownership rights, the question may be to establish ownership in the first instance. When any purchaser uses a third-party trading system, it is an open question to whom the transaction information belongs and who has the right to exploit such information. A large purchaser may be extremely sensitive about detailed exposure of information, as it can be considered a commercial secret. Understandably, Tradezone foresees for the time being that only statistical indicators will be exploited, derived from the underlying detailed transaction information. The question of liability is possibly even more sensitive. When digital information is being charged for, at least some guarantee from the buyer that it has the right to sell could be expected. However, if a service is offered in addition to digital information the situation is less clear. For example, should an auction provider be held responsible for the accuracy of the information provided by sellers, or even for their right to sell? The consumer-auction provider eBay got into a legal clash with Microsoft in February 1999 when it appeared that sales were hosted on eBay's auction of what were probably illegal copies of the MS Office 97 Suite.

Uncertainty about the quality of the information

How can you be sure that the information accurately represents what it claims to? In particular, in B-to-B electronic commerce ensuring the reliability of the information may be critical. This is not only an issue of making sure that the information has not been modified (transmutability). It is also about dealing with the trust gap that is being created as in logistics chains the physical and information flows are increasingly being separated. An example of this was provided by the Infomar case. Questions include:

- Is the information reliable and sufficient? This is determined by the complexity of the product, its value and its uniqueness. Tradezone and

Citius limit (today) their trading to routine supplies, of relatively low value, for which often just a catalogue reference number suffices.

- Is there a need for either physical information about the product or service (being able to see it, touch it, being able to meet the people who provide the service etc.)? With routine supplies the need for information is of course less at the moment of the repeat purchase. First-time purchasers may need more extensive information, such as diagrams, photographs, usage descriptions etc., to overcome the lack of physical feedback. For repeat purchasers a short-cut to ordering should be offered, however.
- Is there a need for complementary information that cannot be provided by the supplier, such as a trustworthy reference? For perishable products like fish or flowers, the appearance and smell can be very important and has a subjective element to it. This type of information and information collecting is not easily digitized. Quality standards can help, but require a trusted third party to manage the standards' definition and their implementation. The Infomar case has demonstrated that there is an emerging need for such a third-party in the fisheries sector.
- Is there a need for complementary information to be provided via other channels, such as TV advertisements?
- Is there a possibility of recourse if information turns out to be of poor quality or even worse?

Pricing of digital information and segmentation and customization

What is the appropriate pricing approach for digital information? Contradictory concepts of digital information need thorough investigation in order to understand their impact on pricing and segmentation. Bakos, Brynjolfsson and Lichtman (1998) provide an interesting example of the surprising conclusions about small-scale sharing of information goods to which such concepts lead. One intuitive notion is that sharing of digital information (as it is very easily copied) will harm producers, as fewer copies will be sold. The other intuitive notion is that digital information (and any other good) increases in value when it can be shared with others, for example with colleagues; that is, in small social groups. The researchers investigated 'small-scale decentralized reproduction of intellectual property' and found that profits can increase through sharing, even if it is more expensive for the customer to copy information than it is for the producer. However, profits can also decrease, even if sharing via the customer is cheaper than producing and distributing additional copies by the producer. This is against conventional wisdom, which says that if the customer can distribute more efficiently than the producer, overall efficiency increases, which will be translated into increased profits for the producer.

However, the situation with digital information goods is different from the conventional situation, as the cost of duplication is virtually zero. The effects that then come into play are 'aggregation' and 'team diversity'. Aggregation is the fact that the variation in the valuation of a social group tends to be smaller than that of the individual members. This is one consequence of an assumption related to the second concept: in a social group the valuation will be the *sum* of the members' valuations. Some of the members will value a good highly, others lower. By aggregating the members the spread will become smaller. The advantage for a producer of digital goods is that a price can be set that does not exclude any part of the market or undercuts profits too much. Suppose that one department, A, in a company is valuing a digital information good at $200, whereas it is worth $150 for another department, B. If sharing is possible, the company will be willing to pay $350. In that case one copy can be sold, and the revenue is $350. If the producer would not allow sharing, it can sell one copy by pricing the good at $200. Alternatively it can sell two copies, by putting the price at $150, with a revenue of $200. Table 7.5 summarizes this. Clearly, it can be attractive to allow for sharing. This can be especially relevant for B-to-B digital content within organizations. In that case no specific segmentation needs to be done.

Team diversity can, however, decrease profits if sharing is allowed. Team diversity is the spread in team size, which is not under the control of the producer. It may be that the same information good will be sold to coalitions of varying size. Let's add another department, C, that is willing to pay $150. Assume that two of the departments share the good between each other and the other does not, for whatever reason. Assume now that the producer has no way to find out how sharing will happen (i.e. does not control team diversity, that is, whether department A will share with B, indicated by A + B; C or any other combination). The producer can do market research to determine the willingness to pay and thus obtain the valuations. The options for price setting and resulting revenue are given in Table 7.6.

Table 7.5 *Example of revenues in cases of aggregation and small-scale sharing*[135]

	Sharing	No sharing	
Price	$350	$150	$200
Number of copies sold	1	2	1
Revenues	$350	$300	$200

Table 7.6   *Example of revenues in cases of team diversity and small-scale sharing*

	Sharing				No sharing	
Team composition	A + B; C		A; B + C		A; B; C	
Price	$350	$150	$200	$300	$200	$150
Number of copies sold	1	2	2	1	1	3
Revenues	$350	$300	$400	$300	$200	$450

In this case the producer should not allow for sharing, if this is possible, and set the price at $150. If sharing cannot be prevented, the price depends on what has been found from market research, and is either $350 or $200. If in this case the producer was able to control the team size, it would have reduced team diversity to just one, namely the team of the three departments together (A + B + C). This team is willing to pay $200 + $150 + $150 = $500 when sharing is allowed, still more than the $450 than can be obtained maximally when no sharing is allowed. The extent of team diversity determines whether profits will decrease or not.

The implication for marketing is the following. When sharing is allowed (or cannot be prevented), but team diversity cannot be controlled and can be widely varying, the digital goods producer should attempt to segment the market of teams and customize the good, so that different prices can be asked for each segment. In this case there would be four different segments and correspondingly four different products, namely A + B (willing to pay $350), B + C (willing to pay $300), A (willing to pay $200) and B (or C, willing to pay $150). In that case it will still be possible to obtain the full revenue of $500, whatever configuration of teams occurs. It is likely, however, that the cost of production also increases and that therefore profits will still go down. Increasing the cost of copying (if at all technically possible) will not lead to a better result.

The relevance of the above for the future of digital content business in B-to-B electronic commerce is that there are likely to be many situations in which such content can be sold to smaller social groups, like departments in a company.[136] The content seller then has to investigate:

- diverse group sizes that could copy the good to each other or otherwise share it;
- valuations of each group member of the digital good;
- possibilities and cost of customization;
- possibilities and cost to prevent copying or sharing.

With this, the seller will be able to develop the most profitable pricing scheme. For example, Citius or Tradezone could start selling transaction information to purchasers, such as a newsletter with average prices and best deals for certain MRO goods. One option is to sell such a newsletter to a central purchasing department with free use for the whole company. No customization or anti-copying protection is being done. Assuming that the central department will ensure full sharing and so team diversity is one, then revenue can be the sum of all valuations. However, if central purchasing cannot buy the newsletter on behalf of the individual departments, then another option is to analyse the purchasing patterns of individual departments and set out to prepare fully customized news-letters for them. If this is possible, the revenue can again be the sum of all valuations. If customization is not possible and no information can be obtained about sharing patterns (team diversity), one has to assume the largest team diversity, that is, settle for the lowest price and hope that the actual team size will not be one. A better option, if possible, in that last case might be to sell newsletters embedded in a copyright-management system that tracks copying and usage, in other words to make sharing controllable.

Customs and taxation related to digital content business

A worldwide moratorium has been agreed for customs applied to digital content delivered online: namely, that they are not subject to customs. That is, until now they have been considered in the same way as services, although there is a debate whether they can indeed be qualified fully as services, rather than as a new category of 'virtual goods'. The WTO is the body that will further pursue the discussion towards an international agreement on customs for online digital content, which would be part of the General Agreement on Trade in Services, GATS. Duty or customs free does not imply that no taxation is levied on digital goods and services, however. Consumption taxation, i.e. sales or value-added tax, is still applicable. The OECD Conference held in October 1998 in Ottawa confirmed that the principle for consumption taxation should be that such taxation is levied in the country of consumption.[137] The EU earlier that year also agreed a set of guidelines, including that there should be no discrimination between online and offline ways of doing business. Therefore no new taxes such as a 'bit tax' should be introduced. It was also stated that taxation should be 'simple', and that taxation in the online world should not cause an undue burden for business.[138] The practical implementation of these principles has not yet been achieved. In October 1998 a three-year tax moratorium was adopted in the USA, stating that until 2001 no new or discriminatory state and local taxes may be introduced on Internet access and related online services.[139]

Business Strategies for Digital Information Business

The previous section has already highlighted a number of marketing-planning considerations, such as pricing, bundling and customization, without attempting to be exhaustive. A number of market opportunities for digital information business were also identified from the case studies and other examples. Taking a step back and looking at the digital information business from the strategic vantage point, it is as usual not only a matter of identifying market opportunities and being able to develop, package, price and deliver the digital products and services. As analysed before for value networks and digital markets, the strategic view also means assessing how the business model will enable key assets to be built and exploited. Table 7.7 provides a number of examples and suggestions for building and exploiting key assets, for 'doing business with digital information' and for 'enabling business with digital information'. Some of the consequences for competitive structure of the industry will be addressed later in this chapter.

What the table shows, *inter alia*, is that digital information is a vehicle for improving access to markets, either through services (e.g. virtual communities that bring customers in a market segment together) or by themselves as a product that is being charged for (e.g. digital textile designs). We can speculate about whether selling digital information can heighten brand awareness. However, digital information allows for better profiling and thus increasing brand awareness (a clear example is targeted advertising on search engines, depending on the search criteria entered by the customer).

Brand image building can be clearly related to digital information. Protecting high-priced digital information can increase the perception of high quality and exclusivity. Responsiveness to customers or an image of customer orientation can be reinforced by using one-to-one marketing techniques based on digital information from past and ongoing interactions between buyer and seller. Digitizing information had a great impact on cost and therefore enabled cost-leadership strategies, for example in the once-expensive encyclopaedia or professional journals business. Digital information is also the basis of self-service, thereby shifting costs away from the seller (and to the buyer!).

Digital information can be very valuable if time dependency is critical, e.g. in stock markets. Digital information is also essential to provide time-critical services, or to provide services where saving time means saving money, such as opportunities-based trading in digital markets. Customers are readily paying for digital content if this enhances their convenience. For example, automatic upgrading of computer and network software is attractive for many companies who can save on maintenance costs. This

Table 7.7   *Building and exploiting key assets in the digital information business*

	Selling digital information	Services from digital information
Access to markets	Customization and appropriate pricing to make digital information interesting for untapped niche markets New ways to address existing markets by enriching the existing offer with digital information	Easy online access to shared information for valud-added services offered into new markets; third-party marketplaces, industry malls, auctions and virtual communities are all examples Exploiting and reinforcing existing market access with services built on digial information from the customer interaction
Brand awareness	The digital counterpart of shirt labels and collectables?	Marketing services based on customer profiling can increase brand exposure
Brand image	E.g. high-quality image: package and protect digital information such that high-quality content remains exclusive	E.g. customer-friendly image: reinforce this image through one-to-one marketing and digital customization
Cost leadership	Reduce production and distribution costs by bringing information online (cf. what happened to Encyclopaedia Britannica)	Shift service towards online self-service, thereby reducing cost (cf. Cisco, FedEx) Auctions to reduce slack in production and inventory
Time to market	Price information according to timeliness, e.g. stock market information, and guarantee response time	Auctions to reduce time to sales, push-based information services to inform about current opportunities
Customer service and convenience	Make customers pay for digital content if it can be delivered when and where they need it and fit for their actual need, e.g. online software upgrading	Charge for online after-sales service according to the level of convenience and assistance required; differentiate from competition through customization
Customer loyalty	Package digital information in chunks that reduce in value over time such that customers return	The essence of online one-to-one marketing: make the relationship with the customer central and extract information digitally to continue offering value to the customer
Network integration	Close business collaboration or mergers in content production and delivery reflecting the convergence of different media and delivery platforms	New services built on information integration in a value network or value chain

example, by the way, holds the middle ground between a digital product and a digital content-enabled service (does one pay for the upgraded software or for the upgrading of the software?). Customer loyalty can be increased through paid-for digital content, if the content is of such a nature that customers will want to come back for more and is priced so that the initial purchase decision is readily made. And, of course, customer loyalty is the goal of one-to-one marketing, which itself is a service that is fully enabled by digital information.

Finally, there are plenty of opportunities in the digital information business to build a key business asset in network integration. In selling digital information, it has almost become natural for IT platform companies to merge with content publishing companies, or for traditional publishing companies to expand into Web delivery, or for telecom companies to team up with content owners, or for IT companies to engage in joint ventures with cable operators etc. All of these mergers and acquisitions and business collaborations, instances of value network configurations or single-company value chains, are driven by convergence and digitization. For the other part of the digital information business, namely business enabled by digital information, the natural tendency is to integrate information across the value chain in order to provide new services, such as the example of MarshallNet/PartnerNet implementing the business model of value-chain integrator.

The Future of Digital Information Business

A variety of trials and commercial ventures are underway in digital content electronic commerce. They often also suggest further exciting opportunities. At the same time, many of them still have to prove their commercial viability. Questions that naturally come up thus include: how will this type of business develop? What will be the business and marketing models for digital content? Which are the new opportunities? For example, will the hope come true that existing content becomes tradeable at large scale through electronic commerce and digital content technologies? Will digital content business mainly be a transposition of existing physical business or will completely new applications arise? What are the conditions for growth of the digital information business in terms of interoperability and legal framework? How and when will critical mass be achieved? What are the implications for competition and industry structure?

An interesting exercise to get an answer to these questions was carried out in 1997 by the Imprimatur project. This project involved European, American and Australian partners from content industries, author organizations and technology companies and set out to build consensus about the technological and legal framework for digital content business. In a workshop involving about 60 experts from various parts of the world, future scenarios were assessed, using possible events, as to their attainability, that is, how likely it is that a scenario will become reality, and as to their desirability, that is, the view of the experts on the attractiveness of a scenario.[140] Four scenarios or 'endstates' for the 2002/2003 timeframe were considered:

Endstate A: physical distribution is still important (possibly via online warehouses) next to digital distribution, in online or offline media.

Endstate B: a one-to-one electronic distribution system for digital content evolves, with highly customized delivery.

Endstate C: increased bandwidth and sophisticated technology for interoperable electronic copyright management with full tracking and direct e-payments from users to content providers.

Endstate D: a broadcasting push environment with differences between B-to-B (customer-specific) and B-to-C (mass-market approach).

The outcome of the exercise was that endstate C was the one considered most desirable but the least attainable. In one exercise in Europe, endstate A came out as most attainable but almost least desirable; a second workshop in the USA identified endstate D in that position. Some of the reasoning included the following:

- Endstate A is closer to the current situation and would meet the concerns of publishers that wish to keep content under control. It would build on electronic trading and delivery systems. As far as copyright protection systems are concerned, these would mostly focus on B-to-B use. We see some of these systems emerging today (e.g. TISSUS mentioned above).

- Endstate C, on the other hand, would require great changes for all the players involved in digital content. Publishers would have to be willing to relinquish more of their control on content. Distributors (intermediaries like telecom operators and ISPs) would have to take on more content mediation but therefore also more liability, and customers would have to become more active in content search rather than being passive receivers. Content creators would be able to disintermediate publishers, but new intermediaries like trusted third parties and rights collectors would gain in importance.

- The differences in perceived attainability of endstate D in the USA and Europe probably reflected the state of the broadcasting market in those regions.

To conclude this section, and perhaps most importantly, we observe that all the considerations until now show that the digital information business is very much an emerging area. Transposition of physical business into digital information business is only one possibility. There are plenty of other opportunities. Some have been suggested, but surely many more still await detection. We have also seen that simple transposition of the rules of physical 'real-world' business may be utterly misleading when drawing up new business models and marketing strategies. In conclusion, 'thriving on information' truly challenges commercial and technical creativity.

Converging B-to-B and B-to-C Electronic Commerce

It is often said that 'on the Internet nobody knows you're a dog'. Paraphrasing this, one could say 'on the Internet no one knows whether you are a consumer or a business customer'. This is certainly not always true, as an Internet supplier–buyer relationship is usually not so superficial that one cannot see the difference between a consumer and a business buyer. Nevertheless, the Internet enables more than any other medium to deal with consumers and businesses in a very similar way, and/or to exploit company assets in B-to-B as well as in B-to-C electronic commerce. Here we will compare B-to-B and B-to-C electronic commerce and see in which aspects they can be made to converge through the Internet and how such convergence can be exploited. We will discuss the markets in which such convergence already happens today or might happen in the near future. Finally, marketing strategies are considered for convergent B-to-B and B-to-C electronic commerce.

Characteristics of B-to-B and B-to-C Electronic Commerce

Dell's Web site asks online customers to indicate whether they are home users or home-based small offices. Independently of which option is chosen, the product pages that follow, and even the ordering and payment methods, are largely the same for both categories. It is only when a buyer indicates that they are representing a corporate or named account that the Web site really changes, emphasizing lifetime cost of ownership and discounts for larger purchases rather than displaying the generic 'best PC offer of the month' approach.[141] Dell manages to keep the processes of the value chain largely identical for its B-to-B and B-to-C operations.

A related example is that of airlines selling tickets online that hardly differentiate between consumer and business buyers. Anyone can look up fares and flight schedules and participate in frequent-traveller or other bonus schemes. A well-designed Web site keeps track of customer preferences and classifies recurrent clients according to their preferences. For example, businesspeople tend to fly during the week, frequently change their plans and have short overnight stays. Consumers tend to go for cheaper deals and more frequently choose a weekend package or a longer stay. With such knowledge about segmenting the market, the airline will offer different options to consumers and businesspeople, suggesting package deals to consumers and flight flexibility to business passengers. Even while responding to different customer profiles, the airline is still maintaining one single Web site. Data mining and one-to-one marketing software help companies to realize mass customization and thus to deal efficiently with customers of any profile—whether businesses or consumers.

Quixell, a UK-based online auction,[142] offers real-time online bidding for bargains, matching sellers with buyers. It emphasizes person-to-person bidding and makes it easy for any consumer to offer a product for sale, or to buy from the auction. In fact, these people need not be consumers at all; they might just as well be business buyers interested in a one-off sale or purchase of a single product. The difference between consumers and businesses as sellers is only visible deep down in the Web site, where businesses are invited to contact QXL off-line if they have a larger amount of products to offer. QXL Exchange, a tool for private person-to-person auctions, is likewise offered to business customers, the Web site stating that 'as a business customer, you can sell items at QXL Exchange just as private individuals can'. QXL assumes that in its online auction businesses behave to a large extent in the same way as consumers do.

Health Online Service (now Multimedica[143]), a German Web medical information service created in 1996, provided information to the medical profession, in particular to doctors. This was information about drugs, therapies and medical conferences, as well as community services such as chat. At the same time, the doctors or other medical personnel were offered leisure information, such as holiday trips, sports information etc. The subscribers were considered at the same time medical professionals and consumers. Similarly, Bloomberg offers financial information to investment traders and analysts. Bloomberg recognized that its customers may earn a lot of money but have very little time to spend it. Therefore the professional information service is enriched by the possibility of buying flowers, clothing and travel online, and get information about real estate.[144] Multimedica and Bloomberg show that customers can be treated at the same time as business professionals and as individual consumers, leading to more sales and increased customer loyalty.

These examples illustrate forms of electronic commerce that are able to deal with consumers and businesses in similar ways, by one or more of the following:

- offering *virtually the same product or service* to both consumers and businesses;
- dealing with both the consumer and the business market through the *same or similar processes*;
- addressing *convergent markets* where the customer is consumer and business at the same time.

It is interesting to contrast this with marketing textbooks that tend to emphasize the differences between consumer markets and business (or organizational) markets rather than stress the opportunities based on their similarities! Consumer markets are usually considered to be mass markets where standardized products with a fixed price are being sold. Business buying, on the other hand, tends to be individualized, with products and services that are custom built and built to specification, and where payment conditions together with product and delivery specifications are often negotiable. Selling to consumers is for the most part indirect, whereas business markets tend to be addressed through direct sales. Direct selling in business markets requires professionals who can communicate on a peer-to-peer level with the buyers, being trained not only in sales techniques but also in the product. Engineers sell to engineers, doctors sell to doctors etc. For direct selling in consumer markets such as door-to-door sales, being a 'good' salesperson is emphasized rather than an academic degree in the product technology. Table 7.8 compares consumer and business markets on product/service characteristics, the steps of the sales process (search, select, order, pay, fulfil, after-sales), intermediaries that are involved and marketing communications, and also suggests how these might change when B-to-B and B-to-C converge.

There is certainly a lot of truth in the good old marketing books. After all, consumers are not buying machinery or airplanes. They do not demand product specificity or lifetime management of relationships as businesses do. They are not purchasing goods worth millions of dollars, so they do not need a variety of financial and risk-management services. Conversely, business buyers are professionals and their personal preferences do not matter. They are not buying on impulse but rather after extensive deliberation. Consumer-oriented advertising is not relevant to influence them. They know their suppliers and the suppliers know them,

Table 7.8   Comparison of consumer and business markets

Characteristic	Consumer *(traditional)*	Business *(traditional)*	Convergence *(in e-commerce)*
Product/service			
Value	Low	High	Business: low-value routine products Consumers: support for high-value purchases, such as house or car
Specificity	Low, standardized	High, custom-made, made to specification	Business: online routine purchases Consumers: mass customization
Market communications			
Media	Mass media, such as TV, national magazines Specialized lifestyle magazines Direct media, e.g. mail	Direct media, such as mail Specialized media, such as trade press, business radio	Business and consumers: e-mail, Web sites (pull and push), infomercials
Relationship supplier-buyer	Often stranger–stranger; one-off and short term	Normally known to each other; long term	Business: unknown, *ad hoc*, one-off partners in dynamic markets Consumers: long term, personalized relationships through one-to-one
Sales Process			
Search	Shop Catalogue	Catalogue Call for tenders	B & C: Web catalogue; third-party marketplace providers supporting B & C for routine products
Evaluate	Consumer reports Peer groups	Test Negotiate	B & C: online evaluation (simulation, 3-D, virtual reality)
Order	Also includes impulse buying	Rational	Impulse buying also in business markets (e.g. SOHO)?
Payment	Cash Credit card Cheque	Bank transfer Purchase card Barter	Business: increasingly using credit cards (purchase cards) B & C: increasingly electronic account-to-account payments

Continued

Delivery	On the spot Postal mail delivery Small package shippers	Specialized logistics/ transport Small package shippers	B & C: increasingly served by companies that offer package delivery of 'any size, any place, any time, any customer'
After-sales	Service is limited or none; consumer pays for service outside warranty	Service can be extensive and charged for Aims at repeat buy or modified buy Buyer evaluates supplier performance	B & C: lifecycle management of products and of customer relationships
Intermediaries			
Sales	Retail Direct for small suppliers	Direct Professional resellers (VAR)	B & C: bypassing intermediaries
Financial	None or indirect (credit-card company, bank)	Direct involvement of bank for credit letter, collateralized bill of lading etc. Insurers	B & C: both served by credit card companies
Logistics	Postal service Small package shippers	Logistics companies	B & C: global package delivery companies like FedEx, UPS, TPN

so they buy an open account rather than through a credit card or advance payment or payment on delivery.

Or is this consumer-business dichotomy really too simple? Does the future consumer deserve or demand customized products and truly personalized service? And might consumers be of more value if they are always considered as prospects (Silverstein, 1998), that is, if the relationship with them is managed as a lifetime relationship (lifetime value, LTV, see Chapter 6) or if purchases are considered as a lifetime opportunity for upgrading and maintenance whenever necessary or desirable? And could it be that consumers are better served if their purchasing is supported by several financial options such as buying on credit or opening an account or access to an open bank account, especially if there is a recurrent relationship with the supplier? Could it be that more value might be extracted from business purchasers by knowing their personal preferences, perhaps even up to the colour of products? Could it be that business buyers too are attracted by the one-off, unique opportunity offer that can only be bought *now*? After all, even a business purchaser is a person. And could it be that professional decisions to buy are influenced by what is seen at home, or with friends, or in the super-market? And finally, is business perhaps as interested in the convenience of credit and debit cards as the average consumer?

The examples mentioned before suggest that the answer to at least some of these questions should be a clear 'yes'. Perhaps, then, we should conclude that consumer and business markets have more in common than we traditionally tend to assume.

The drivers for the convergence of business-to-business and business-to-consumer electronic commerce are twofold. One driver is new information and communications technology, and derived from this the convergence of media. The other driver is the convergence of markets. Let's look at each of these in turn.

Technology as a driver

To exploit the commonalities between B-to-B and B-to-C, we need to have the means available to treat them alike in a more efficient or more effective way than treating them differently. Such means are now becom-ing increasingly available with the Internet, the Web and electronic commerce technologies like data mining, electronic payments and copy-right-protection software. They enable the convergence between B-to-C and B-to-B to be exploited in new online business models. They copy marketing strategies from the consumer world to the business world or vice versa. They exploit the similarities by identifying business processes for the design and delivery of consumer products with the corresponding business processes for business products, such that the B-to-B value chain and the B-to-C value chain are more identical than was ever possible before. They make it possible to address new markets where consumer and business customers are one and the same. The obvious result is lower investments, higher efficiency and increased economies of scale.

As well as rapidly emerging and ever higher-performing electronic commerce technologies, it is also the convergence of information and communication technologies that enables marketing strategies for business and consumer markets to come closer. Delivering across a multitude of platforms (PC, TV, CD-ROM, printed media), the same message enables the potential customer to be influenced at any time and any place. This can become a critical factor in the adoption of electronic commerce, as business buyers are often uncertain about the usefulness of these new technologies for their own business. It lends credibility to electronic commerce as a new way of doing business when the business buyers see in their immediate environment that friends, neighbours and children are already using very similar technology for personal use. Mass media are perfectly suited to bring this message (literally) home, such that the business buyer cannot escape from the impression that electronic commerce and the Internet are really becoming perfectly 'normal'.

Market convergence as a driver

The other driver for the convergence between business and consumer-oriented electronic commerce is the increasing overlap between home and business activities, that is, the fact that work and non-work are becoming intermingled for many people. With the rise of portfolio working (Handy, 1994) and with the increase in mobile and teleworking and with more flexible working hours, new markets arise where the business and consumer customer are one or at least very close to each other.

- The rise of SOHO companies (small office, home office), the largest growing segment of new companies today, is a reflection of this. SOHO businesses have created most of the new jobs in the US economy over the last 20 years and SOHO workers earn 28% more than the average office worker. It is an attractive market, mostly of one-person companies, where the owner is a consumer and a businessperson at the same time. Many of them depend on telecommunications facilities to telework with their clients. They are ready customers for Internet facilities and they will move easily into buying over the Internet, not being held back by conventional purchasing departments and procedures.
- Increasing consumer convenience by moving part of routine consumer shopping into companies is now being experimented with. ICL's employees can shop for groceries at the workplace, using their intranet. They thus save time in evening and weekend shopping. It may be an attractive proposition for the employees but is certainly also interesting for their employer, as employees will be under less pressure to deal with the hassle of supermarket shopping and thus be able to work better or longer. It is, of course, also an attractive proposition for the selected online groceries that will be allowed on the intranet. Conceptually it is then only a small step towards offering public services over the company's intranet, saving employees time in dealing with the public authorities.
- Business buyers can be profiled on their personal preferences as well as their company's buying patterns and preferences. La Redoute (http://www.redoute.fr), the largest French consumer catalogue company, has launched a reward programme aimed at business customers (as part of its B-to-B catalogue service, Redoute

Enterprises). Company employees are awarded with personal bonus points, which they can use to buy products from the Redoute Enterprise catalogue. This kind of convergence between the business buyer as a professional and the same person as a consumer is not necessarily a new phenomenon, but companies find new marketing strategies, enabled by technology, to exploit its commercial potential that was left untapped until now.

Opportunities for Convergent B-to-B and B-to-C Electronic Commerce

The classical Ansoff product–market matrix (Ansoff, 1988) is a useful tool for exploring business opportunities along the dimensions of products and markets. Opportunities are first in products that can be offered without much modification to both consumers and businesses. Examples are PCs, software and travel. Secondly, we would be looking for new markets in which consumers and businesses can to a large extent be treated alike. Examples are the SOHO market, but also markets like managers who buy professional information not only for consumption during working hours but also to absorb in their free time (such as this book, hopefully!). However, as we have seen, the analysis of opportunities for convergent consumer and business electronic commerce also addresses the dimension of 'process'. Therefore, we should also investigate the opportunity to make business processes identical for consumer and business markets, or to replicate ways of dealing with consumers in the business market or vice versa. Examples are in applying consumer-type mass-market customer interaction to the business world, or in personal product design support for consumer users.

Figure 7.8 gives an extended opportunity matrix along those three dimensions of product–market–process. Each of the eight boxes in this matrix has to be analysed as in the usual Ansoff type of analysis. This means determining the opportunities *in convergent B-to-B and B-to-C electronic commerce*, given the assumption that product or market or process changes *due to the convergence* between business and consumer electronic commerce. A few possibilities are also indicated in the diagram. For example, we have sold PCs to consumers, but we wish to tap into a new market that emerges because of the fact that the consumer and business customer roles start to overlap. We could then consider addressing the SOHO market or the market of independent professionals such as doctors, while still selling essentially the same PCs as before and with essentially the same sales approach, only adding that the PCs are a business tool too. This is more or less Dell's approach towards small businesses. As a next step, consider the box where the process approach changes, while the market and the product stay the same, for example, by

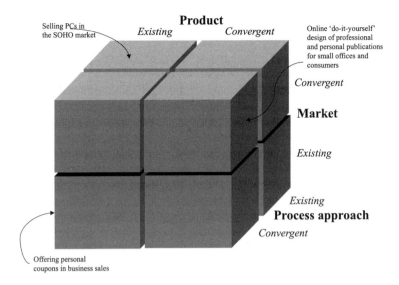

Figure 7.8 *Products–markets–processes opportunities when B-to-B and B-to-C converge*

introducing consumer-type sales processes such as personal coupons into business sales. Finally, consider the box where the product/service, as well as the market and the process approach, are all new. We could be looking, for example, for offering professional publishing to individual consumers who also run their own small business, using as a new process approach a self-service publication design facility. Clearly, this is addressing a new emergent market, with a new service (professional publishing) and through a new process approach (online design).

Identifying and choosing opportunities are closely related to market segmentation, targeting and positioning. Table 7.9 compares these steps for the 'traditional' approach and the approach in convergent electronic commerce. As an illustration, suppose as a furniture manufacturer you have identified similar benefits sought by both business and consumer buyers, notably in the SOHO market. The targeting could then be to address the buyers in this market who see their office work at home as an integral part of their private lifestyle. Positioning relative to competitors could be achieved by addressing the customer in both roles at the same time, that is, taking into account all of the customer's preferences, whether professional or consumer, in all sales. An example would be to stress that the office part of the house is designed in harmony with the (private) living part of the house. The result is something that Chan Kim and Mauborgne (1999) call 'creating new marketspace'. Instead of trying to compete head to head within the same product–

Table 7.9   *Segmentation, targeting and positioning when B-to-B and B-to-C converge*

Characteristic	Consumer (traditional)	Business (traditional)	Convergence (in e-commerce)
Segmentation	Demographics, lifestyle, personal benefits	Industry sector, business benefits	Segmenting can also include SOHO that is a mix of lifestyle and industry sector dimensions; or looks at combinations of business and personal needs that are associated to the same potential customer
Targeting	Either/or (exclusive)	Either/or (exclusive)	Both (inclusive)
Positioning	Relative to B-to-C competitors	Relative to B-to-B competitors	Serving the customer in any role and in both roles at the same time: depositioning traditional competitors

process–market box, the challenge is to move to a new marketspace that is found by looking across buyer groups (new markets), or across functional or emotional appeal to buyers (new process approach), or offers complementary products (new products).

Subsequently the marketing mix can be developed to arrive at the marketing model, as defined in Chapter 3. Table 7.10 provides these steps. The offer is to include furniture for both the office and private part of the house. Taking over customization practices from the B-to-B world, (mass) customization can be implemented. By offering self-service online design or online customization, the burden of customization can be shifted to the customer, at the same time increasing profiling possibilities. Near-realistic simulation onscreen would give the customer a better feel for what is being purchased—although lack of physical evidence may long remain a weak link in the chain. Pricing then also becomes much more fluid, depending on the customization but possibly also on trade-offs between price and quality or delivery time, which the customer can negotiate. Price lists are not very useful any more, as they suggest too much that 'one size fits all'.[145] Repeat sales stimulated by coupons can also be factored in, as part of the ultimate price determination.

Table 7.10 *Marketing mix (4P/7P) when B-to-C and B-to-B converge*

Characteristic	Consumer (traditional)	Business (traditional)	Convergence (in e-commerce)
Product/service	Mass-market	Custom	Mass customization
Delivery (place)	Shops/direct at home	Direct in company	For SOHO direct at home is the same as direct in the company For online products delivery is wherever the customer is online
Price	Fixed price lists; planned or regulated sell-outs/mark-down periods	Negotiated Fixed price lists	Negotiated or customized Disappearing price lists Auctions any time for anyone
Promotion	Promotional items are coupled to the specific purchase Mass-media advertising	Product bundling as promotion Specialist media advertising information based	Personalized advertising based on buying profile rather than on the distinction between consumer/business buyer—assume the business buyer is as keen on a good buy as the consumer Person-related incentives such as coupons can be coupled to business purchasing (with consideration of ethics!), especially for SOHO
People (supplier staff role)*	Selling oriented	Advice oriented	At least a basic level of personal advice to be provided (e.g. through a call centre); selling task left to Web site
Process*	Consumer often assumed to be passive	Business actively involved in specifying	Always active customer involvement (self-servicing) to increase efficiency for supplier and opportunities for profiling
Physical evidence*	Ambience, outfit etc. Importance to create confidence	Personal visit of salesperson Company visits, reference customer visits	Virtualize physical evidence, through simulation, virtual reality, and automated sales assistants ('personal agents') Enhance feeling of presence through virtual community of buyers and by integrating Internet interaction with phone, fax and offline physical presence e.g. paper ads

* As a service (online sales) is always also being provided, these factors are to be included next to the traditional 4P marketing mix.

The business models in Chapter 3 address ways to organize the flow of information, products and services. The preceding analysis provides insight into at least part of those flows, namely where the 'process' dimension is being addressed. Using the extended Ansoff matrix and considering segmentation, we can also get an impression of promising products/markets, which provides a starting point for determining benefits and sources of revenue. Continuing this way, we can then design business models that exploit the convergence between B-to-B and B-to-C electronic commerce. Taking into account targeting, positioning and the marketing mix, we ultimately arrive at marketing models for convergent B-to-B/B-to-C electronic commerce. Conversely, we can also take the 11 business models that were explicitly identified in Figure 3.1 and analyse whether they are appropriate for convergent B-to-B/B-to-C electronic commerce. Without going into a detailed analysis, the conclusion is that for most of these models examples can indeed be imagined or are already being implemented that exploit the convergence between B-to-B and B-to-C electronic commerce.

We conclude that the convergence of B-to-B and B-to-C electronic commerce is already becoming a reality for certain products, markets and value-creation and value-exchange processes. This convergence appears to be a persistent trend, driven by technology and by societal changes that lessen the strict separation between the personal and the professional life. Plenty of opportunities will be emerging, but to exploit them requires a rethink of traditional marketing.

New Technologies, New Business Models, New Policies: New Rules?

In this section we will not consider yet another scenario for future business-to-business electronic commerce, but instead try to take a helicopter view.

Internet electronic commerce is probably the most extraordinary economic phenomenon of recent years. Its growth is described in superlatives. Whole industry sectors are enthusiastically adopting the concept, while Internet entrepreneurs who exploit the new technologies and audaciously experiment with new business models are shaking other sectors to their very foundations.

The Internet is also increasingly having an impact as a social phenomenon, enabling people to engage in new forms of communication, in new relationships, in new forms of organization. It has become a political phenomenon too, having caught the interest of the highest political levels around the world. Politicians are excited about these new social and economic opportunities and at the same time worried about national sovereignty and security, harmful use, loss of cultural values, and ultimately loss of identity. Intense international activity is underway to come up with new policies that should help the economy and the society at large to move into the information age.

There is no end to the technological revolution that is the driver behind this. Computing and communications performance continues to improve as if driven by an iron hand. Moore's Law, which states that chip density will double every 18 months, still holds true. Optical computing is around the corner, with bio-computing and DNA computing already visible on the horizon. Quantum computing receives intense research interest although its feasibility is still highly speculative. At the system software and application level, the pace of change is very high too, although new versions are not always experienced as an improvement. Promising software and hardware are emerging in novel user interfaces, in new interaction models that are more natural and entertaining, in security support, in information management and navigation, as well as in business process interaction such as negotiation support, in knowledge management and learning, and in distributed business and work management. Public- and private-sector research 'thinktanks' have identified many exciting areas of future R&D in electronic commerce. For example, the European Union has created a targeted R&D/pilot programme on 'New Methods of Work and Electronic Commerce' as part of the Information Society Technologies Programme in the 5th Framework Programme.[146] The well-known Bled conference on electronic commerce has initiated collective brainstorming exercises about key research issues in electronic commerce.[147]

Looking at all of these developments from a distance, it is striking that there is a strong interdependence between new technologies, new business models and new societal thinking and policies. When this interdependency leads to mutual reinforcement it can become a virtuous cycle, delivering large benefits to business and consumers. Alternatively, if there is no such virtuous match the risk is real that there will be a great deal of wasted effort and capital and sometimes large-scale frustration or fear among businesses or citizens.

The interplay between technology, legislation and business practice is increasingly recognized in international and national policy making in the private and public sector.[148] Currently, electronic commerce is driven by rapid technology development. Yet, to exploit the new technologies, the legislative framework needs to be favourable and clear, and the appropriate business and social models need to be found. Legislation for business operations should facilitate rather than obstruct the deployment of new technology. An example of this is in legislation for the protection of copyright in the digital, networked environment. This has to take into account the emerging technology for electronic copyright-management systems (ECMS). Once this technology can be deployed on a worldwide scale (and there is still a lot of work to be done in terms of interoperability before this is achieved), the necessity reduces to compensate authors for private copying, for example by flat levies on information carriers.[149] Business cooperation can further help to create viable exploitation of emerging technologies by means of codes of conduct that create trust, and by promoting interoperability and best-practice examples.

It is not hard to think of similar cases where the interplay between technology, business practice—including self-regulation and codes of conduct—and if necessary also legislation can create certainty and at the same time provide an incentive to the supply side of the market. Example areas are security, privacy protection, taxation, certification and electronic contracting. The challenge to legislators is to maximize economic and social opportunities through a proactive approach that is well informed about technology scenarios. This will require thinking far ahead in view of the relatively long timescales of the legislative process, striving for technology-neutral legislation, making few assumptions about the most likely competitive industry configuration and maintaining a balance with industry self-regulation.[150]

The previous chapters have extensively addressed emerging business models and the experimentation that is going on to find such models and appropriate marketing strategies. To enable low-cost and fast experimentation of new business models in electronic commerce, new technology approaches will be required. In fact, it cannot be emphasized enough how much technology is the key driver for new business models. This is clear from the Internet explosion itself, driven particularly by WWW technology and by the integration of new technologies (Web/Internet) with the old (logistics and warehouse management) to build complete and very effective shopping systems. Emerging technologies that could change the rules of the game also include new devices (PDAs, WebTV, WebPhone), smart cards, embedded intelligence in products and processes and mobile e-commerce technologies. They also include e-commerce services technologies such as electronic payments, including micro-payments and digital cash, intellectual property management and negotiation support. New business-management technologies are required such as business objects and semantics management, value network and dynamic market builders, lightweight ERP and knowledge management. And finally, new interaction technologies, such as visualization technologies, may bring a revolution to electronic commerce including virtual reality, 3D, simulation as well as natural language support and e-commerce/ entertainment technologies.

Another key theme in this respect is convergence: the confluence of information technology, telecommunication technology and media technology. This is leading to giant acquisitions, mergers and joint ventures between broadcasters, telecom operators and information technology companies. Other companies with privileged access to the home such as energy companies are joining the pack. Such industry reorganization represented 15% of the total global acquisitions and mergers value in 1996, which was US$1 trillion.[151] Convergence is driven by the combination of digitization and exponentially growing computing and communications power. From a user point of view, convergence will lead to the same services being delivered on alternative platforms, such as phone over the Internet (Webphone) and WWW access via the TV (WebTV). It also leads to new services on which research is being conducted now, such as smart mobile phone applications or Internet-enabled cars. The PC as the dominant platform may have had its longest day. EACEM, the European Association of Consumer Electronics Manufacturers, points out that the WWW is increasingly developing as an entertainment and information facility for households and sees the TV as the more natural and social alternative.[152]

Rapid business model development could be a next phase in electronic commerce development and deployment, anticipating the globalization of legal frameworks, thousandfold increases in performance of technologies, and much better economic dynamics (Timmers, 1998f).

It is also striking that more than ever before the rules of the game seem to be changing on the basis of these new technologies, new business models and new policies. Whether in business or in politics, it is risky to assume that the current position is secure and certain. Visionaries are pointing to new rules for the digital economy. Others are emphasizing that sound business practice should nevertheless not be forgotten. In the current cases indications have been obtained of both.

Some of the new rules that we have seen in this book are as follows:

- The importance of network effects and, related to this, thinking in terms of interoperability.
- Moving fast—the 'fast and small can eat the big and slow'.
- Let the customer work for you—the rise of self-service and online environments built from customer contributions; this is also a road towards close customer–supplier relationships or, to put it less positively, it can lead to customer 'lock-in'.
- Rather than location ('place') it is the set of relationships ('space') that matters, as in value networks and dynamic markets.

Of the 'old rules' that still hold but that take on a new dimension, the cases and examples analysed here illustrated, among others, the following:

- Exploiting first-comer advantage and riding the experience curve have always been important, but with the hypergrowth possible in the Internet they become even more critical.
- Customer orientation, or 'think customer' or, as Kelly (1998) calls it, 'feed the Web [of customers] first' is foremost in lasting business success—it takes on a new dimension through the one-to-one philosophy.
- Market segmentation (and positioning) continues to be central to strategic marketing from which price, packaging etc. (4P or 7P) follow—even when economic rules seem counterintuitive, as is the case at times for digital content.
- Trust, as always, is the foundation for growth in the mass market— this holds for B-to-C as well as B-to-B electronic commerce. Brand presence and reputation continue to be the most powerful means to achieve trust—but old brands cannot assume that they also have the upper hand in electronic commerce.

It can be debated for a long time whether and which rules of the digital economy are different from those of the past. What is observably changing, however, is the competitive landscape. Already established companies are seeing new competition entering what they considered to be 'their' markets. Some contenders for the same market could be seen coming from far away: they are companies for which extension into neighbouring markets is a logical consequence of new technology or trends such as convergence and globalization. Often these are companies that are outgrowing their current market. Hungry for new sources of revenues they seek to extend their offering by closely related products and services or moving into nearby markets. However, other contenders are coming out of the blue. They are the dark horses. They are newly created companies that do not live by the rule book, that manage to change the rules of the market radically. In the electronic commerce industry, it is not uncommon to hear that what has to be feared most is not the biggest competitor but rather the competitor that does not yet exist!

Who are in B-to-B electronic commerce the incumbents, who are the can-be-expected contenders, and who are the may-be-competitors— the dark horses? Table 7.11 details some guesswork about potential competition in each of the scenarios that have been presented before. This is necessarily an incomplete overview of competition, as we can only speculate about the companies that do not yet exist today and that may be the key competitors of tomorrow.

Table 7.11 *Competition in B-to-B electronic commerce*

	Incumbents	Contenders	Dark horses
Value networks	• VANs like GEIS, EDS • DBMSs: Oracle, Informix etc. • SAP, Baan • Platform providers like Microsoft, HP, SUN • Integrators like Computer Associates, Logica, Origin ... • Sector-specific companies with EDI experience, Sterling, Harbinger, Kewell, EDI-TIE etc.	• Telecom operators • Banks • Independent third-party marketplace providers • E-malls such as Industry.Net, VerticalNet etc.	• Trust service providers • Information brokers, cataloguers such as Reed Elsevier, IHS, etc • ISPs • Internet auctioneers seeking value-added
Digital markets	• None	• Internet auctioneers • Third-party marketplaces • Virtual community providers • Independent matchmakers	• Agent technology companies • ISPs • Catalogue companies • New opportunity brokers equipped with Web-based analysis technology
Digital information business	• Market research companies like Gartner, Forrester, IDC; Reuters, Bloomberg; Dun & Bradstreet • Training companies • Consultancy companies like Andersen, CMG, Gartner etc. • Sector-specific information providers, such as Bertelsmann/Burda in healthcare; specific catalogue providers	• Information brokers with search engines, agent technology such as Acses, Jango, ZD-Net etc. • Information providers such as Pointcast, CNN, Netscape etc. • Data mining, such as NCR, Oracle etc.	• Startups in online training • Electronic commerce repositories/e-commerce portals • 'Convergent' companies, Microsoft, AT&T, Bertelsmann ...
B-to-B and B-to-C	• Telecom operators • Banks • SOHO equipment and service providers • Travel agencies	• Microsoft; Oracle • SOHO equipment providers branching out into related services such as finance • Virtual banks and insurers	• Yahoo, AOL, Amazon • Consumer electronics/entertainment, Sony, Philips • SOHO virtual communities

CONCLUSIONS

The conclusions listed here fall into two categories, namely those that address the two main hypotheses underlying this book, and those that bring together the main conclusions of the various chapters.

Hypotheses

The hypothesis set out in the introduction to this book, namely that existing strategic marketing theory and business economics are valid for the analysis of Internet electronic commerce, is broadly supported throughout this book. Applying these theories led to interesting new insights, such as about the relationship between transaction theory and the product/service offering of Internet B-to-B electronic commerce systems and an assessment of exploiting the characteristics of the Internet to build competitive advantage. However, marketing communications theory seems to be incomplete, in the sense that there is not yet an integrated marketing communications model for business-to-business electronic commerce. Market research also faces new challenges. Furthermore, the understanding of the networked organization of strategic business collaboration and competition needs to be deepened. New topics for research could therefore be identified, including:

- support for negotiation and contracting related to transaction cost theory;
- supporting trust structures in electronic commerce, such as quality systems;
- the relationship of electronic commerce systems with legal frameworks, public policies and private-sector collaboration;
- integrated marketing communications for business-to-business electronic commerce;
- networked market research;
- market process organization, as part of business process organization in dynamic markets.

The second hypothesis, that the business models classification and terminology developed in Chapter 3 are applicable to actual business cases, is well supported. As the conclusions of Chapter 4 about the case studies show, all cases could be mapped into the business model classification, and it has been possible to apply the terminology developed for business models throughout the descriptive and analysis chapters. Moreover, the distinction between business models and marketing models has been found useful in order to distinguish between the 'mechanics' of electronic commerce systems and the commercial strategies of those that operate these systems.

Summary of Main Conclusions

The main conclusions and results of this book can be summarized as follows.

Chapter 2 concluded that:

1. The Internet is radically different from any other sales channel because of its combination of ubiquitous and global presence, multimedia and immediate interactivity, digitization and integration, yet individualized handling of information.
2. It is also much more than a sales channel; it is a versatile tool for building key assets and exploiting new ways to create and deliver customer benefits. It is also a threat, as it increases competition and reduces switching costs for customers.

Chapter 3 provided:

3. The terminology and classification of business models, whose applicability has been mentioned before. It also introduced the concept of the marketing model, which combines the business model and marketing strategy.

Chapter 4 provided:

4. Detailed descriptions of the eight cases and it successfully mapped these in the business models classification scheme.

Chapter 5, about market structures, concluded that:

5. The companies in the case studies seek to build competitive advantage in global brand building and/or in profound knowledge of the specific industry with a central role in a network of business partners.
6. While technology is critical to realize the business model, it is usually not considered as the key sustainable competitive advantage.
7. Dynamic value network configurations are expected to emerge but are not (yet) realized in all cases. They require a convincing approach to building trust, loyalty and affiliation.
8. Transaction cost theory points to the need for negotiation and contracting support, possibly with third-party arbitration for flexible and *ad hoc* business relationships.

Chapter 6's conclusions and achievements include:

9. A customer benefits segmentation scheme for providers or operators of electronic trading systems which aim to build competitive advantage by delivering such benefits.
10. These benefits are different for routine and non-routine products trading, as well as different for the suppliers and buyers who trade through such systems.

11.   The Internet as a distribution channel for services or digital products supports most of the functions of traditional distribution channels, as well as new functions such as automated information brokerage and virtual community participation.

12.   Integrated marketing communications for Internet B-to-B electronic commerce are still poorly understood.

13.   The Internet as a communications channel is used, but to a limited extent only.

14.   Related to the threats and opportunities of the Internet mentioned before, it is considered important to address customer retention explicitly from the point of view of marketing communications.

15.   One-to-one marketing is relevant for business-to-business electronic commerce, but it is concluded that this approach is still only very limited applied in the cases studied here.

Chapter 7 focused on strategy development and scenarios for the future of business-to-business electronic commerce and showed that:

16.   New approaches to market research are needed to deal with the turbulent electronic commerce world. These may have to exploit the networked nature of the phenomenon itself.

17.   Adaptation of legal frameworks to global electronic commerce is progressing, but the challenge is to cope with the fast changes of technology. New entrepreneurs do not wait for all the legal rules to be in place.

18.   Many companies, especially market incumbents, are caught in a strategic dilemma, having to carry along their legacy and yet having to decide for a new strategy in the midst of high uncertainty.

19.   Value networks are here to stay and will evolve much further through Internet electronic commerce; dynamic markets are near. Both are at the heart of competitive strategy development.

20.   Digital information business is everywhere and opportunities are plentiful—but the successful business models are not yet clear. Digital information business forces us to rethink segmentation, pricing, packaging and other elements of the marketing mix.

21.   The convergence of B-to-B and B-to-C enabled by electronic commerce is an opportunity in certain product/markets/processes to reduce costs and address new markets. It also reflects societal trends.

22.   Is the networked economy governed by new rules? To some extent this seems to be the case—particularly striking is the increased importance of network effects and of relationships. Are the old rules of strategic marketing still valid? To a large extent the answer seems to be 'yes, provided that they are reinterpreted for electronic commerce'.

Bibliography

Ansoff, H.I. (1987) *Corporate Strategy*, 2nd edition, Harmondsworth: Penguin.

Ansoff, H.I. (1988) *The New Corporate Strategy*, New York: John Wiley & Sons.

Ansoff, H.I., McDonnel, E., Lindsey, L. and Beach, S. (1993) *Implanting Strategic Management*, 2nd edition, Englewoods Cliffs, NJ: Prentice Hall.

B2B journal (1998), February, http://www.b2b.com.

Bakos, Y., Brynjolfsson, E. and Lichtman, D. (1998) 'Shared Information Goods', http://ccs.mit.edu/erik/sig.pdf. August.

Benjamin, R.I. and Wigand, R.T. (1995) 'Electronic Markets and Virtual Value Chains on the Information Highway', *Sloan Management Review*, Winter, 62–72.

Blankenhorn, D. (1997) 'Crain Communication case study', Netmarketing, http://www.netb2b.com.

Bloch, M., Pigneur, Y. and Segev, A. (1996) 'On the Road of Electronic Commerce—a Business Value Framework, Gaining Competitive Advantage and Some Research Issues', March; Proceedings of the Ninth International EDI-IOS Conference, Bled, Slovenia, June; also online at http://www.stern.nyu.edu/~mbloch/docs/roadtoec/ec.htm.

Bollier, D. (1996) *The Future of Electronic Commerce*, The Aspen Institute, Queenstown, MD.

Bons, R. (1997) 'Designing Trustworthy Procedures for Open Electronic Commerce', dissertation Erasmus University Rotterdam.

Booz·Allen and Hamilton (1997) report prepared for the European Commission for the G7 Global Marketplace for SMEs Annual Conference, Bonn, April, available at http://www.ispo.cec.be/ecommerce/doc2.html.

Brynjolfsson, E., Malone, T., Gurbakani, V. and Kambil, A. (1994) 'Does Information Technology Lead to Smaller Firms?', *Management Science*, Vol. 40, No. 12, also at http://ccs.mit.edu/CCSWP123/CCSWP123.html.

Brynjolfsson, E., Renshaw, A.A. and Van Alstyne, M. (1997) 'The Matrix of Change: a Tool for Business Process Reengineering', January, http://www.mit.edu/.

Buckley, E., Faux, I., Kesteloot, P., Sauer, A. and Stewing, F.-J. (1997) 'GEN—Turning Engineering Knowledge into an Accessible Corporate Asset', *ISFAA-97 Electronic Forum*.

Chan Kim, W. and Mauborgne, R. (1999) 'Creating New Market Space', *Harvard Business Review*, January–February, 83–93.

Chapman, K. (1979) '*People, Pattern and Process: an Introduction to Human Geography*', Edward Arnold, London.

Choi, S.-Y., Stahl, D.O. and Whinston, A.B. (1997) *The Economics of Electronic Commerce*, Macmillan Technical Publishing, Indianapolis.

Coase, R.H. (1937) 'The Nature of the Firm', *Economica*, IV, 386–405; reprinted in Putterman, L. (1989), *The Economic Nature of the Firm: a Reader*, Chapter 5, Cambridge University Press.

CommerceNet (1998) '1998 eCommerce Barriers and Inhibitors', March, see also http://www.commerce.net/.

Cool, K. (1997) 'The Competitiveness of European Industry', inauguration speech for the BP Chair in European Competitiveness, INSEAD, 3 June.

Cordella, A. and Simon, K. (1997) 'The Impact of Information Technology on Transaction and Co-ordination Cost', *Proceedings of the 20th IRIS Conference*, Hankø, Norway, August.

Coulson-Thomas, C. (1997) *Business Process Re-engineering: Myth and Reality*, London: Kogan Page.

Datamonitor (1997) *Business-to-Business Electronic Commerce: Exploiting Market Opportunities in the Extranet Age*, Datamonitor.

Dibb, S. (1994) Services marketing survey and interview questionnaire internal paper, Warwick Business School.

Dibb, S., Simkin, L., Pride, W. and Ferrell, O. (1991) *Marketing, Concepts and Strategies*, Houghton Mifflin, Boston.

Dolfsma, W. (1999) 'Consumers as Subcontractors on Electronic Markets', *First Monday*, Vol. 4, No. 1, 1 March.

DTI (1997) 'Moving into the Information Society—an International Benchmarking Study', study by Spectrum Strategy Consultants, UK, published by the Department of Trade and Industry, UK, as part of the Information Society Initiative, August.

ECOM (1996) Electronic Commerce Association of Japan.

Egan, C. (1995) *Creating Organizational Advantage*, Butterworth Heinemann, Oxford.

Electronic Commerce Weekly (1997) 12 May.

European Commission (1996a) *Summary of the Proceedings of the Business on the Web Conference*, http://www.cordis.lu/esprit/src/busweb.htm. For the full proceedings contact the European Commission, DGIII, ecommerce@dg3.ce.be.

European Commission (1996b) *European Electronic Commerce Initiatives*, http://www.ispo.cec.be/infosoc/promo/seminar/eeci.html.

European Commission (1996c) *Introduction to Electronic Commerce*, DGIII/F/6, http://www.ispo.cec.be/ecommerce/whatis.html.

European Commission (1997a) *Electronic Commerce Better Practice*, case study book published by the European Commission as part of the G7 Global Marketplace for SMEs Project. A Web version can be found at http://www.ispo.cec.be/ecommerce/bonn.html.

European Commission (1997b) presentations as prepared by the European Commission, Directorate-General III/F/6, 1997.

European Commission DGXIII (1997c) 'The Evolution of the Internet and the WWW in Europe', study by IDATE, TNO, Databank Consulting, October.

European Commission (1998a) *Synopses of Technology for Business Processes and Electronic Commerce Projects*, June, also available online at http://www.cordis.lu/esprit/src/tbp-home.htm.

European Commission (1998b) *Accelerating Electronic Commerce in Europe*, 2nd edition, November, also available online at http://www.ispo.cec.be/ecommerce/ecbook.html.

European Commission (1998c) *Business Transformation through Technology, 21 Striking Cases from Technologies for Business Processes.*

European Union (1996) *Basic Statistics Data, 1996.*

Everett-Thorp, K. (1997) 'Web Advertising Secrets', *C-Net*, 16 Dec, http://www.cnet.com/Content/Builder/Advertising.

Fariselli, P., Oughton, C., Picory, C. and Sugden, R. (1997) 'Electronic Commerce and the Future for SMEs in a Global Marketplace: Opportunities and Public Policy Requirements', http://www.ispo.cec.be/ecommerce/doc4.html.

Financial Times (1998) 21–22 March.

Forrester Research (1997) *Sizing Intercompany Commerce*, 28 July.

Forrester Research (1998a) 'Resizing On-line Business Trade', December.

Forrester Research (1998b) 'The Commerce Threshold', *Forrester Reports on Business Trade & Technology Strategies*, Vol. 2, No. 4, October.

G7 Global Marketplace for SMEs Project (1997) Reports from workshops held in the European part of the Project, http://www.ispo.cec.be/ecommerce/g7init.html.

Gartner (1997) 'Electronic Marketplaces: Management and Technical Implications', *Inside Gartner Group This Week*, 2 April.

Gebauer, J. and Segev, A. (1998) 'Assessing Internet-based Procurement to Support the Virtual Enterprise', *Proceedings of 21st Century Commerce 1998 Conference*, Long Beach, 26–29 Oct.

Goldfinger, C. (1997) 'Intangible Economy and its Implications for Statistics and Statisticians', *International Statistical Review*, Vol. 65, No. 2, 191–220.

Goldhoff, R. and Skoog, D. (1996) 'FedEx on the Web', *Proceedings Business on the Web Conference*, Paris, May, European Commission.

Grabowski, H. and Pocsai, Zs. (1997) *Electronic Marketplace Beyond the Vision*, Universität Fridericiana Karlsruhe.

Hagel, J. and Armstrong. A. (1997) *Net Gain: Expanding Markets through Virtual Communities*, Harvard Business School Press, Boston.

Hammer, M. (1996) *Beyond Reengineering*, HarperCollins Business, London.

Hammer, M. and Champy, J. (1994) *Reengineering the Corporation*, HarperCollins Business.

Handy. C. (1994) *The Empty Raincoat*, Random House, London.

Hoffman, D. and Novak, T. (1995) 'Marketing in Hypermedia Computer-Mediated Environments: Conceptual Foundations', July, http://www2000.ogsm.vanderbilt.edu.

Hoffman, D., Novak, T., and Chatterjee, P. (1995) 'Commercial Scenarios for the Web: Opportunities and Challenges', *Journal of Computer-Mediated Communication*, Vol. 1, No. 3, Dec.

IDC (1998) as presented at its Monaco Conference, 8–10 May.

Jelassi, T. and Lai, H.-S. (1996) 'CitiusNet: the Emergence of a Global Electronic Market', Society for Information Management, http://www.simnet.org. See also http://www.citius.fr.

Johnson, J. (1997) 'Global Information Infrastructure Commission (http://www.gii.org)', as presented at the *G7 Global Marketplace for SMEs Policy Group* meeting of 16 Sept in Ottawa, Canada.

Kalakota, R. and Whinston, A. (1996) *Frontiers of Electronic Commerce*, Addison-Wesley, Reading, MA.

Kelly, K. (1998) *New Rules for the New Economy: 10 Ways the Network Economy is Changing Everything*, Fourth Estate, London.

Kerridge, S., Slade, A., Kerridge, S. and Ginty, K. (1998) 'SUPPLYPOINT: Electronic Procurement Using Virtual Supply Chains—An overview', *International Journal of Electronic Markets*, Vol. 8, No. 3, 28–31.

Klein, S. (1996) EDI und Internet.

Kopriwa, A. (1997) 'Electronic Commerce and the Internet', GartnerGroup Briefing Presentation.

Kotler, P. (1991) *Marketing Management, Analysis, Planning, Implementation and Control*, Prentice-Hall, Englewood Cliffs.

KPMG (1997) *Survey of UK Business*.

KPMG (1998) Analysis of e-Christmas at http://www.kpmg.co.uk.

Kraut, R., Steinfeld, C. and Plummer, A. (1997) 'The Impact of Interorganizational Networks on Buyer-Seller Relationships', *Journal for Computer Mediated Communication*, Vol. 1, issue 3.

Kroll, L., Pitta, J. and Lyons, D. (1998) 'World Weary Web', *Forbes Home*, 28 December.

Lee, H.G. (1997) 'AUCNET: Electronic Intermediary for Used-Car Transactions', *International Journal of Electronic Markets*, Vol. 7, No. 4, 24–28.

Leerink, J. (1998) 'De virtuele fabrikant', *Proceedings of the ECP.NL National Electronic Commerce Congress 1998*.

Lipsey, R.G., Steiner, P.O., Purvis, D.D. and Courant, P.N. (1990) *Economics*, 9th edn, Harper & Row, New York.

McDonald, Malcolm H.B. (1997) *Marketing Plans: How to Prepare Them, How to Use Them*, Butterworth-Heinemann, Oxford.

Michalski, J. (1995) 'People are the Killer App', *Forbes ASAP*, June 5, 120–122.

Mougayar, W. (1997) *Opening Digital Markets, Advanced Strategies for Internet-driven Commerce*, Cybermanagement Publications, Toronto.

Mowshowitz, A. (1997) 'Virtual Organization', *Communications of the ACM*, Vol. 40, No. 9, Sept.

Norman, R. and Ramirez, R. (1993) 'From Value Chain to Value Constellation', *Harvard Business Review*, July–August, 65–77.

OECD (1997) OECD Paris, Committee for Information, Computer and Communications Policy, OCDE/GD(97)185, 1997. See also http://www.oecd.org.

Peppers, D. and Rogers, M. (1997a) *Enterprise One to One: Tools for Competing in the Interactive Age*, Bantam Doubleday Dell, New York.

Peppers, D. and Rogers, M. (1997b) *The One to One Future: Building Relationships One Customer at a Time*, Bantam Doubleday Dell, New York.

Porter, M. (1980) *Competitive Strategy, Techniques for Analyzing Industries and Competitors*, Free Press, New York.

Porter, M. (1985) *Competitive Advantage*, New York. Free Press.

Porter, M. and Millar, V. (1985) 'How Information Gives You Competitive Advantage', *Harvard Business Review*, July–August, 149–160.

Price Waterhouse (1998) *Annual Technology Forecast*, 26 March, http://www.pw.com/.

Quinn, J.B. (1980) *Strategies for Change: Logical Incrementalism*, The Irwin Series in Management on Behavioural Sciences, Richard D. Irwin.

Radeke, E. (1997) GENIAL—Global Engineering Networking Intelligent Access Libraries, GEN White Paper, August.

Radeke, E. and Seifert. L. (1998) GENIAL: Enabling Intelligent Access to Internal and External Engineering Information, paper presented at CAD '98 Tele-CAD Produktentwicklung in Netzwerken, Darmstadt, Germany.

Rayport, J.F. and Sviolka, J.J. (1995) 'Exploiting the Virtual Value Chain', *Harvard Business Review*, November–December, 75–85.

Report on Electronic Commerce (1998) Vol. 5, No. 4.

Rethfeld, U. (1994) 'Manufacturing and the Information Highway', keynote address at the *ESPRIT-CIME, 10th Annual Conference*, 5–7 Oct, Copenhagen.

Rethfeld, U. (1997) 'Global Engineering Network: Vision, Status and Demo', *Procedures the 2nd Symposium on Global Engineering Networking (GEN'97)*, Antwerp, April.

Rogers, E.M. (1962) *Diffusion of Innovations*, New York: Free Press.

Salminen, V., Buckley, E., Malinen, P., Ritvas, J., Silakoski, S. and Sauer, A. (1997) 'Global Engineering Networking—Turning Engineering Knowledge into an Accessible Corporate Asset', *International Conference on Engineering Design—ICED 97*, Tampere, August 19–21.

Sarkar, M., Butler, B. and Steinfield, C. (1995) 'Intermediaries and Cybermediaries: a Continuing Role for Mediating Players in the Electronic Marketplace', *Journal of Computer-Mediated Communication*, Vol. 1, No. 3, December (http://www.ascusc.org/jcmc).

Schwartz, E. (1997) *Webonomics: Nine Essential Principles for Growing Your Business on the World Wide Web*, Broadway Books, New York.

Shapiro, C. and Varian, H.R. (1998) *Information Rules: a Strategic Guide to the Network Economy*, Harvard Business School Press, Boston.

Silverstein, B. (1998) *Business-to-Business Marketing*, Maximum Press.

Snow, C.C., Miles, R.E. and Coleman, H.J. (1992) 'Managing 21st Century Network Organisations', *Organisational Dynamics*, Vol. 20, No. 3, 5–20.

Steinfeld, C. and Klein, S. (eds.) (1999) 'Local versus Global Issues in Electronic Commerce', *International Journal of Electronic Markets*, Routledge, Vol. 9, No. 2, May.

Strong, E. K. (1925) *The Psychology of Selling*, New York: McGraw-Hill.

Tapscott, D., Lowry, A. and Ticoll, D. (eds.) (1998) 'Blueprint to the Digital Economy', McGraw-Hill, New York.

Teunissen, W. (1997) 'Doing Electronic Components Distribution Business Online', *Proceedings G7 Global Marketplace for SMEs Conference*, Bonn, April, European Commission.

Timmers, P.H.A. (1997a) *Electronic Commerce Policy and Industry Involvement*, Hungary: Hiradástechnika.

Timmers, P.H.A. (1997b) 'Internet Electronic Commerce Business Models', November, http://www.ispo.cec.be/ecommerce/busimod.htm.

Timmers, P.H.A. (1998b) 'Electronic Commerce Business Models—New Ways of Doing Business with the Internet', in *WHO-IS* (who-is-who in electronic commerce), April, Duesseldorf: Empirica.

Timmers, P.H.A. (1998c) 'Electronic Commerce and the European Commission', in D'Haenens, L. (ed.), *Canada-EU in Cyberspace: Cyberidentities*, Antwerpen.

Timmers, P.H.A. (1998d) 'Business Models for Electronic Markets', *International Journal of Electronic Markets*, Vol. 98, No. 2, July, 3–8.

Timmers, P.H.A. (1998e) 'Information Society Technologies in the Fifth Framework Programme of European Union R&D', *Journal of Strategic Information Systems*, Vol. 7, No. 4, December.

Timmers, P.H.A. (1998f) 'The Future of Electronic Commerce', *Proceedings of 21st Century Commerce 1998 Conference*, Long Beach, 26–29 October.

Timmers, P., Stanford-Smith, B. and Kidd, P. (eds) (1998) 'Opening Up New Opportunities for Business', *Proceedings of the G8 Global Marketplace for*

SMEs Electronic Commerce Conference, Manchester, September, Cheshire Henbury, Macclesfield, UK.

Timmers, P. and Van der Veer, J. (1999a) 'Europa speelt tweede viool in elektronische handel', *Automatiseringgids*, 5 March, 17.

Timmers P.H.A. (1999b) 'Think Global-Act Local: The Challenge of Thriving in the Global Digital Economy', *Proceedings of 12th Bled International Electronic Commerce Conference*, Vol. II, Bled, June, Moderna Organizacija.

Tradezone (1998) Website http://tradezone.onyx.net/ and internal company documents 'Tradezone Outline Technical Specification' and 'Tradezone Business Concept' presentation.

Upton, D.M., and McAfee, A. (1996) 'The Real Virtual Factory', *Harvard Business Review*, July–August, 12–133.

Uyttendaele, K. (1998) 'Internet Business and SMES: Catalysts for the New Nerwork Economy' in Timmers, P., Stanford-Smith, B. and Kidd, P. (eds) *Opening up New Opportunities for Business, Proceedings of the G8 Global Marketplace for SMEs Electronic Commerce Conference*, Manchester, September, Cheshire Henbury.

Van Alstyne, M. (1997) 'The State of Network Organizations: A Survey in Three Frameworks', *Journal of Organizational Computing*, Vol. 7, No. 3.

Varian, H.R. (1997) 'Differential Pricing and Efficiency', *First Monday*, No. 2, http://www.firstmonday.dk/.

Vassos, T. (1996) *Strategic Internet Marketing*, Que Corporation, Indianapolis.

Venkatraman, N. (1994) 'IT-Enabled Business Transformation: from Automation to Business Scope Redefinition', *Sloan Management Review*, Vol. 35, No. 2, Winter, 73–87.

Vittet-Philippe, P. (1998) 'US and EU Policies for Global Electronic Commerce— a Comparative Analysis of the US "Magaziner Paper" and of the EU Communication "A European Initiative in Electronic Commerce"', *Computer Law & Security Report*, Vol. 14, No. 2.

Warwick (1998) Warwick Business Process Resource Centre, http://bprc. warwick.ac.uk.

Whittington, R. (1993) *What Is Strategy—and Does It Matter?*, London: Routledge.

Wigand, R.J. and Benjamin, R.I. (1995) 'Electronic Commerce: Effects on Electronic Markets', *Journal of Computer-Mediated Communication*, Vol. 1, No. 3, December.

Williamson, O.E. (1985) *The Economic Institutions of Capitalism*, New York: Free Press.

Williamson, O.E. (1986) *Economic Organisation: Firms, Markets and Policy Control*, Harvester Press.

Wyckoff, A. (1997) 'Imagining the Impact of Electronic Commerce', *The OECD Observer*, No. 208, October/November.

Yankee Group (1997) data as quoted in internal documentation provided by Globana.

Young, K., Malhotra, A., El Sawy, O. and Gosain, S. (1996) 'The Relentless Pursuit of "Free. Perfect. Now": IT-Enabled Value Innovation at Marshall Industries'; Society for Information Management, http://www.simnet.org/ public/programs/capital/97paper/paper1.html.

Endnotes

1. For this definition and a comparison of traditional and electronic commerce, see chapter 1 of the European Initiative in Electronic Commerce, European Commission, April 1997, http://www.cordis.lu/esprit/src/ecomcom.htm; as well as related publications at http://www.ispo.cec.be/Ecommerce/.
2. For example see Forrester Research report, *Sizing Intercompany Commerce*, 28 July 1997, see also http://www.forrester.com.
3. McDonald (1997), notably the marketing planning framework of Chapter 13, as summarized on p. 432.
4. EDI take-up in Europe is referenced in 'Introduction to Electronic Commerce', http://www.ispo.cec.be/ecommerce/whatis.html, and in Kalakota and Whinston (1996), p. 334.
5. NUA, 2 March 1999, http://www.nua.ie.
6. Grainger study referred to in Chapter 3 of the US government's *The Emerging Digital Economy* report (1998), http://www.ecommerce.gov/emerging.htm.
7. CyberAtlas, 11 December 1998, http://www.cyberatlas.internet.com/professional/mro.html.
8. Forrester Group (1998), as reported by InternetNews.com on 18 December 1998; Yankee Group December 1996; Price Waterhouse *Annual Technology Forecast*, 26 March 1998, http://www.pw.com/; IDC, as presented at its Monaco Conference, 8–10 May 1998.
9. For the Information Society Technologies (IST) Programme and other EU programmes, see http://www.cordis.lu. A short description of the IST Programme and specifically of its Key Action about 'New Methods of Work and Electronic Commerce' can be found in Timmers (1998e).
10. Stefan Klein, in *EDI und Internet*, compared the cost of EDI via a value-added network service provider (VANS) and via an Internet service provider, for a company with 15 business partners, having 135 transactions/week, as $12 300 versus $447 per annum.
11. As an example, hosting a Web site and giving the company its own domain name (i.e. address on the Internet) is being offered for a set-up cost of £200 and annual fee of £250.
12. James Roper, Interactive Retail Management Group IMRG UK, private communications.
13. The contest Les eLectrophées was organized in 1998–99 by the French Ministry of Economy, Finance and Industry, http://www.finances.gouv.fr/electrophees.
14. See 'Introduction to Electronic Commerce', published by the European Commission DGIII, and available at http://www.ispo.cec.be/ecommerce/whatis.html; Booz-Allen-Hamilton, report prepared for the European Commission for the G7 Global Marketplace for SMEs Annual Conference, Bonn, April 1997, available at http://www.ispo.cec.be/ecommerce/doc2.html; CommerceNet, '1998 eCommerce Barriers and Inhibitors', March 1998, see also http://www.commerce.net/.

15. See reports from workshops held in the European part of the G7 Global Marketplace for SMEs Project, http://www.ispo.cec.be/ecommerce/g7init.html; and the European Initiative in Electronic Commerce.

16. KPMG analysis of e-Christmas, as presented to the European Commission, March 1998. The KPMG report is also available at http://www.kpmg.co.uk.

17. Andersen Consulting, 'eEurope', a survey among about 350 European and 40 American companies, 1998.

18. Details per country are provided by IDATE in the World Atlas of the Internet (http://www.idate.fr).

19. Chapman (1979) highlights the importance of our spatial perception for decision making.

20. Private communication, M. Gnat, European Association of Purchasers.

21. These trends were pointed out to me by Jeffrey Baumgartner.

22. http://www.mitsukoshi.co.jp. According to a Mitsukoshi representative there is a convenience store within a few hundred metres of most Japanese people.

23. Strong (1925). A somewhat different analysis of the stages of product/service adoption is presented in Chapter 6, see also Table 6.7.

24. Bloch, Pigneur and Segev (1996), also online at http://www.stern.nyu.edu/~mbloch/docs/roadtoec/ec.htm.

25. Upton and McAfee (1996). They report on aircraft manufacturing where the cost of transfers of designs has fallen from $400 to $4 by using the Aerotech Service Group Internet-based network.

26. http://www.andrew.cmu.edu/user/kc53/history.htm.

27. *Financial Times*, 21–22 March 1998.

28. B2B News: http://www.doyle.com.

29. http://nanothinc.com/Nanothinc/ChairmansIntro/businessmodel.html.

30. La Redoute, the largest French consumer catalogue company, has recently launched a new reward programme aimed at business customers (Redoute Enterprise). Company employees are awarded bonus points which they can use to buy products from the Redoute Enterprise catalogue. Through personalized catalogues and the bonus point scheme they tie in the customer and make it more difficult to switch to another supplier. From 'Consumers or Business to Business or Both Changing Side?', *Catalog & Mail Order Business*, Issue 4, March 1996, p. 3.

31. Strategic Marketing Course, Warwick Business School.

32. Quote from marketing representative of the Internet Shopping Network at the Milan Electronic Commerce Conference, September 1996.

33. For European electronic commerce R&D and pilot projects, see *Accelerating Electronic Commerce in Europe*, European Commission (1998b), also available at http://www.ispo.cec.be/ecommerce/ecbook.htm. For information about the clustering of these projects around themes such as security, payments, IPR, agent technologies, transaction management, retail, tourism, logistics, techno-legal issues, awareness and other topics, see http://www.ispo.cec.be/ecommerce/clusters.htm. For detailed summaries of other ESPRIT projects, see also http://www.cordis.lu/esprit/home.html.

34. The inventory of European electronic commerce-related projects captured in *Accelerating Electronic Commerce in Europe* (http://www.ispo.cec.be/ecommerce/ecbook.htm) was a particularly useful tool to identify business models and classify projects accordingly.

35. One of the challenges in electronic commerce is to define the building blocks of business, that is, business objects and business processes, and to develop a widely accepted description or language for them. Several industry consortia have taken up the challenge, including the Object Management Group OMG, Open Buying on the Internet OBI, EBES and CommerceNet.

36. A well-known example like Amazon.com is not just an e-shop, as it critically depends on a new organization of inventory and logistics management; and also adds virtual community-type value by means of book reviews, readers' opinions etc.

37. Private communications BT, Onyx.

38. See synopsis of ESPRIT Technology for Business Processes and Electronic Commerce projects, European Commission (1998a), also at http://www.cordis.lu/esprit/src/tbp-home.htm.

39. See in particular the ESPRIT HPCN projects addressing the automotive, aerospace and space sectors.
40. For an evaluation of this experiment, see http://www.kpmg.co.uk.
41. 'CitiusNet: The Emergence of a Global Electronic Market', Tawfik Jelassi, INSEAD and EAMS, Han-Sheong Lai, CitiusNet SA, Society for Information Management, 1996, http://www.simnet.org. See also http://www.citius.fr.
42. See projects references on http://www.cordis.lu/esprit/home.html.
43. *Business Week*, 21 December 1998.
44. The recent evolution of Industry.Net is a counter-example to the trend towards more integration. The new owners of Industry.Net, IHS, have decided to take it back to its roots as an industry mall. It thereby does not pursue the repositioning of Industry.Net as a third-party marketplace, which was initiated by the previous owner Perot (who was implementing a tight integration between transactions and marketing).
45. ABN-AMRO, Bank of America, Chase Manhattan, Deutsche Bank/Bankers Trust, Citibank, Barclays and HypoVereinsbank AG announced in October 1998 that, together with Certco Inc, they would offer global digital certification services (informally known as the Roosevelt alliance).
46. An example in the consumer area is SeniorNet (http://www.seniornet.com), which offers members for a yearly fee of $35 access to the virtual community as well as a quarterly newsletter, discounts on computer products and access to computer classes.
47. *Internet News*, 23 July 1998,
    http://www.internetnews.com/ec-news/1998/07/2301-onsale.html.
48. http://www.netb2b.com.
49. For a summary of the proceedings of the Business on the Web conference, see http://www.cordis.lu/esprit/src/busweb.htm. For the full proceedings, contact the European Commission, DGIII, ecommerce@cec.be.
50. Kerry M. Young; Marshall Industries; Arvind Malhotra, University of Southern California; Omar A. El Sawy, University of Southern California; and Sanjay Gosain, University of Southern California, 'The Relentless Pursuit of "Free. Perfect. Now"': IT-Enabled Value Innovation at Marshall Industries', Society for Information Management, 1996,
    http://www.simnet.org/public/programs/capital/97paper/paper1.html;
    Wim Teunissen, SEI, 'Doing Electronic Components Distribution Business Online', *Proceedings G7 Global Marketplace for SMEs Conference*, Bonn, April 1997, p. 199, European Commission; *Electronic Commerce Better Practice*, case study book published by the European Commission as part of the G7 Global Marketplace for SMEs Project. A Web version can be found at http://www.ispo.cec.be/ecommerce/bonn.html; Bob Edelman, Marshall, private communication; Mougayar, (1997), pp. 201–11.
51. http://www.m1to1.com/success_stories/ss_bt_19.html.
52. Joshua Macht (1996), p. 34 illustrates this with the Baron Messenger Service in Miami, a small, $1.5 million courier who initially invested $60 000, with $15 000 yearly upgrades. The company reschedules their drivers while they are on the road, for fast local delivery. By capturing customer information there is minimal need for customers to provide tedious details, and at the same time a customer information base is being built up for marketing purposes. This company is claimed to be faster and of better quality than large delivery companies.
53. Quote from Vernon Keenan, Zona Research, Mountain View, CA in a Dec 1997 Crain Communication case study by Dana Blankenhorn published by Netmarketing at http://www.netb2b.com.
54. *Electronic Commerce Weekly*, 12 May 1997.
55. Although its number of 'buying members' increased from 200 000 to 450 000, these are not paying, nor necessarily active, buyers. Instead, the 'seller members', who do pay, seem to have defected in large numbers. The data quoted here are from 1996 information provided by IndustryNet for the CommerceNet VIP Award Nomination, and from February 1998 information by IHS on the Industry.Net Web site.
56. Amazon works with global shipping companies, such as DHL, which may be able to fulfil this last requirement. This is a *de facto* market dominance choice. The alternative of working with local logistics companies is not feasible as this would require global interoperability of logistics systems, which does not (yet) exist. There is no global

inventory company, nor global compatibility and interconnection of inventory management systems. Therefore there are still barriers for Amazon to become a global bookstore in the wide sense.

57. They thus can get 45% + 15% = 60% as revenue on their own list price of their books.
58. http://web.iese.edu/Subirana/DOCS-V1/princip.htm.
59. 'CitiusNet: The Emergence of a Global Electronic Market', Tawfik Jelassi, INSEAD and EAMS, Han-Sheong Lai, CitiusNet SA, Society for Information Management, 1996, http://www.simnet.org; *European Electronic Commerce Initiatives*, 1996, http://www.ispo.cec.be/infosoc/promo/seminar/eeci.html.
60. Interview with Mrs Ilse van Rijsbergen, founder and Marketing Manager of CitiusNet Belgium, January 1998 who kindly made available the information and diagrams in this section.
61. Economic study into Citius benefits (Mrs van Rijsbergen).
62. Intershop is a 200-person company, led by a 28-year-old entrepreneur (1998), and based in Jena (east part of Germany). Intershop supplies business-to-consumer and business-to-business Internet shopping technology.
63. Private communication, 14 January 1998.
64. The Interbanks Standards Association ISABEL is a privately funded initiative that originates from the banking sector in Belgium. The country has a very advanced electronic banking system. 64 000 companies of the approx. 250 000 companies in Belgium were using electronic banking in 1997. It is also a home market where 70% of the companies do not export or import. The electronic banking network puts a strong emphasis on a multibank approach, which deploys common international standards, and on security issues between the customer–bank and customer–customer relationship. ISABEL offers to all companies in Belgium in the first instance secure Internet access to accounts, and in the second instance trading services such as certification and digital signatures. It is open to companies from the non-banking sector to share the high development costs. ISABEL expects that in four years' time 60% of the Belgian companies will be connected to the ISANET server. It is mainly a national initiative, although it aims at expanding the project to serve neighbouring countries where several Belgian banks have subsidiaries. See also http://www.ispo.cec.be/ecommerce/invencom.htm#isabel.
65. Web site http://tradezone.onyx.net/, and internal company documents 'Tradezone Outline Technical Specification' and 'Tradezone Business Concept' presentation; 'Tradezone International, an Electronic Commerce Case Study on Business to Business Third Party Trading Services Using the Internet, From a Service-provider's Perspective', Dr David Horne, CommerceNet Global Summit, November 1998, Madrid.
66. In particular the ESPRIT projects E2S, MULTIPLEXC, CASBA, see http://www.cordis.lu/esprit/home.htm.
67. Michael Jeffries, personal communications, November 1997 and February 1998.
68. In the *NRC Handelsblad* of 4 March 1998, Albert Heijn's president of the board Van der Hoeven announced that the retailer would start to offer banking services. He stated that 'after all we get many more people in our shops than banks in their offices', and that it would build on its reputation 'which inspires confidence, means quality'. The banking services would fit in the one-stop shopping that consumers want and with the daily shopping (implying that no services would be sold that require a lot of explanation).
69. Rethfeld (1994). At the conference Mr Rethfeld introduced for the first time the core ideas of the 'GEN concept, then called the 'European Engineering Network'. During a panel discussion, at the suggestion of G. Metakides, Director of the ESPRIT Programme, 'European' was changed to 'Global'. For an extensive set of references to recent manufacturing research see the Warwick Business Process Resource Centre, http://bprc.warwick.ac.uk.
70. Procat-GEN can be found at http://www.c-lab.de/procat.
71. Interviews with Dr Ulrich Rethfeld, Globana, February 1998 and January 1999.
72. Rethfeld (1997); 'Electronic Marketplace Beyond the Vision', H. Grabowski, Zs. Pocsai, Universität Fridericiana Karlsruhe; Radeke and Seifert (1997); Radeke (1997). See also ESPRIT electronic commerce-related projects GEN, GENIAL, AGENTISME at http://www.ispo.cec.be/ecommerce/ecomproj.htm; Buckley *et al.*

(1997); 'Technologies and Architectures for Electronic Commerce', report from workshop at the IST'98 conference, 2 December 1998, Vienna, also available at http://www.ispo.cec.be/ecommerce/agresults.htm.
73. PartNET: 'Parts Information Network', http://www.part.net.
74. E.g. ISDN penetration is 12 per 1000 population (1995) in Germany, and has been provided largely by Deutsche Telekom (compared to 9 in 1000 in the UK, 6 in 1000 in France, 2 in 1000 in Japan and 1 in 1000 in the USA). Data from 'Moving into the Information Society—an International Benchmarking Study', a study by Spectrum Strategy Consultants, UK, published by the Department of Trade and Industry, UK, as part of the Information Society Initiative, August 1997.
75. See synopsis of ESPRIT Technology for Business Processes and Electronic Commerce Projects, European Commission (1998a), also at http://www.cordis.lu/esprit/src/tbp-home-htm.
76. Interview with Luc Schelfhout, February 1998.
77. Infomar, 'European Seafood Marketing Comes of Age', paper presented at the TBP-IIM Advisory Committee by Luc Schelfhout, 6 February 1998.
78. See http://www.fastparts.com.
79. *International Journal of Electronic Markets*, Vol. 7, No. 4, Winter 1997/98.
80. SCS Web site contains several examples of its electronic auction systems, including screenshots that illustrate the bidding processes, http://www.schelfhout.com.
81. 'Auctions and Bidding on the Internet, an Assessment', Efraim Turban, *International Journal of Electronic Markets*, Vol. 7, No. 4, Winter 1997/98.
82. Ingram launched this PrimeAccess program in fall 1998. On the one hand it increases revenues for Ingram, on the other hand it may reinforce the reseller network.
83. For example in the ESPRIT IMPRIMATUR project, http://www.imprimatur.alcs.co.uk/imprimatur/.
84. Broad consensus consists among public policy makers worldwide that electronic commerce would benefit from a light legal framework; see e.g. the 1997 policy papers from the USA ('A Framework for the Global Information Infrastructure'), the European Union ('European Initiative in Electronic Commerce'), about 35 European countries (Bonn Declaration, July 97) and Japan (Ministry of International Trade and Industry, 'Towards the Digital Economy'). A similar view is expressed by industry, as can be expected, for example in the November 1997 Declaration on Electronic Commerce of the Transatlantic Business Dialogue, and in the Conclusions of the OECD Conference in Turku, Finland, November 1997, 'Removing the Barriers to Global Electronic Commerce'.
85. Classical contract law considers the identity of parties irrelevant, carefully delimits the nature of the agreement and gives preference to formal descriptions rather than relying on third-party participation for remedies, avoiding open-ended consequences for non-performance.
86. Providing such guarantees and more generally clarifying the application and applicability of legislation to electronic commerce is an area of active policy making in the EU and in other regions of the world. In principle, for intra-EU trading the problems are far less than for transactions between trading blocs.
87. The challenge is to offer online negotiation support. Projects like MEMO and CASBA attempt to address this.
88. Chrissafis, A., European Commission, Directorate-General III, Industry, private communications, March 1998.
89. 'Electronic Marketplaces: Management and Technical Implications', *Inside Gartner Group This Week*, 2 April 1997, pp. 7–9.
90. See e.g. Wilson, R.F., *Web Commerce Today*, Issue 10, 15 May 1998.
91. Aspen report, Bollier (1996).
92. *European Union Basic Statistics Data*, 1996. In 1994 European Union GDP was €6189 billion. Imports from within the EU were €861 billion, exports to other EU countries were €895 billion, total intra-EU trade was therefore €1756 billion. Imports from outside the EU were €519 billion, exports to outside the EU were €524 billion, total trade extra-EU trade was thus €1043 billion. Total trade was €2799 billion which is 45% of GDP.
93. E.g. the CASBA and MEMO projects, ESPRIT programme, European Commission, http://www.cordis.lu/esprit/src/home.htm.

94. Although FedEx VirtualOrder is described as an example of one-to-one marketing by Peppers and Rogers on their Web site, http://www.m1to1.com, there is little evidence provided that FedEx has a specific marketing programme to enhance 'life-time value' of its VirtualOrder customers.

95. An interesting recent case has to do with patents awarded by the US Patent Office to OpenMarket for rather generic elements of electronic trading systems. Even though they are granted under US law only, due to the fact that electronic trading systems increasingly need to work globally and since they apparently have a wide definition they might affect many third-party marketplace providers.

96. Kotler calls this 'physical possession', which includes storage, movement and delivery. In this context we are talking about intangibles (services and electronically stored information) where the delivery aspect is most evident. However, storage, transmission and caching of information may be important functions of the channel too, cf. the Tradezone case where franchisees need to provide servers (i.e. computer systems) for proxying.

97. George Colony, CEO Forrester, November 1997, private communications.

98. This is based on the innovation adoption work of Rogers (1962).

99. It will be interesting to monitor Tradezone's approach to public relations, its primary market being the USA.

100. The ESPRIT project CyberBrand experiments with multiple online representation of a brand, based on online customer feedback and analysis. Such technology might become part of the one-to-one marketing toolset. See http://www.ispo.cec.be/ecommerce/ecomproj.htm.

101. An example is the failure of the same online shopping malls mentioned elsewhere in this book and discussed in detail in Schwartz (1997), pp. 93–6.

102. The OECD study also notes that many of the data providers are at the same time consultants, whose business is well served by an increased interest in the Internet and electronic commerce.

103. Chapter 1 of the European Initiative in Electronic Commerce, European Commission, April 1997, http://www.cordis.lu/esprit/src/ecomcom.htm; as well as related publications at http://www.ispo.cec.be/Ecommerce/.

104. N. Negroponte at EITC'97 conference, Brussels, 25 November 1997.

105. CommerceNet, '1998 eCommerce Barriers and Inhibitors', March 1998, see also http://www.commerce.net/.

106. Nick Mansfield, Shell Information Security Services, private communications, 1997.

107. For an assessment of the readiness for electronic commerce in the European Union, see also Timmers and van der Veer (1999a).

108. An overview of national policies and action plans can be found at http://www.ispo.cec.be/ecommerce/legal.htm and http://www.ispo.cec.be/ecommerce/relpol.htm.

109. Final Report of the G8 Global Marketplace for SMEs Pilot, as presented at the Dallas Seminar, 16 April 1999, see also http://www.ispo.cec.be/ecommerce/g7init.htm.

110. E-CLIP ESPRIT project at http://www.jura.uni-muenster.de/Eclip.

111. M. Bangemann at the IST'98 conference, 30 November 1998, Vienna, *Automatiseringsgids*, 2 December 1998.

112. Examples are France Telecom, Telecom Italia, KPN in the Netherlands and BT. See also 'The Certification Game', Annelise Berendt, in *Telecommunications*, December 1998.

113. S. Van der Velden, InTouch, private communication.

114. The person-based scenario has been analysed in more detail by Northeast Consulting, http://www.ncri.com/.

115. For examples of the impact of business process engineering, see e.g. European Commission (1998c), also available at http://www.ispo.cec.be/ecommerce/tbpbook.html.

116. For more information about Klotz's requirements see http://www.agentisme.com/en/smes/expectations.html.

117. RosettaNet (http://www.rosettanet.org) is a project supported by a wide industry consortium and managed by CommerceNet since 1998.

118. Ontology.org (http://www.ontology.org) is an industry and research forum supported by CSC focused on the application of ontologies in Internet commerce, to address the

problems that affect the formation and sustainability of large electronic trading groups. An ontology is a vocabulary of basic terms and specification of their meanings, which allows for the composition of meaningful higher-level knowledge.

119. Forrester has given the name 'dynamic trade' to trading that has these first two characteristics ('satisfying current demand with customized response'). See *Forrester Business Trade & Technology Strategies Report*, May 1998, Vol. 1, No. 11.

120. http://www.acses.com provides a comparison of book prices.

121. Jango's technology, http://www.jango.com, integrated into Excite, provides price comparison for consumer goods like PCs, sportswear or CDs delivered by a range of (pre-selected) Web sites.

122. *Forrester Business Trade & Technology Strategies Report*, March 1998, Vol. 1, No. 9.

123. http://www.wehkamo.nl is originally a mail order company, which has for several years held an online Dutch auction for surplus items (restricted to the Netherlands in order to guarantee payment by the consumers through their bank account).

124. COBRA is an ACTS project, http://www.infowin.org/ACTS/RUS/PROJECTS/ac203.htm.

125. For references and links, see for example http://www.insead.fr/calt/Encyclopedia/ComputerSciences/Agents/, http://www.iig.uni-freiburg.de/telematik/projekte/telos/, and http://www.haas.berkeley.edu/~citm/nego/. See also *International Journal of Electronic Markets*, Vol. 7, No. 4, Winter 1997/98.

126. ECOM Electronic Commerce Association of Japan, 1996; EU 97, presentations as prepared by the European Commission, Directorate-General III/F/6, 1997. The input of Mrs Rosalie Zobel of the European Commission is gratefully acknowledged and has been essential.

127. In the defence, aerospace and shipbuilding industry lifecycle management is well-known. CALS, Computer Aided Lifecycle Support, is the concept for this that is implemented through a set of methodologies, standards and technologies. It remains to be seen whether the CALS experience is also useful in light manufacturing, services and information industries.

128. Research issues in value networks and dynamic markets were identified at the December 1998–April 1998 CEC workshops, Brussels, http://www.ispo.cec.be/ecommerce/docs/consolidatedreport.zip, and at the September 1998 NSF Workshop, Center for Research in Electronic Commerce, University of Texas, Austin, http://crec.bus.utexas.edu/.

129. See http://www.pixelpark.de and the ESPRIT project PEP-PRO.

130. This argument may not always hold true, however, as the introduction of coordination technology also affects business organization and skills management. Internal organizational inertia or lack of coordination skills may make internal coordination more expensive than external. This is a consideration for outsourcing.

131. Hall, D. (1999) 'The Call of the Web', *Telecommunications*, January, using data from Datamonitor.

132. Condrinet study, 'Content and Commerce Driven Strategies in Global Networks', European Commission DGXIII, INFO2000 programme (1998).

133. See The Industry Standard (IDG), 1 Jan 99, http://www.thestandard.net/. IShip can be found at http://iship.com.

134. See http://www.cordis.lu/esprit/src/ep20718.htm for the TISSUS project description, and http://www.lyon.cci.fr/musee-des-tissus/tissus01.htm for the Lyon Textile Museum, one of its users.

135. The examples are modelled after Bakos *et al.* (1998). Readers are referred to the original paper for a much more profound explanation.

136. The assumption that the group valuation is the sum of the members' valuations should still approximately hold. This may not always be true; for example it may be easier to exchange digital goods by making a copy and sending that to a peer in another company than to share the budget between those companies and have one purchaser pay the sum of the valuations.

137. http://www.oecd.org/dsti/sti/it/news/ottrepor.htm.

138. http://www.ispo.cec.be/ecommerce/legal.htm#ecommerce.

139. According to the text of the Internet Tax Freedom Act (S.442), no new taxes may be imposed on 'communications or transactions using the Internet' and on 'online

services or Internet access'. Online services are those that are bundled with Internet access. The Act would therefore not appear to exclude taxation on digital goods delivered via the Internet.

140. The workshops were following the Futures Mapping® approach of Northeast Consulting Resources Inc, see http://www.ncri.com.

141. At the same time Dell virtualizes for small businesses some of the services that were previously only accessible for large accounts, such as product briefings. It calls this the 'Virtual Account Executive' programme. Likewise, it has an online 'Breakfast with Dell' programme for small businesses to be briefed about information technology for their company. Thus we see not only a trend towards convergence based on electronic commerce and Internet technologies between Dell-to-consumers and Dell-to-small businesses, but also with Dell-to-corporates.

142. http://www.quixell.co.uk/. It was claimed that Quixell (or rather QXL) received the largest single venture capital investment in Europe to date (*Financial Times*, 1 March 1999).

143. The 'multimedica' online medical service, created in 1997 (following the merger of the Burda group's Health Online Service and the similar service operated by Bertelsmann AG and Springer Verlag), expected to have around 30 000 subscribers by the end of 1998.

144. The Bloomberg case is analysed in more detail in Chan Kim and Mauborgne (1999).

145. This point is also made in 'Good-bye to Fixed Pricing?', a *Business Week* Special Report of 4 May 1998.

146. Details about the European Unions R&D/pilot programme in 'New Methods of Work and Electronic Commerce' can be found at http://www.cordis.lu/ist.

147. Resulting on 1998 in a White Paper about 'Key Research Issues in International Electronic Commerce', 11th International Bled Electronic Commerce Conference, http://ecom.fov.uni-mb.so.

148. The relevance of such systemic thinking for the design of public R&D programmes is addressed in Timmers, P. (1999) 'Designing Effective Public R&D Programmes', *Proceedings Portland International Conference on Management of Engineering and Technology, PICMET'99*, July, http://www.emp.pdx.edu/picmet.

149. This has been an element in the discussion about a 'Directive on Copyright Rights and Related Rights in the Information Society' from the European Commission, proposed in COM(97)628, http://europa.eu.int/comm/dg15/en/intprop/intprop/index.htm.

150. This stream of thinking is also having its impact on higher education. In April 1997 it was proposed to the G8 Global Marketplace for SMEs Pilot, an international collaboration to promote electronic commerce for small companies, to create a new master-level programme in global electronic commerce. The programme, which is jointly developed by universities, business schools and policy institutes in the USA, Europe and Asia, takes an integrated approach to technology, policy and business for electronic commerce.

151. European Commission, 'Green Paper on Convergence of Telecommunications, Media and Information Technology Sectors, and the Implications for Regulation. Towards an Information Society Approach', COM(97)623, 3 December 1997, http://www.ispo.cec.be/convergencegp/.

152. EACEM, position on the Green Paper on Convergence, May 1998.

Index

A

Acses, 43, 125, 192, 243
Actra, 94
ACTS. *See* EU Programmes
Ad-hoc markets, 191
Advertising
  banners, 155, 157
  focus on brand building, 156
  income from, 36, 40
  Internet, online, 25
  traditional, physical, offline, 11, 16, 45,
    153, 157
Aerospace industry, 22
Aerotech, 22, 186, 256
Agent technology, 11, 17, 25, 43, 168, 191,
  193, 203, 243
AGENTISME Project. *See* EU Programmes
Agriculture, 105
AIDA—Awareness-Interest-Desire-Action.
    See also product adoption process,
    17
Albert Heijn, 85
AltaVista, 13, 43, 178
Andersen Consulting, 9, 171, 204, 256
Assets, 20
AT&T, 56, 59, 243
Automotive industry, 21, 94, 99, 122, 126,
  187

B

Baan, 243
Banking
  competition, 243

competition in e-commerce for telecom
    operators, 178
  Internet/home, 85
  Isabel, association, 44
  trusted party, 85
  virtual, 243
Banners, *See* Advertising
Behaviour
  customer, 28
  decision making. *See also* processual, 175,
    193
  dynamic. *See also* Business organization,
    210
  purchasing, 145
  transaction cost theory and, 200
Belgacom, 67, 69, 76, 77, 95, 118, 176
Belsign, 40, 44
Bertelsmann, 243
BIAC—Business and Industry Advisory
    Committee (of the OECD), 174
Bilateral contracting, 127, 129
Book retail sector, 38
Brand(ing)
  advantage of large companies, 12, 23
  as a key asset, 20
  as third party marketplace feature, 39
  asset of established telecom operators,
    178
  brand to protect the business model, 29
  building
    Amazon, 156
    banners for, 157
    Citius, 77
    customer loyalty, 26, 140
    FedEx, 124

GEN/ICS, 101
Industry.Net, 59
marketing communications objective,
    152
Tradezone, 88
competition in the industry/barrier to
    entry, 117
digital information and, 223
digital information and (*table*), 224
electronic mall
    brand reinforcement, 36, 143
importance of global, 12, 55, 77, 152
in dynamic markets and value networks,
    196, 208
quality, 187
transaction cost theory and, 210
British Telecom, 44
Broadvision, 17
BT—British Telecom, 44
Bundling
information, 159
product/services, 159, 237
transactions, 190
Business models
classification, 41
definition, 32
degree of innovation, 41
e-auction
    auction models (Dutch/English), 193
    auctioning advertising space, 193
    auctioning computer parts, 193
    auctioning production capacity, 37, 91,
        194, 197
    auctioning surplus stock, 197
    business-to-consumer, 228
    improving access to markets, 223
    new competition, 242
    optimization of business operations,
        198
    person-to-person, 228
e-shop, 35
examples, 42
information brokerage, 40
integration of functions, 41
trends, 44
trust services, 40
value chain integrator, 39
value chain service provider, 40
virtual communities, 38
Business organization
external, 115, 132, 133, 135, 137–138

(dis-)intermediation, 2, 52, 115, 133,
    135
affiliation, loyalty, trust, 136
Amazon, 60
Citius, 137
dynamic, 52, 136
dynamic markets
    definition, 181, 189
GEN/ICS, 137
hub and spoke, 136, 141, 192, 207, 209
junction box, 49, 136
Marshall, 1376
strategy, 196, 197, 199, 206
Tradezone, 137
value constellations, 136, 138
value networks
    definition, 181, 183, 185
    integration, 19
    virtual organization, 136
internal, 132, 133

C

CALS—Computer Assisted Lifecycle
    Support, 3, 195
CASBA Project. *See* EU Programmes
Cases, 47
Amazon Association/Advantage, 60
Citius Belgium, 66
FedEx, 52
Global Engineering Network/Industrial
    Cooperation System, 90
Industry.Net, 55
Infomar, 103
Marshall Industries, 49
Tradezone, 80
Certification agent. *See also* Trust, 131
Chain reversal, 187
Channel(s)
channel mix, 11
communication channel, 150–152, 155
communication via TV, 219
complementarity between, 11
conflict, 140
direct, 133, 140, 148
distribution channel, 59, 139,
    148–150, 163, 198, 246
functions, 148, 150
marketing channel, 35, 133, 148
multiple, 140
physical/virtual, 39, 148

synergy/coherence/integration, 140, 151,
    156, 163
Cisco, 6, 23, 204, 224
Classical planning. *See also* strategies, 175
CMG, 54, 243
CNN, 243
Coalitions, buyer or seller, 191
Coalitions, digital information pricing and,
    220
COBRA Project. *See* EU Programmes
Collaboration
    between auctions, 104
    in value networks and dynamic markets,
        136, 181–182, 210 platforms. *See*
        Business models
    supplier-buyer in project-based business,
        160
CommerceNet, 9, 170, 250, 256
Compaq, 13, 204
Competition
    business models analysis and sources of,
        119
    Citius, 70
    collaboration and, 97
    competitive forces and barriers to entry,
        116–117, 122, 126, 138
    FedEx, 54
    for telecom operators as e-commerce
        companies, 178
    GEN/ICS, 94
    global, 12
    in digital information business, 224
    in value networks and dynamic markets,
        136, 181, 182, 210
    increase of customer choice and more, 22
    incumbents, contenders, dark horses, 243
    Industry.Net, 57
    Infomar, 106
    Internet characteristics and, 118
    market research, 20, 77
    market share, 23, 86
    Marshall, 51
    one-to-one marketing and, 160
    positioning, 20, 58, 117
    price-based, 69
    protecting the business model, 29
    standards wars, 8
    strategic focus, 52
    third party marketplace providers, 117
    third party marketplace providers, 119
    threat of substitution, 123

time-based/time-to-market, 49, 69, 189
Tradezone, 82
Competitive advantage, 79
Competitive strategies, 20, 123–124, 134,
    246
Competitive structures, 115, 137, 223
Computer Associates, 243
Construction industry, 69, 74, 94, 141, 208
    negotiation and contracting, 127, 191, 208
Consumer protection, 173
Convergence
    as driver for industry restructuring, 224
    marketing mix, *See* Marketing mix of
        B-to-B and B-to-C, 141, 181, 227,
        232, 238
    drivers for, 233–234
    of communications, information
        processing, media, 15
    of markets, 232
    of media, 232
    of technology, 10
Coordination costs. *See* Cost(s)
Coordination technology, 203
CORBA—Common Object Request Broker
    Architecture, 170
Cost
    increasing returns to scale, 15
Cost base, 20, 21
Cost concerns, 8
Cost leadership, 75, 123, 208, 224
Cost of ownership, 227
Cost(s)
    breakdown of total, 199
    coordination, 126, 133, 199, 201–203
    for access to electronic commerce, 7, 87
    Internet to lower transaction, 134
    of telecommunications, 9
    reduction of purchasing, 143
    savings, 7, 15, 21, 68
        business models and, 35, 37
    switching, 7, 20, 26, 27, 29, 137, 154
    value networks and reduction of, 181
CPM—cost per 1000 impressions, 157
Customer
    loyalty, 20, 26, 154
    one-to-one marketing and value for, 159
    retention, 154
Customer benefits, 19, 143
Customer orientation, 24
Customer relationship management, 198,
    231

Customers
    benefits, 20
    loyalty, 26
    orientation, 20, 24, 242
Customers of electronic commerce systems,
        144
Customs, 173, 222

D

Data mining, 243
Datamonitor, 4, 263
Dell, 204, 227, 234, 264
Differentiation strategy, 124, 125
Dis-intermediation, 52, 133
    cases, 134, 135
    in electronic components distribution/
        Marshall, 51
    marketing mix, 134
Distribution
    online, 22, 34
Domain names, 173
Dun & Bradstreet, 23, 243
Dynamic business organization. *See*
        Business organization
Dynamic market
    Amazon Associates, 61
Dynamic market characteristics, 182
Dynamic product/service bundling, 191
Dynamics dimension in value creation
        (illus.), 211
Dynamics in business environment, 177
Dynamics in technology development, 166,
        168

E

EACEM—European Association of
        Consumer Electronics
        Manufacturers, 241
e-Christmas, 9, 39, 54, 121, 168, 256
E-CLIP Project. *See* EU Programmes
ECR—Electronic Customer Relationship
        management, 187
EDI providers, 71
EDI, *See* Electronic Data Interchange
EDI-TIE, 243
EDS—Electronic Data Systems, 71, 94, 95,
        122, 243
Electrical engineering, 94
Electronic commerce definition, 3

Electronic components industry, 50, 145,
        153
Electronic Data Interchange
    'lite' EDI, 71
    Citius, 66
    Citius, 67
    contracts, 127
    EDI vs Internet
        lock-in, 121
    EDI vs Internet, 67
    standard, 169
    usage, 3
    versus Internet
        cost, 7
        global standards, 12
        interactivity, 16
        lock-in, 72
        sector-specificity, 7
    XML and EDI, 13, 71
EMB—Electronic Mall Bodensee, 36
Energy industry, 56
Engineering industries, 57
ESPRIT, *See* EU Programmes
EU Programmes
    ACTS
        COBRA, 193
        ACTS Programme, 6, 170, 193
    ESPRIT
        AGENTISME, 187
        CASBA, 40, 118
        E-CLIP, 174
        GENIAL, 39, 95, 260
        Internet Megastore, 14, 39
        LOGSME, 28
        MEMO, 40, 193, 202
        SUPPLYPOINT, 192, 208
        TISSUS, 215, 226
        TRANS2000, 40
        VIVE, 187
        ESPRIT Programme, 6, 14, 28, 39, 40, 80,
            84, 103, 170, 187, 193
    Telematics Applications Programme, 6
European Information Technology
        Observatory, 4
Extensible Markup Language, 13, 71, 195
Externalities, 17

F

FastParts, 38
Fedex, 22, 52, 53, 54, 55, 59, 82, 135, 153

Fisheries, 104
Fleurop, 36
Flowers sector, 104
Focus strategy, 123
Forrester, 4, 5, 81, 151, 171, 172, 192, 216, 243, 255, 261
Franchising, 13
Frequency of transactions/purchasing, 126, 127
Fuzzy markets, 191

G

G7 (now G8), group of industrialized countries, 156, 256, 258, 262, 264
GartnerGroup, 23, 133, 151, 215, 243, 261
GBDe—Global Business Dialogue on Electronic Commerce, 174
GEIS TPN Register, 58, 82, 85, 95, 141, 144
GEIS-GE Information Services, 71, 94, 95, 96, 122, 243
GENIAL Project. *See* EU Programmes
GIIC—Global Information Infrastructure Commission, 174
GlobalSign, 44
Grainger, 5, 9, 58, 82, 255

H

Harbinger, 243
Harmful content, 173
Hewlett-Packard, 23, 57, 83, 84, 86, 87, 88, 120
Hospital supplies/medical goods sector, 69, 125

I

IBM, 5, 8, 23, 36, 37, 92, 96, 99
ICC—International Chambers of Commerce, 174
IDC—International Data Corporation, 5, 7, 215, 243, 255
IMRG—Interactive Media in Retail Group, 7, 255
Industrial competitiveness
  barriers to entry, 86, 108, 116, 117
  internal competition, 108, 117–118
  new entrants, 116, 118–119, 121, 179
    business models, 119
  power of customers, 121

power of suppliers, 120
substitution, 122
Information Handling Systems, 56, 59, 82, 121, 243
Ingram Micro, 120, 192, 193
Intermediaries, *See also* Business organization, 133
Internet
  features, 10
  size, 6
INTERNET MEGASTORE Project. *See* EU Programmes
Intershop, 71, 73, 82, 99, 259
Isabel banking association, 44
ISP internet service provider, 9, 81, 84, 91, 99, 110, 177, 178, 255

J

JAL—Japan Airlines, 36
Jango, 192, 243
JIT—Just In Time, 22, 49

K

Kewill, 28, 243
Key competitive/business/success factors, 117, 138, 189, 200
Klotz, 187–188
Knowledge management, 181, 239–240
KPMG, 9, 256, 256

L

Language
  extensible markup—XML, 13, 71, 195
  for electronic commerce, 165
  formal business language, 193
  influence or support of language/culture, 13, 50, 63, 65, 140
Legacy
  integration with legacy systems, 9, 19, 118
  organizational, 122, 165, 176, 179
Legal framework
  digital information business, 217
  EU-US (*table*), 173
  for electronic commerce, 171
  global, 241
  overview of issues (*table*), 173
  relationship to technology, 246
  uncertainty, 8, 177

Liability, 218
Lifecycle management, 196, 205
Lite EDI. *See* Electronic Data Interchange
LocalEurope, 39
Logica, 54, 243
LTV, *See* lifetime value

M

Marginal cost, 15, 161, 200
Market research
    difficulties in emerging markets of, 167
    networked, 168
    quality of, 166
    value network versus dynamic market,
        197
Marketing
    new characteristics of B-to-B, 140
    traditional B-to-B, 139
Marketing mix
    convergence of B-to-B and B-to-C, 237
    digital information business, 217
    dis-intermediation, 134
    GEN/ICS, 101
    Infomar, 111
    marketing models, 32
    Tradezone, 87
Marketing model
    definition, 32
Marshall, 50–52, 150
Mechanical engineering, 94
MEMO Project. *See* EU Programmes
Merck, 36
Microsoft, 8, 9, 27, 71, 99, 120, 122, 243
Microsoft Merchant Server, 54
Mitsukoshi, 14, 256
MRO—Maintenance, repair and
    operations, 5
Muddling through. *See also* strategies, 124,
    175
Multichannel, 140

N

NatWest Bank, 80, 83, 86
NCR, 243
Negotiation
    assisted, intelligent agents, 118, 142
    bilateral, 129
    business-to-business, 140
    coordination technology, 204
    direct. *See also* dis-intermediation, 113

electronic, online, 36, 131, 150, 162, 168
    information brokerage and, 40, 193
    price, 105
    third party arbitration/assistance and,
        138, 191
    transaction cost theory and, 128
Netscape, 8, 23, 71, 120, 122, 169, 243
Network
    effects, 10, 17
    externalities, 17
    market research, 168
Networked market research, 168
Niche strategy, 123

O

OBI—Open Buying on the Internet, 170
Occasional transactions, 127, 128, 129
OECD—Organization for Economic
    Cooperation and Development,
    166, 174, 222, 260, 261
OMG—Object Management Group, 170
ONSALE, 45
Onyx, 80, 83, 84, 86, 118
OpenMarket, 71, 82
Oracle, 120, 243, 243
Origin, 243
OTP—Open Trading Protocol, 170

P

PDM—Product Data Modeling, 189
People factor, 102
Perfect competition. *See* competition
Personal agents. *See also* Agent technology,
    237
Personal selling, 152
Person-based sales, 140
Philips, 243
Pixelpark, 203
Place versus space, 241
Portfolio analysis, 197
Portfolio working, 233
Post-mass-production, 94
Price-differentiation. *See* Pricing
Priceline, 45
PriceWaterhouseCoopers, 5, 252, 255
Pricing
    Citius, 79
    digital information, 217
    dynamic markets, 209

GEN/ICS, 102
Marshall, 49
one-to-one marketing, 161
price differentiation/individual pricing/
    marginal pricing, 70, 126,
    161–162
purchaser-dependent in 3rd party
    marketplace, 76
strategies for, 78–79, 133
Tradezone, 89
Privacy
legal framework, 173
Product
adoption process, 153
Promotion
chain owner and shop owner, 39
in B-to-B markets, 140
mix, 155
multimedia, 15
when B-to-B and B-to-C converge, 237
Publishing industry, 74, 141

Q

Quixell, 228

R

Reed Elsevier, 243
Retail sector, 3, 14, 230–231
Return on investment, 7
Reuters, 215, 243
RosettaNet, 13, 170, 188

S

SAP, 102, 104, 243
Scenarios
for impact of Internet on transaction
    costs, 134
for substitution of physical goods by
    intangibles, 123
for the future of B-to-B electronic
    commerce, 179
Security
anonymity, 161
barrier to electronic commerce. *See also*
    Trust, 9
Citius, 73
credit card, 201
in dynamic markets, 196

legal framework, 173
sensitive personal and business data, 8
Tradezone, 81, 90
Segmentation
benefits, 75, 163, 246
convergent B-to-B and B-to-C, 235, 236
digital information, 219
geographical, 84, 111
micro-markets, 190
product-market, 74, 141, 142, 143
purchasing markets, 142
Selling agent. *See also* intermediaries, 106,
    110
ServiceNet Project. *See* EU Programmes
SET—Secure Electronic Transaction
    protocol, 18, 87, 170
Shell, 209
Shopping bots. *See also* Agent technology,
    192, 201
Siemens, 95, 96, 103
Small Office—Home Office, 230,
    233–237
Sony, 243
Standardization
business process terminology and, 33
global supply chains and, 12
integration and, 18
STEP—Standard for the Exchange of
    Product Data, 189
Sterling Software, 243
Strategies
critical assumptions, 165
dilemmas for telecom operators, 177
generic, 123, 176
global, 12, 14
local, 14
organization, 196–197, 200, 208
strategic fit, 174
Suppliers
assets, 20
SUPPLYPOINT Project. *See* EU
    Programmes

T

TABD—Trans-Atlantic Business Dialogue,
    174
Taxation, 173
Telematics Applications Programme, *See*
    EU Programmes Tesco, 6, 85
Textiles, 215

TISS, 36
TISSUS Project. *See* EU Programmes
Trade procedures, 128
TRANS2000 Project. *See* EU Programmes
Transaction cost(s)
 brand building and the theory of, 210
 governance, 126
 key dimensions, 126
 theory, 126
 trust and, 201
Transient markets, 191
Transport sector, 141
Travel sector, 134
Travelocity, 36
Trust
 brand and reputation, 37, 84
 business organization and, *See also*
  Business organization, 185
 certification authorities, 40, 195
 channel function to provide, 149
 codes of conduct, 240
 customer loyalty, 207, 208
 digital information and 'trust gap', 217,
  218
 digital signatures, 171, 178
 enhancing technologies, 201
 globalization strategy and, *See also*
  Strategies, 43
 labeling and quality schemes for, 201
 lack of trust and confidence as a barrier, 9
 legal framework, 172
 new competition and trust service
  providers, 244
 telecom operators and trust services, 178
 transaction costs, 210
 transaction costs and, 201
Trust enhancing technologies, 42
Trust services, *See also* Business models, 40
Trusted third parties, 19, 40, 185, 226

U

UN/EDIFACT, 169
UNCITRAL—United Nations
 Commission on International
 Trade Law, 173, 174

Unilever, 209
UPS, 9, 40, 50, 54, 55, 65, 124, 214, 231

V

Value chain
 analysis, 32
 de-construction, 33
 re-construction, 31, 33
Value network
 Amazon Advantage, 61
Value network characteristics, 183
Value network. *See also* Business
  organization, 183
Verisign, 40, 44
VerticalNet, 45, 213, 243
Virtual banks, 243
Virtual catalogue, 80
Virtual factory, 186
Virtual goods, 222
Virtual presence, 14
Virtual reality, 196, 230, 237, 240
Virtual supply chains, 192, 193
Virtual teams, 4
Virtual Vineyards, 53
Visa, 87
VIVE Project. *See* EU Programmes
VPN—Virtual Private Network, 98

W

Wine sector, 70
WTO—World Trade Organization, 173,
 174, 224

X

XML/EDI. *See also* Electronic Data
 Interchange, 13, 71

Y

Yahoo, 13, 40, 70, 120, 178, 243
Yankee Group, 5, 92, 255

Z

ZD-Net, 243